FIGHTING
PROGRESSIVE

FIGHTING PROGRESSIVE

A Biography of Edward P. Costigan

By FRED GREENBAUM

Public Affairs Press, Washington, D. C.

To Ann, Jonathan, Rose,
Theodore, and Dave

Copyright 1971, by Public Affairs Press
419 New Jersey Avenue, S. E., Washington, D. C.

Printed in the United States of America
Library of Congress Catalog Card No. 70-168553

PREFACE

In many ways this is an old fashioned biography. There is no attempt at retroactive psychoanalysis. Such an approach would not be valid since the correspondence of Edward Costigan was invariably impersonal, business-like, and concerned almost solely with politics and ideas.

Many people do not engage in personal correspondence, and this explains nothing about their psyche. Even if Costigan's letters were personally revealing, it is of questionable value to try to explain ordinary political phenomena in psychological terms. Political movements, whether formed to pursue an ideology or patronage, attract followers with a full range of mental attitudes; the politics of paranoia is, of course, an exception. Unless the subject displays characteristics outside the norm such an examination can be a fruitless and misleading pursuit.

Similarly, it is far more important to examine the socio-economic origins of political movements than of their leaders, for such leadership, in this country, is almost invariably a middle and upper class affair. While some politicians appear to be motivated by economic interests, it is more likely that their stands on issues and their economic interests both spring from a particular socio-economic view, rather than the former being derived from the latter; simple economic self-interest is just too naive. And particular philosophical perceptions, though more dominant in one class than another, are present in all classes in our society.

Economic factors are instrumental in generating ideas, which modify and are modified by past concepts, and become part of the general ethos from which we draw our own view of life. It is this perspective which motivates men, determines their economic activities, personal behavior, political affiliations and friendships. A man supports an expanding military arsenal and an aggressive foreign policy not because he derives his income from the military-industrial complex, but he engages in all three because they conform to his concept of the world. Consequently, where Costigan's actions are interpreted, they are explained in terms of his political philosophy with no effort to find the derivations of this ideology other than to say that he lived in a particular country, within western civilization, in a given historical era during which these ideas, in varying combinations, were prevalent among a large number of people.

CONTENTS

I Mainstream America	1
II Denver	9
III Progressivism at its Apex	25
IV The Election of 1914	55
V Epilogue to the Progressive Movement	75
VI The Tariff Commission	88
VII The Election of 1930	105
VIII Relief for the Unemployed	119
IX The Jones-Costigan Bill	143
X The Costigan-Wagner Anti-Lynching Bill	160
XI Postscript	
Notes on Sources	181
Index	188

CHAPTER I

MAINSTREAM AMERICA

If American history is conceived of in the broadest possible terms, there are two principal strains. One derives from the neomercantilist conviction of Alexander Hamilton, that government must promote the interests of the commercial and industrial elite, since they are the catalyst that generates the nation's economic well-being. This conception was injected into our legal system by Hamilton's southern ally, John Marshall, and has been pursued by such illustrious figures as Daniel Webster, Roscoe Conkling, Nelson Aldrich, Herbert Hoover, Robert Taft, and, in our own day, Richard Nixon. Thomas Jefferson, on the other hand, sought to prevent government from being used by urban capitalists to advance their own interests at the expense of all other elements in the society.

While at first Jefferson hoped to accomplish his objective by limiting the powers of government, he was not consistent in applying this means, abandoning it whenever it clashed with his more important goals. The Jeffersonians tried to promote the full development of the potentials of the ordinary citizens, the yeomen of the early years of the Republic, and sought to protect the rights of the many rather than the privileges of the few. This conception has emerged in many forms. Jefferson saw the need for adaptation, for recognizing that one generation should not be bound by the formulas of the previous generation. In subsequent years Jeffersonian democracy was reworked by the Jacksonians, the populists, the progressives and the liberals. Its proponents have included such notables as Justice Roger Taney, Walt Whitman, William Jennings Bryan, Senator Robert M. LaFollette, Franklin D. Roosevelt, and, in our own day, Senator George McGovern.

Edward Prentiss Costigan was completely immersed in the Jeffersonian tradition. He was willing to use Hamiltonian means only for Jeffersonian ends, unwittingly drawing from the populists before him and mirroring his contemporary, Herbert Croly. Like many urban based progressives, Costigan did not recognize his affinity for rural populism. In the process of rejecting their highly visible provincialism, anti-urban rhetoric, and preoccupation with currency inflation, he ignored their anti-monopolistic social and economic programs. But in reality, progressives shared their fundamental values with the populists, many of whom joined the insurgent ranks. Both were anti-trust, pro-capitalism, anti-boss, and pro-democracy. Just as the populists differed from the progressives on important programmatic details, so the progressives diverged among themselves.[1] And some rejected the third major reform impulse of their lifetime, the New Deal.

Why did Costigan adapt to the changing application of Jeffersonian values and assume a position to the left of the New Deal? There are several reasons. An excellent lawyer, Costigan did not see the Constitution as a rigid document to be preserved intact as first conceived by the founding fathers. Like Francis Bacon, who saw the Greeks as being in the infancy of knowledge, he questioned the assumption that genius lay only in the past. "The fathers of the Republic saw as through a glass, darkly," he commented. "We see face to face." As an elastic, liberating charter, the Constitution was capable of interpretation to meet the needs of an industrial society. Costigan agreed with Lincoln's reaction to an unfavorable decision by a contemporary court: the composition or opinions of the court could be changed. Alternately, the Constitution could be amended. As early as 1923 he drafted a general welfare amendment to permit legislation, resubmitting it after adverse social decisions crippled the New Deal; and he helped draft a child labor amendment. While he felt that precedent, like habit and custom, was essential to the functioning of men and society, he considered precedents an aid, not an end, and when they failed to meet society's needs it was necessary to return to the first principles upon which they had been based. The Constitution, then, he saw as an inspiration for life, not the stifling hand of the past, and he endorsed the broad interpretations of constitutional provisions expounded by the New Deal. His followers continued to adapt to an expanding conception of governmental functions. Oscar Chapman and Charles Brannan served in Truman's cabinet. John A. Carroll was carrying the banner of Colorado liberalism in the United States Senate when John F. Kennedy was elected. And Costigan's executive secretary, Lee F. Johnson, opened New Frontiers as Denver's public housing administrator. While Costigan shared the progressive view of government as an instrument removed from class interests, he refused to panic during labor-capital strife and join conservatives who sought to make the state an instrument of class oppression. On the contrary, he was actively pro-labor, not just paternalistic. Like many progressives, he rejected Samuel Gompers' fear of government and supported a wide range of measures to improve the conditions of all workers, organized and unorganized. But when in 1914 the violence accompanying the Ludlow mine strike frightened large segments of the Colorado Progressive Party, Costigan, then Progressive candidate for governor, continued to serve as special counsel for the United Mine Workers of America. To his colleagues' cry for law and order, he responded that the coal operators had for years disregarded laws that they considered disadvantageous to their interests. Law and order, he contended, was meaningless without justice, an argument still valid today as an answer to politicians who use this slogan to suppress those dissatisfied with the status quo.

In a world of collective capital, Costigan argued, workers must organize; "collective capital has no right to decline to confer with collective labor." In the struggle between employers and employees, the rights of society were supreme, but when he had doubts he always resolved them in favor of labor. He never viewed the New Deal as too favorable towards trade unions and felt that FDR did not do enough for unorganized workers. He endeavored to protect the interests of farm labor in a tradition that has most recently surfaced with liberal participation in a boycott of California grapes in order to support Cesar Chavez's "Huelga."

Costigan's desire to improve society was deep rooted—not just a moralistic crusade to be blithely swept aside by the next emotional outburst such as Teddy Roosevelt's drive for preparedness and war, or A. Mitchell Palmer's hysterical anti-radicalism. "War," he said, "is the sum of all villainies," and one reason he supported Wilson in 1916 was the latter's refusal to take the easy path to hostilities in American disputes with Mexico and Europe. To his way of thinking the appeal to arms was the result of anarchistic nationalism, economic misery, and inequality. Hence he advocated American entrance into the League of Nations and the World Court. Hence he concerned himself with living and working conditions, here and abroad. Hence he backed broad economic and social reform in the United States, and the reduction of international tariff barriers to a level that compensated for differences between American and foreign costs of production. He was a humanist, concerned with the well being of citizens of other lands, but he was unwilling to impose our will on others. His views were similar to those who today oppose our southeast Asian adventure, the growth of the military-industrial complex, and the general arrogance that has characterized our cold war responses.

Costigan's faith in democracy and civil liberties was unshaken by the Red scare of the 1920s. Each individual was precious. Each had the right to express unpopular ideas. Each was entitled to a fair trial, free from the pressures of popular prejudice; to equal treatment regardless of the minority status of his religion, race, or beliefs; and to the protections guaranteed by the Constitution's Bill of Rights. Thus, he asked FDR to release all conscientious objectors jailed during the First World War. He fought to obtain reconsideration of the conviction of Tom Mooney for allegedly throwing a bomb during a Preparedness Day parade. He insisted that Rosa Schwimmer should have been naturalized despite her pacifism. And he championed anti-lynch legislation though Colorado had few Negro voters and many former southerners. A staunch libertarian, he warmed the embers for those who resist the repressive tactics of the McCarthys and Agnews. He lighted the way for those who, since the Fair Deal, have picked up the torch of the Reconstruction Radicals and have sallied forth to extend Jefferson's concept of citizenship to all minority groups.

Costigan did not fear a government under the direct control of the people. To ensure a responsive representation he advocated party primaries (still an issue in some states), the Australian secret ballot, the short ballot, direct election of Senators and the President, referendum, initiative and recall, and, above all, vigilance before, during and after elections. His trust in popular jurisdiction rested on his faith in the capacity of men to rise above narrow self-interest: "The economic motive is only one of the weapons in the human arsenal. Alone it does not . . . explain either the sacrifice of love or the self-denying achievements of science, literature and the wonderful arts."

Costigan had the confidence in the average man that underpins the contemporary struggle for participatory democracy and community control. It rested on his faith in a democratic education process, devoted to service to the community, devoid of any elitist institutions such as fraternities, an educational process that was never finished. To ensure proper education he advocated federal aid to education and subsidies to underprivileged students. His concern for mass education derived from a heritage common to Jefferson and Horace Mann which has its most recent advance in open enrollment in the City University of New York.

A commonwealth controlled by the people, limited by a concern for civil liberties, Costigan insisted, could act for the general welfare. Prejudice against an active sovereignty, after all, derived from the monopoly granting practices of the English Parliament. And an inactive administration, in effect, ceded power to the special interests. The governmental sphere, in fact, has been extended into one area of social concern after another. Medicare may have prepared the way for public entrance into another area of the private sector's inadequate performance.

In a corporate world, Costigan realized, even an active authority could not hope to restore nineteenth century atomistic competition. Giant companies must be regulated, not only in their own interest, but in the interest of the community. During the progressive era he sought the regulation of public utilities through state commissions which would determine rates on the basis of physical valuation. When the New Deal sponsored business cooperation through the National Industrial Recovery Act, he greeted the experiment favorably but with a critical eye; he attempted to ensure that the provision for collective bargaining be worded to prevent the creation of company unions; persistently, he demanded a greater role for, and concern with, the interests of consumers and labor. As a result of the Panic of 1929 he strongly favored governmental control of the securities exchanges, the guarantee of savings deposits, and minimum standards for banking operations. He could not forsee the failures of the progressive and New Deal efforts at corporate control. He could not forsee a day when massive railroad complexes, greater than those the progressives tried to harness, would attempt to dip their hands into the public till to support high paid, inefficient management, while the agencies created to supervise industry would become the tools of these very industries and necessitate a reexamination of American political and economic conceptions about private enterprise.

In a corporate world, Costigan thought, workers should organize to bargain collectively with collective capital wherever possible. When this could not be accomplished the government must intervene in the interest of the disadvantaged: "A workmen's compensatory law, throwing the burden of industrial accidents on organized industry, rather than on its victims; laws safeguarding the lives and health of all workers in hazardous employment; an eight hour law for women, level with our civilization; a mothers' compensatory law, enabling children to be decently born; a minimum wage law, making honest living and respectable dying alike possible."

The most helpless of all were children "stunted in body and mind by early hire." He made every effort to eliminate child labor in factory and field. Never content with the limitations of charity — "Social, industrial, and Governmental justice are more important than charity"—

he led the struggle for federal grants-in-aid to state relief programs when the prolonged depression drained state resources. He not only supported New Deal social security legislation, but he insisted that those excluded from its coverage be provided low value annuity bond insurance in sums smaller than those private insurance companies were willing to underwrite. One wonders what language Costigan would have employed had he viewed an arm of the federal government, the military, increasing their purchase of grapes to help sustain grape growers in their effort to prevent the unionization of some of the most poorly paid workers in the country.

But the responsibility of the republic was not limited to restraints on corporate conduct. The state was responsible for the land and those who lived on it. During the twenties he supported efforts to aid the export of farm products; he hoped to reopen European markets by a saner tariff policy. During the thirties he endorsed the Agricultural Adjustment Act and succeeded in extending its benefits to the sugar industry. Nevertheless, he refused to accept the farmer's blindness to the needs of those they employed. He fought to end exploitation of children by sugar beet farmers. He insisted that field hands and agricultural laborers receive a reasonable share of the benefits of New Deal agricultural programs. Further, those who benefited from the nation's natural resources were obligated to future generations. Federal conservation, Costigan believed, "permits use without destruction." Federal authorities could best oversee the use of the public range, forests and water sites to prevent the destruction of soil surfacing and to permit reclamation and irrigation. And now the heirs of the conservation struggle, with even greater concern about the price of failure, are fighting the battle to preserve our ecology.

Under certain circumstances Costigan advocated communal ownership of production facilities. He strongly favored public power: "Our streams and rivers can easily be coined into human happiness by government, as surely as they can be transformed into gold by monopoly." Not only would the individual projects be useful, but they would serve as yardsticks to determine rates for private firms who used holding companies and inflated debt structures to disguise real costs and thus complicated the process of rate making. An early partisan of municipal ownership of municipal utilities, he expanded his horizons when midwestern farmers experimented with state-owned businesses through the Non-partisan League, and endorsed their efforts. Whenever regulation based on physical valuation proved inadequate, as in railroads, he was prepared for government ownership. As with many contemporary progressives, he was gradually convinced of the advantages of a mixed economy, a concept still very much under discussion.

Finally, Costigan felt taxes must be based on ability to pay. During the progressive era he supported a graduated income tax and an assessment on the unearned emolument from the land. During the depression he resisted an excise on sales for it was levied in inverse proportion to earnings; he preferred additional revenue from increased rates on income and corporations. And today the battle continues as the sales tax proliferates and the Nixon Administration prepares to replace revenue from a lapsed income surtax with a regressive value added or turnover duty. Costigan proposed a Constitutional amendment to permit levies on tax-exempt securities. He supported the younger LaFollette's fight for income tax publicity and he was a firm advocate of the purposes of Roosevelt's impost on wealth to restore prosperity with funds from those who benefitted most from the commonweal, and to redistribute wealth, rather than our modern practice of exempting society's beneficiaries from their fair share of its costs. Even through its tax policy the government was to attempt to further the welfare of its citizens.

Since Costigan was very much a product of the twentieth century, since he believed in a flexible, responsive government that took the initiative to improve the conditions of its citizens, since he refused to be hampered by the ideas and constitutional interpretations of a dead era, he espoused both major reform impulses of his era, the progressive movement and the New Deal. He recognized the increasingly corporate nature of society and the weakness of the solitary individual. Thus, he proposed to tame the combines by encouraging the development of trade unions and by the actions of a government, directly controlled by its citizens, which used its power to improve the lot of all. He pursued Jefferson's essential goal, that the object of government is to secure the pursuit of happiness for all its citizens. However, he was flexible enough not to get bogged down in the formulas derived from this tradition.

Motivated by these ideas, Costigan inspired devoted support in like minded followers. Yet, uncompromising, unwilling to appear ambitious, and unconcerned with the details of political organization, during a career spanning forty years he rarely sought office and was elected only during the Democratic victories of 1930. Nevertheless, Costigan was a political power in Colorado during the progressive era and the New Deal and an influential figure in the national capital during the the late 1920's and early 1930's. He was at the center of

Denver reform, the acknowledged leader of the Denver progressive Republicans and Colorado Progressive Party, an important factor in Wilson's victory in 1916, the last of the Wilson appointees to the Tariff Commission to abandon the effort to take the tariff out of politics, and the heart of Colorado's New Deal faction. In one term in the Senate he made important contributions to the progressive caucus and the New Deal. Had his career not been cut short by a stroke, this able, humane, charming and dedicated figure might have fulfilled his great potential.

Costigan's story is an interesting one in itself. In its narration the issues and events, the aspirations, accomplishments, and failures of the progressive movement and the New Deal unfold. The battles he fought did not end with his death, but have been refought in each decade on both the state and national levels. Only a few years ago descendants of his foes poured a fortune into a Colorado Senatorial election and succeeded in defeating his follower, John A. Carroll. The tides of Hamiltonianism and Jeffersonianism ebb and flow, but each time a larger portion of the citizenry has disembarked on the fertile soil of full participation. Costigan's place in the eddies of history has been assured by his life of dedication.

1. For a full discussion of the differences among progressives and the difficulty of defining progressivism see Fred Greenbaum, "Progressivism: A Complex Phenomenon," *New Politics*, VI (1968): pp. 85-90. For the purposes of this study progressives, using the lower case, refers to those who espoused a general political position then so identified, having in common a desire to lessen the economic and political power of big business and their allies among machine politicians; Progressive, using the upper case, refers to members of the Progressive Party.

Chapter II

DENVER

In 1877 the United States was in crisis. Not until March, amid cries that the Civil War be renewed, was the Presidential contest between Tilden and Hayes resolved. At the same time, in the fourth year of one of the nation's most severe depressions, one-fifth of the work force was unemployed and two-fifths was partially employed. In June a leader of the terroristic coal miners' group, the Molly Maguires, was executed. In July a new round of wage cuts led to a spontaneous nationwide railroad strike; during its course an infuriated Pittsburgh mob drove militiamen into a roundhouse, besieging the building until it burst into flames, workers seized control of East St. Louis, and everywhere railroad property was attacked with such fury that armories were erected in the new urban frontier.

Simultaneously investors were struggling for dominance over the sources of wealth. In the nation's capitol, Colis Huntington of the Southern Pacific and Thomas Scott of the Pennsylvania Railroad were in furious competition. In Colorado, the newest state of the union (1876), the Atchison, Topeka and SantaFe and the Denver and Rio Grande battled for the right to tap the mineral wealth of the western slope of the Rockies. In this year George Purcell Costigan Sr., a young Irish lawyer, led his family into this promising region of the state.

Edward Prentiss Costigan, the second son born to George, and his Spanish wife, Emilie Sigur, was but three when his family moved from the Virginia tideland to the mountainous southwest Colorado, residing first in Lake City, and then in Ouray and Telluride. His father became a leading citizen in this mining area. A successful law practice led to a county judgeship, a post he could afford to hold because his investments in mining ensured the comfort of his family for many years. The Judge, as his children often referred to him, finally settled the family in Denver where both his youngsters excelled in their studies. George Jr., Edward's brother, was to become a professor of law and an editor of case books.

Physically, Edward was not prepossessing. He was asthmatic, short in height, and slender, though his shoulders were large for his size. Even in his youth his sharply etched features were not handsome.

Edmund Wilson once referred to "his Spanish hatchet-face and his dry yellow skin." When he spoke, however, he became a compelling figure. His voice was deep, his accent precise; he sounded his "h's" "as if they were strokes from a bell of bronze."

Costigan early displayed the oratorical skills he was to use so effectively in later life; he was singled out to deliver graduation orations at East Denver High and Harvard University. On the stump "the smooth and even cadence of his voice and ready vocabulary commanded close attention." During the New Deal days he was considered one of Washington's three best radio speakers. His spellbinder's voice, was complemented by a sharp, incisive mind expressed so eloquently that some of his meticulously crafted speeches are models of rhetorical excellence. Journalist Robert G. Allen said in 1932:

"I have covered the Senate for six years during which time I have heard hundreds of addresses. But I want to say that in all my experience here, without exception, your speech on Wednesday was one of the most beautiful and telling I have ever heard. It was a gorgeous piece of work.

"It would have to be, to move a pretty hard-boiled and speech weary reporter."

Like many of his progressive contemporaries, Costigan embraced his political philosophy with a self-righteous fervor, an uncompromising certainty in the validity of his views. Yet his advocacy of a position never descended into personal attacks. Firm in his beliefs, he was personally tolerant of others. Still, when forced to choose between personal friendship and his singleminded devotion to political principle, friendship was unhesitatingly sacrificed. While he recognized that no reformer could achieve even a modicum of success if he completely eschewed political practices, his career was marked chiefly by a dedication to his ideas.

Even in his first national campaign Costigan chose to follow his convictions rather than political expediency. In the 1896 and 1900 Presidential elections he and his brother canvassed the silver states of Colorado and Utah in behalf of Republican orthodoxy—gold and protection. Edward backed the conservative junior Senator, Edward Oliver Wolcott, although Colorado's insurgents were supporting senior Senator Henry Teller, the Republican Party's leading silver spokesman. Wolcott advocated silver coinage, but Costigan, more orthodox on fiscal matters at that time, strode into the Lake City mining district to attack the "silver fetish." [1]

His strong sense of social justice and total commitment to democracy guided him throughout his career as a progressive Republican, a Progressive, and a New Deal Democrat. As Progressive candidate for governor in 1912, he refused to consider a possible coalition with Republicans that might have placed him in the statehouse at the expense of his fledgling party. Two years later, though again a gubernatorial candidate, he sacrificed middle class support in order to aid striking coal miners whose cause he considered just. He was the chief sponsor of an anti-lynching bill though Colorado had few Negroes and many transplanted southern whites. And he voted to reduce the sugar tariff while a resident of the nation's leading sugar producing state. It was such dedication to principles that Costigan brought to the corporate and machine dominated politics of Denver.

By the end of the century the United States was the world's leading industrial power. Resurgent farmers, led by William Jennings Bryan, twice were thwarted by the election of William McKinley. The Spanish-American War committed the nation to a policy of Empire. Passage of the Gold Standard Act laid the silver issue to rest while increased gold production, the growth of urban markets, and the return to prosperity eased rural pressures. Many Americans, however, were disturbed by the growing concentration of economic power and wealth and Ida Tarbell had already begun delving into the questionable history of Standard Oil. Together with Lincoln Steffens' revelations about urban politics her articles were to stir the cauldron of resentment that simmered into the progressive movement. While Steffens did not include Denver in his articles, he had assured interested residents, during a visit, that the Speer machine was a match for those of the cities he had publicized.

During this decade of a nation's transformation, Edward Costigan graduated from East Denver High in 1892 and attended Harvard College until an extended illness interrupted his studies. He travelled through Europe for a time and then joined his brother in Salt Lake City, where he campaigned for McKinley in 1896 and was admitted to the bar the following year. His return to Denver was preceded by the completion of his work at Harvard.

Costigan returned to a new life in a new Denver. Personal affairs were drastically altered when he married Mabel Corey, a high school classmate who was to be his active political companion as well as a devoted wife. In later years she was to achieve prominence in her own right in such movements as the National Consumer's League and the

Progressive Party of 1924. The Costigans were a happy and distinguished young couple.

Since the senior Costigan had considerable status in the community, Edward experienced little difficulty in launching a successful law firm with an old family friend, Frank Goudy. They had a typical western law practice—general law, incorporation of small firms, and mining claim cases. Edward supplemented his income through investments in real estate and mining. His legal skill attracted attention and, with George J. Kindel, he promoted the interests of Denver in freight rate cases. Soon he was known as an outstanding western expert on rate problems.

Talent and inclination brought Edward and Mabel Costigan into local politics and they quickly assumed a position of leadership in Denver's reform movement. While Edward had been absent from the city for some years, in his high school days he had been elected class president and Mabel served as class secretary. In Denver, as in other small cities, there was considerable continuity in social circles; the Costigans figured prominently in those circles.

Denver's reform movement resembled a repertory company. Its members held different positions in various organizations, but the cast on the letterheads remained the same. Edward Costigan became the president of the Civil Service Reform Association, a member of the executive board of the State Voters League and the Church Federation Against the Saloon, a precinct captain in the League for Honest Elections, a member of the Committee for Commission Government of the Chamber of Commerce, an investigator of vice for the Denver Law Enforcement League, an active member of the Anti-Saloon League and the League for Municipal Ownership, the Director of the Juvenile Improvement Association and a prime mover of the Citizen's Party. Together with Ben Lindsey, County Court Judge and founder of the nation's first Juvenile Court, former Senator T. M. Patterson, publisher of the *Rocky Mountain News*, and banker James Causey, Costigan labored tirelessly for Denver's regeneration.

Municipal Government Problems

When Costigan left for Harvard, Denver was still in the hands of a Republican machine that catered unabashedly to selfish private interests. Responsibility for Denver's affairs was divided between the state and the city, making it difficult to enact municipal legislation in the badly splintered state legislature. At the turn of the century, however, the Democratic machine of Robert W. Speer was well entrenched, having ousted the non-partisan reform administration of T. S. McMurray. Speer was a shrewd politician with a genius for both political organization and municipal administration. His followers were so adept at ballot box stuffing that they were collectively nicknamed "the big mitt." While in the beginning Speer leaned upon Democratic governors Alva Adams, C. S. Thomas, and James Orman, by the time that the insurgents pressed for enactment of a home rule charter drafted in part by Costigan, Speer's own strength was formidable.

Costigan and other reformers wanted a small unicameral city council. Speer had a large bicameral body enacted. They proposed the short ballot, initiative, referendum and recall. All they could obtain was inadequate referendum and initiative provisions, without recall. And the state legislature passed unsatisfactory election, civil service, franchise and public service measures. To complete the rout of Costigan and his friends, Speer was elected the first mayor under the city's new charter; he remained in this position for the rest of the decade.

Costigan found that Speer, like his predecessors, ran the town to suit the special interests, differing from his Republican predecessors only in his greater efficiency. In vain did Costigan object to the protection of prostitution, gambling and illegal drinking as well as the cozy relationship with the public utilities—the traction, water, electric, and gas interests.

Organized vice was offensive to Costigan and his fellow upper and middle class reformers. Denver's prostitution was flagrantly evident on "an artificial street lined on both sides with cubicles in which half-naked women sat for sale beside soiled beds and dirty washbowls. When a customer mounted the short flight of steps, a corrugated shutter was pulled down." Gambling was open and saloons freely ignored the legal closing time. In 1907, when Costigan and his fellow attorneys for the Christian Citizenship Union forced Governor Buchtel to close the gambling houses and enforce the Sunday and midnight closing laws for saloons, they found that the syndicate operated at least four gambling houses, 66 "policy" shops, 45 poker games in saloons and cigar stores, and 10 segregated poker and crap games for Negroes.

Most of Denver's residents were so anxious to acquire the conveniences of municipal transportation, lighting and heating that companies had been granted extensive privileges to provide them although the city government was offered little financial compensation and minimal assurance of performance. Some reformers insisted upon contracts fairer to the city's interests, while others, including Costigan, called for municipal ownership of municipal facilities. The utilities responded with unusually heavy campaign contributions to friendly politicians such as Speer in return for franchises, rights of way, and permission to extend their highly profitable business activities. The tramway company had financed Speer's first successful campaign when the McMurray administration insisted upon a percentage of gross receipts rather than a small increase in the firm's compensation to the city. At the same time the Denver Union Water Company resorted to the courts to prevent a rate reduction and municipal ownership. The utilities were not to be deeply disturbed for another decade.

The Speer machine did its work well. On the rare occassions when a dissenter was elected to local office, the machine was usually able to win him over with fat legal fees and easy campaign financing. If anti-corporation laws were passed, the chief clerk could manage to lose their text to prevent the registration necessary for them to become effective. When companies were sued for accidents caused by their negligence they somehow managed to escape payment through deadlocked juries. But the easiest way to protect Speer's clients was to prevent the election of opponents by tampering with election results.

Costigan's awareness of election fraud was heightened in 1902 when he became one of the "big mitt's" victims. Having failed to receive a nomination for the State Senate, he ran for the Assembly. The Republicans anticipated fraud and tried to supply enough poll watchers for Denver's fifteen worst precincts. Costigan was assigned a precinct in District F. At about 1:30 p.m. on election day a rough crowd gathered at the polls in his precinct. One tough approached Costigan, snatched his list of voters, and crumbled it while another threw ink that stained the candidate's hands. A "deputy" then told Costigan that he was making a disturbance; despite his protests, he was put out. A nearby policeman was unperturbed by the scene. In testimony before a Grand Jury, another Republican poll watcher reported that every time he challenged a suspected "floater" he was thrown out by a policeman. At the same hearing, a Democratic election judge admitted offering cash payments ($2) for each Democratic vote.

When the ballot boxes were opened over 5000 fraudulent ballots were found, including 1700 in Costigan's district alone. This evidence served as the chief basis for claims by Costigan and other Republican candidates from Arapahoe County (Denver and its suburbs) to the seats to which they felt they were entitled. The maneuvering that awaited them in the state legislature was an experience they did not soon forget.

The Republicans had a majority in the Assembly, but the preponderance of Democrats in the Senate was sufficient to give the latter control of a joint session. If the Republicans from Arapahoe County were seated, the balance would tip and a Republican would be sent to the Senate. Since the Republicans dominated the Assembly they could determine who was to be seated from Arapahoe, but the Republican followers of State Senator Goudy wanted to defeat Senator Wolcott more than they wanted a Republican Senator.[2]

Of the fifteen Arapahoe claimants, nine supported Wolcott—enough to elect him. Costigan had spoken from the same platform with him when many Republicans had pretended previous engagements, and he refused to pledge his opposition to the ex-Senator in order to be seated.

The Arapahoe delegation consisted of eleven representatives from Arapahoe County and four "float" representatives from Arapahoe and part of the adjoining counties. Of the fifteen Republican claimants Costigan had the largest vote; his claim was thus the strongest. Yet he was not seated and others were. The Speaker, an anti-Wolcott Republican elected with Democratic aid, chose a committee on elections consisting of five anti-Wolcott Republicans and four Democrats. After some hesitation the Republican majority recommended the removal of all fifteen Arapahoe Democrats and two Democrats from Las Animas County. When the matter reached the floor three Republicans from the southern counties defected and voted against seating any of the Republicans from Arapahoe proper. Only the "floats" and the two Las Animas Republicans were seated. A deal had been made, Costigan charged, because he had refused to commit the vote of the Arapahoe delegation against Wolcott.

The Republicans now had a majority of the combined houses but not a majority of the Senate. The Democratic Senate ousted two Republicans over the protest of the presiding officer (the Republican Lieutenant Governor) and gained control of a joint session once again. When the angry Republican Senators refused to sit with the Democrats, there were two Senates. The anti-Wolcott Republicans refused to meet with the Republican Senate, and after the first ballot for Senator by individual houses they called for an adjournment. The law called for a joint session once the balloting had started. Wasting no time, the Democratic members of the two houses, constituting a quorum, met alone. After some bickering they elected the former Republican leader of the silver forces, Henry Teller, while the anti-Wolcott Republicans prevented the Republican legislators from taking any action. Although Wolcott considered this reprehensible, he felt it was legal and he refused to contest the seat.[3]

Costigan was not a mere partisan when he rejected a political deal. He was completely sincere in what he said to the contesting Arapahoe delegation on November 18, 1902: "In these contests, we shall ask of the courts and of the legislature nothing but the strictest justice—no justice to ourselves merely, but justice to the great voting population of this country, whose will it has been sought fraudulently to frustrate."

Although Costigan was anxious to pursue a political career, he consistently rejected purely personal advancement. In 1911 he hesitated to allow progressive Republicans to use his name as a potential candidate because he felt individual fortunes "ought to be entirely subordinated to the very definite principles in which we are interested. Success for the cause means much; personal advancement is of no moment; and it would be grievous indeed, were the latter allowed to interfere with the former." However, his reluctance in this connection caused some very real concern to his associate, Merle D. Vincent: "It is to be regretted that Costigan does not have more personal ambition. For I do not consider ambition as inconsistent with good principles, and when the two are united in a man of ability, the result is an effective man.... Once we get Costigan where he is looked upon generally as one of our leaders and he realizes that he has assumed the duties of leadership, the responsibility, not-withstanding his lack of personal ambition, will cause him in my opinion to meet our expectation."

Despite the efforts of his partisan supporters, Costigan ran for no political office in the decade after 1902. He concentrated on redeeming Denver, attempted to convert the Colorado Republican Party into a vehicle for progressivism, and tried to advance the career of his good friend Ben Lindsey.

Ben Lindsey the Bantam Battler

One of the first of the Colorado progressives to risk his political career in the fight for honest and effective government, Benjamin B. Lindsey was a small, slight man but his fervent convictions and depth of feeling compensated for any lack of physical stature. He had lost a nomination for District Attorney because of his refusal to agree to limit gambling prosecutions to a token number. As County Judge he was unwilling to fire competent clerks in order to make room for "deserving Democrats." When he investigated a conspiracy to overcharge the courts for supplies he opened a hornet's nest. The machine harassed him by cutting off his electricity and denying him janitorial services. His enemies even tried to entrap him through prostitutes. An aroused *Rocky Mountain News* finally forced a trial of the court's profiteers, but it resulted in mocking fines of ten dollars per defendant.

Although frustrated, and treated as a political leper, Lindsey's natural sympathy for youthful offenders and his flair for publicity made him a national figure as the founder of the nation's first Juvenile Court, a court to which he devoted a quarter century of his life. A subject for numerous magazine articles, he focused the spotlight on corruption in Denver and became a natural center for reform politics. Consequently, he became the prime target for political extinction.

The Democratic machine quietly undercut Lindsey as early as 1901 but a major effort to defeat him came in 1904, when he tried to run as a non-partisan candidate for a non-partisan court. Already angered by his sniping at the existing system, the bi-partisan machine initially decided to deny him both nominations. An outcry by the Womans Club of Denver and the newspapers forced the Democratic leaders to nominate him lest Republicans place his vote catching name on the opposition ticket. After bipartisan nomination, he was endorsed by the Prohibitionist Party and the Peoples Party and was easily elected in the May municipal election.

But Costigan and other young Republicans cautioned their Democratic ally that the home rule charter had made the spring election invalid and that he would have to run again in November. Forewarned of another effort to deny Lindsey both nominations, Costigan, Causey, and J. S. Temple led Senator Wolcott's faction in a fight to control the Republican convention. A gallery of hooting and cheering Lindsey partisans intimidated the delegates into nominating the "kid's judge" and he was endorsed by all parties except the Socialists. Refusing to accept defeat, agents of the machine attempted to remove Lindsey's name from the election rolls as having been elected in the spring. Through invalidation of the spring election Lindsey could be replaced by the Board of Supervisors. The plot was foiled by a decision of the Colorado Supreme Court. Lindsey was the only Democrat to survive in the fall election.

As President Theodore Roosevelt continued to move to the left, progressive activity in Colorado was intensified. In 1905, inspired by the Illinois Legislative Voters' League, Lindsey organized the non-partisan State Voters' League to campaign for specific legislation—particularly the direct primary. Costigan became one of the League's most active members. In the following year he was deeply involved in forging a number of progressive alliances that were to come to fruition in the next decade.[4] He helped organize non-partisan support on specific issues in several elections. He was the close adviser and backer of Lindsey when the judge pursued the governorship on an independent ticket. And he was the Denver leader of the Republican caucus formed to enact progressive legislation.

Vice and Law Enforcement

Early in 1906, the Denver Law Enforcement League investigated commercialized vice. Costigan, as a member of the investigating committee, drafted a report in which it was charged that saloons were open all night in violation of law and that "Chili Parlors" were dens of iniquity. "Wine rooms," the report added in Victorian tones, "were and are in constant operation in violation of the law, and little girls are enticed into them, given knockout drops, ruined, and finally end in houses of ill fame." Gambling was open and well organized, while authorities looked on without concern. One night in February a patrolman shot and killed a man in a saloon two hours after the legal closing time; they had argued while shooting dice to decide who was to pay for the drinks. When the Denver Law Enforcement League complained about the matter, Mayor Speer responded that he had not been elected by the church element. The district attorney was equally deaf to their grievances.

The Municipal Election in 1906

The 1906 Denver municipal election was fought over the issue of new franchises for public utility corporations. Costigan served on the Law Committee of the Independent Citizen's Party in an investigation of the requests for franchises. The Denver Tramway Company, unable to obtain clear court support for its contention that it had a perpetual franchise, proposed a new charter in which it would extend its lines and pay the city $1,200,000 for municipal improvements. If it won its court case it could just ignore the new grant. One group of reformers urged a second streetcar charter as a means of forcing the Tramway into conceding better terms. Another, less controversial, proposal would have granted terminal facilities and some rights of way to the Union Pacific. Finally, the Denver Gas and Electric Company requested a twenty-year franchise and the transfer of the city-owned Lacombe plant to the company. In return, the Gas company offered the city only $50,000 annually, or about half what it then received from the city for gas and electricity.[5]

Even the self-interested Denver Post volunteered evidence against the demands of the utilities. It singled out the Tramway Company for particular criticism. The paper compared Denver's situation with that of other cities. In Denver the tramway used the streets gratis while paying taxes only after litigation and rebates. Kansas City annually received $400,000 in tramway compensation; Toronto was reimbursed by twenty percent of tramway gross receipts. Kansas City children were given free transportation; full fare was exacted from Denver's children. Toronto even had control over the routing of cars as well as an option to purchase tramway facilities at its physical valuation a year before franchise renewal.

Having considered such evidence, the majority of the Law Committee supported only the Union Pacific application. Edward Costigan, in a minority report, opposed all of the franchise requests. The Gas and Electric Company and the Denver Tramway Company, he contended, offered inadequate compensation. He rejected the suggestion that the city surrender its $100,000 interest in the Lacombe Lighting Plant to the Electric Company. As for the Union Pacific, its proposal conflicted with those of the Municipal Traction Company and the Denver Tramway Company to use the same streets.

The stakes were high; Costigan and his allies expected fraud. Having failed to prune the voting list of fraudulent registrants, aware that the district attorney had just dismissed charges against machine politician Billy Green of paying a registrar to fix the registration books, three days before the election, Costigan and Lucius Hoyt, attorneys for the League for Honest Elections, secured a temporary injunction from the reforming District Judge Frank T. Johnson, commanding that the Board of Fire and Police ensure an honest election. Judge Johnson appointed a full list of watchers and challengers for each precinct. The precautions were unavailing. Two watchers, Lucius Hoyt and James Causey, were ejected from the polls by a Democratic district captain. In an election marred by fraud, the public utility franchises carried by narrow margins.

Judge Johnson followed his injunction by seizing the ballot boxes in order to begin an honest recount. The City Attorney of Denver and the Election Commission obtained a temporary writ of prohibition against Judge Johnson from Chief Justice Gabbert of the Colorado Supreme Court and blocked Johnson's efforts.

Not to be totally denied, the insurgents succeeded in convincing Judge Mullins to hold an open grand jury inquiry into the election. Despite the obdurate silence of the chairmen of the Democratic and Republican parties, much evidence of fraud was uncovered. Only taxpayers could vote in a franchise election; consequently bogus tax receipts were distributed to his subordinates by the purchasing agent of the Tramway. The general manager of the Gas Company bought seven hundred lots on the prairies within city limits in order to ensure another seven hundred taxpayer's votes for his cause. Billy Green, who had been sent to jail after the previous election for ballot box stuffing, admitted ignorance of the location of a piece of land that he was supposed to own, although his right to vote was based on ownership of this land. The grand jury found 1073 bogus tax receipts—certainly enough fraudulent votes were cast to supply the 185 vote margin for the Tramway franchise and the 615 vote margin for the Gas franchise.

The battle between the reformers and the machine shifted to the Colorado Supreme Court. Costigan, as chief attorney for Judge Johnson, tried to prevent the city attorney from obtaining a permanent writ against the crusading judge. His success would have permitted the imposition of contempt of court sentences on those who engaged in election fraud. Judge Johnson had based his decision on the 1904 Tool Case, in which the Supreme Court had intervened to supervise the election. The city attorney distinguished between the original jurisdiction of the Supreme Court and the District Court, arguing that the higher court was a common law descent from the King's Bench, and as such could supervise an election. The lower court had no such power. In a presentation that won him statewide recognition, Costigan insisted that the District Court, not the Supreme Court had such original jurisdiction, for the Colorado Supreme Court was essentially a court of review. It had exceeded itself in 1904. Only the District Court was not restricted in its original jurisdiction. Fraudulent elections, he warned, were better than judicial subversion of the law. It was the citizens' responsibility, not the courts, to reassert the inviolability of the suffrage. "Judicial Revolution is not preferable either to executive despotism or the temporary rule of the mob," he declared. Unfortunately, the court sustained the City Attorney.

Emergence of the Progressive Republicans

While the Democratic and Republican reformers struggled against the Denver Democratic machine, the Colorado Republican progressives, inspired by the example of LaFollette and the fiery language of President Roosevelt, sought control of the state party by capturing city, town and county conventions. And in many counties they were to meet with success. Costigan led the most important struggle, the fight against the Denver machine; without control of the Denver delegation the progressives could never hope to capture the state Republican machinery. "Denver, corrupt and contented," Costigan declared, "can veto an otherwise triumphant Republicanism in Colorado."

The Republican machine in Denver was forged after the decline of Senator Wolcott as a power in the city and the county. Simon Guggenheim, a powerful industrialist who used his fortune to become United States Senator from Colorado, was one of the machine's chief financial backers. The machine was led by Bill Evans and A. M. ("Archie") Stevenson (the latter was to be instrumental in ensuring the renomination of Taft in 1912). The Republican machine cooperated with the "big mitt" of Boss Speer so that the corporations would have no fear about electoral results. In fact, Boss Speer undercut the 1906 Democratic state ticket, allowing two Democratic ward heelers to be jailed for continuing their normal ballot box stuffing despite contrary orders. The Denver Republican machine was well entrenched and had an effective working alliance with its Democratic counterpart. The Denver progressives were going to find it a tough opponent.

In May, 1906, Merle D. Vincent, a Paonia lawyer influential in Delta County and on the western slope, and one of the leading progressive Republicans in the state, agreed to lead a struggle for the progressive program, concentrating on the direct primary as the chief issue. He planned a campaign that would not be limited to 1906. Expecting severe opposition he insisted that they must be well financed if they were to attract any sort of effective support (and additional contributions). Each county, he suggested, must be canvassed so that at least one person prepared the county's work on local issues, candidates, and lists of people who would be receptive to literature. Progressive activity, he felt, should be concentrated in the most favorable counties—Mesa, Montrose, Boulder, Larimer, and Weld—and there engage in extensive education, agitation and large mass meetings. If properly organized, they could convince a bloc of legislative candidates to pledge themselves to the direct primary; with a nucleus of eight to ten effective legislators in the major party much could be accomplished, he predicted. The groundwork for a systematic campaign against the Republican Party machine had been laid.

Independent Judiciary

The action of the Colorado Supreme Court, preventing Judge Johnson's recount of the May election ballots, led to a concerted effort to elect a judiciary concerned with the needs of the people of Colorado rather than the interests of the corporations—the fight for an independent judiciary. This non-partisan movement was led by the Democratic "kid's judge," Ben Lindsey, and the Republicans Edward Costigan and J. S. Temple. Costigan stated the issue succinctly:

"Soon or late the courts touch all men intimately; soon or late the judiciary has an opportunity greatly to advance or vastly to interfere with the welfare of our individual citizens.

"Historically bad judges and bad judicial findings, and good judges, and good judicial findings have always been closely associated."

It was time, they felt, to replace judges who represented the special interests with judges who were public servants.

Unfortunately, the insurgents did not concentrate all of their political activity into the effort to elect non-parisan judges. When Ben Lindsey decided to run for governor the reformers dissipated their energies with internal bickering. While Alva Adams, the leading Democratic candidate, showed due reluctance to seek the office until sufficient sentiment for a draft had been created, well meaning Lindsey sympathizers fed his gubernatorial fever. Costigan, and other friends, failing to discourage him, remained loyal. Unable to capture the nomination but supported by the Denver *Post*, Lindsey decided to pursue an independent race. Costigan, Causey and Temple tried to convince him to withdraw for he was confusing the issues and endangering his career, but nevertheless, campaigned for their adamant friend. Unfortunately, Judge Frank Johnson, a Republican and a key figure in the franchise fight, declined to run for the Supreme Court on Lindsey's ticket lest the election of Democrats be promoted (and Lindsey had confided to an acquaintance that he expected his candidacy to foster the election of a Democratic legislature). Statewide Democratic candidates, who had been added to Lindsey's ticket at their own request, withdrew under pressure from Alva Adams. Lindsey's campaign was a fiasco. Even in Denver he drew few votes and the Republican machine swept the state.

Lost in the wreckage was Costigan's primary concern, the fight for an independent judiciary. All Republican candidates for the Supreme Court were victorious.

Judge Lindsey Challenged Again

Lindsey's poor showing in the gubernatorial election revitalized his opponents. In 1908 they so thoroughly controlled both county coventions that it was useless to seek renomination. Yet he could not relinquish without a fight the county judgeship he so cherished. Despite the overwhelming odds, despite contrary advice from his closest friends, Costigan, Causey and Temple, Lindsey (financed by a wealthy woman) determined to run for reelection on an independent ticket. The election law deliberately encouraged voting a straight ticket. Voters who wished to support an independent had to scratch the name of his opponent off the ticket and then vote for the independent. It was necessary to find the manpower to teach the voters how to scratch the tickets.

Lindsey polled his usual sources of support, and found that only Costigan would campaign actively. J. S. Temple did not participate, though he cast his vote for the judge. James Causey felt the pressure of the interests when he was dropped as director of his bank. Since he was away during the campaign period, he contributed only his vote to Lindsey's cause. Even the church coterie in Denver, with whom Lindsey had long been identified, disappointed him. He received some aid, but one rich church cancelled a prohibitionist meeting in its building when it found that he was to speak. Most of the leaders of the women's clubs succumbed to corporate pressure and abandoned him.

At first Lindsey was almost without newspaper support. The Denver *Post* would not even accept his paid advertisements; the Denver *Republican* was the mouthpiece of the Republican machine. Fortunately, Costigan and Causey had just convinced E. W. Scripps to establish the Denver *Express*, particularly to support Lindsey's work. And the Patterson press, which published both the *News* and the *Times*, endorsed Lindsey later in the season so that he had strong newspaper support before the campaign ended.

Still, Lindsey lacked an organization to do his legwork. Upon the recommendation of Toledo's reform mayor, Brand Whitlock, and Lincoln Steffens, he went to the labor unions for help. Their response amazed him; they canvassed voters, taught them how to scratch a ticket, held numerous meetings, and on Election Day mobilized his vote. The local youngsters, who loved the judge of the Juvenile Court, played hooky on Election Day to distribute literature. When the votes were tallied, Lindsey had won by 15,000 votes despite 5,000 invalidated ballots due to faulty scratching, and had outpolled his combined opponents. No one had doubted that the people supported him. Now the reformers were heartened by the knowledge that even stacked election laws could be overcome.

The Fight for the Direct Primary

With the taste of victory still fresh, Costigan and the Denver progressive Republicans threw their weight behind Merle Vincent. With continued financial support from Boyd Gurley and James Causey, Vincent began a systematic campaign against the party machinery in 1908 in an effort to enact a direct primary. He was stalled in his own county, for despite victories in the local primaries he was defeated in the county convention by the application of the unit rule. As a good Republican who still felt that more could be accomplished within the party than outside it, he declined to make the fight as an independent. While the progressive forces were beaten in the state convention by the Guggenheim-Evans machine, Senator Guggenheim's own defeat in the November elections made Vincent feel that there was still hope for the progressive Republicans. He could have added that the defeat of conservative Republicans in Ohio, Indiana, Minnesota, North Dakota and Montana, while Taft carried these states, indicated a groundswell of progressive sympathy. Thus, as the national party leadership shifted from Theodore Roosevelt to his handpicked successor, William Howard Taft, the Colorado progressive Republicans girded themselves for the battles to come, confident of continued inspiration on the national scene.

---

1. As a Senator, Wolcott was a conservative Republican. Although, like Mark Hanna, he supported the right of labor to organize and he backed labor's demand for immigration restriction, he opposed the eight hour day for government employees. A former railroad attorney, he opposed the safety appliance bill of 1893 and supported a bill to lessen the restrictions of the Interstate Commerce Act on pooling. He was not too concerned about the tariff, but he accepted the Republican high duty policy. As an occasional speculator he opposed a tax on grain options and futures despite the demands of Colorado grain interests. In 1904 he led a group of reform Republicans in a successful effort to nominate Ben B. Lindsey for County Judge and thus prevented the machine from defeating him. The Democrats then felt compelled to renominate Lindsey.

2. In addition, President Theodore Roosevelt opposed the election of Wolcott. Roosevelt had his friend, Philip Stewart, use Presidential patronage to weaken Wolcott, an ally of Mark Hanna. Roosevelt wanted a clear path to the 1904 nomination.

3. Costigan and the Wolcott forces claimed that Teller was elected as the result of a deal between the Democrats and the Goudy Republicans.

4. For a fuller analysis of the events of this year see Fred Greenbaum, "The Colorado Progressives in 1906," *Arizona and the West*, VII (1965): pp. 21-32.

5. With the aid of Judge Palmer a delinquent tax claim of $61,919 was settled between the city and the Tramway for $25,000. The valuation of the Tramway and Water Companies was then reduced by twenty per cent.

Chapter III

PROGRESSIVISM AT ITS APEX

It was during the administration of William Howard Taft that progressive Republicans on the national scene began to coalesce—in the House of Representatives in an effort to strip Speaker Cannon of his dictatorial powers and in the Senate to fulfill Taft's pledge for tariff revision.

Taft took the oath of office amid high hopes on the part of the progressive Republicans. He had been chosen by Teddy Roosevelt, an inspiration to most progressives, and his campaign speeches and inaugural address had strengthened their expectations. His competence had been proven during a distinguished career. A widely quoted and admired judge (albeit somewhat anti-labor) he had been considered for the United States Supreme Court at the age of thirty-two. So skillful had he been in pacifying the Philippines that even former rebels demonstrated against an effort to recall him for a Supreme Court nomination. As Roosevelt's Secretary of War he had been the Administration's international trouble shooter. Unfortunately, as President he proved to be indolent and lacking in political skill.

Taft first aroused the ire of the progressives in the fight against "Uncle Joe" Cannon, Speaker of the House. Cannon had used the very considerable powers of his office to save the country from the "wild ideas" of Teddy Roosevelt and his followers. Nevertheless, Roosevelt had convinced Taft that no program could be passed without the help of Cannon. Drawing upon the support of the President, Cannon deftly parried insurgent efforts to dilute his power both in the 1909 regular Congressional session and the special session called by Taft to revise the tariff.

Initially, when Taft called for tariff adjustment he had indicated a revision downward. Since the House—passed Payne bill lowered more rates than it raised, it did not meet serious insurgent resistance. Confident of Taft's assistance, Senate progressives expected to reduce rates further. Much to their surprise and displeasure, the President veered between support and opposition of their efforts, and finally used his patronage against them. Then, at Winona, he analyzed both the strengths and weaknesses of the bill and concluded, in an ill-chosen phrase, that it was the best Republican tariff that had ever been passed. The progressives were furious.

As if to complete the break, the Pinchot-Ballinger controversy within the administration boiled to the surface and provided the insurgents with two martyrs. Gifford Pinchot, the leading exponent of Roosevelt's conservation policy, condemned Secretary of Interior Richard Ballinger for his handling of the Cunningham claims to Alaskan coal fields. Whether these claims were only technically deficient, as Ballinger's proponents maintained, or morally deficient, as charged by Louis Glavis, a minor Interior Department official, is not important here. Glavis' pursuit of the issue even after Taft had overruled him, his recruitment of Chief Forester Pinchot as an ally, and his exposé for *Colliers Weekly*, resulted in the dismissal of Pinchot and himself, and precipitated a Congressional investigation. While the administration was exonerated, the disclosure that Attorney General Wickersham had predated a memorandum brought charges by dissidents that corruption had been whitewashed.

The progressives had misjudged the rotund President. Taft had never intended to break new ground, but to complete and perfect Roosevelt's program. Hampered by a judicial temperament, Taft lacked Roosevelt's flamboyance and his political acumen. While there were few progressives in Congress during Roosevelt's tenure, Taft was faced with a strong minority within his own party and a resurgent Democracy. Unable to recognize the shift in the temper of the country, he greeted the opponents of his Congressional leaders with anger, although they were more responsive to his program than Cannon and Aldrich. Disappointed, the progressives were not disheartened, and led by George Norris, they returned to the attack in 1910. First, on January 7th, the House adopted his resolution to choose the committee to investigate the Ballinger-Pinchot controversy rather than to permit its choice by the Speaker. Then, on March 15th the appropriation for automobiles for the Speaker and Vice-President was eliminated. And finally, with some brilliant parliamentary maneuvering, Norris succeeded in stripping the Speaker of his power to appoint the members of the all-powerful rules committee. Cannon was beaten and an effort to unseat him was only thwarted by Norris' intervention.

The lines of battle were being clearly drawn. Taft drifted towards the conservative Congressional leadership while progressives formed a center of political power separate from the Executive and the traditional Congressional leadership. Every move by Taft drove the insurgents into more vigorous opposition. When he attempted to amend railroad regulations they completely rewrote the Mann-Elkins bill. His efforts, in 1910, to purge the Republican party of progressive legislators backfired; they were reelected and many conservatives defeated. His convening of a special session in 1911 of the new Democrat-controlled Congress in order to pass the Canadian Reciprocity Treaty stimulated agrarian opposition to the reduction of rates on agricultural products in order to export more industrial goods. Taft triumphed, only to have the treaty rejected by the Canadian legislature. Despite the enactment of considerable forward-looking legislation the special session had damaged Taft's image even further. Disregarding the revelation of a slush fund, the Senate seated William Lorimer of Illinois. And the President rejected tariff reductions on items purchased by farmers. Finally, he vetoed statehood for Arizona and New Mexico since a provision for judicial recall dared "to pass upon questions involving the judicial interterpretation of the law," challenging the democratic commitments of such insurgents as Costigan.

The Fight for Municipal Ownership

While dismayed by Republican polarization in Washington, Costigan continued the progressive fight in Denver and Colorado. Inspired by Lindsey's victory in 1908, Costigan and the reformers no longer feared political activity independent of the two major parties. Emboldened by the publicity following Lindsey's revelations about Denver corruption in *Everybody's*, they demanded municipal ownership of the water plant and put candidates in the field for alderman, supervisors and election commissioners.

In 1910 the franchise of the Denver Union Water Company was to expire. Three years before, the Speer Administration and the Denver Union Water Company, implementing the charter's recapture clause, chose a five man board which returned an appraisal of $14,440,000 in 1909. Yet a year later the company's tax assessment was only $2,200,000 and many citizens grew angry. When the Water Company requested a new franchise that offered little to the city, anger was transformed into a campaign for municipal ownership.

Costigan and the reformers formed the Citizen's League to spark the drive for municipal ownership by initiating an amendment to the city charter. The League proposed to create a three member public utilities commission with full power to acquire and operate a waterworks system for the city (the amendment designated the members of the first commission). Since the city engineer had estimated the cost of duplicating the water plant at $8,000,000, the amendment empowered the commission to submit a bond issue to the electorate for that amount for capital equipment, unless the company was willing to sell its plant for $7,000,000. At the same time, the Citizen's League supported three candidates for election commissioners and proposed an amendment for the initiative, referendum and recall.

The 1910 campaign was fought with fervor. Costigan had rejected the nomination for election commissioner but speaking at various meetings throughout the city, he campaigned vigorously for the League's proposals. His labor was rewarded. Despite the company's efforts to confuse the issue with two misleading amendments, the Citizen's Party won a sweeping victory. Their amendment was adopted while the projected franchise of the Denver Union Water Company was overwhelmingly defeated. They elected all three water commissioners, two aldermen, and two of the three election commissioners.[1]

The 1910 Republican Convention

While progressives, Republican and Democratic, were engaged in a united struggle in Denver, Merle Vincent continued the drive to capture the statewide Republican Party. In correspondence in early 1909, Costigan and Vincent had agreed that important issues could not be sidetracked for party harmony, but that personal attacks on Republican bosses were meaningless unless the rise of future Republican bosses could be prevented. On June 11, 1910 Vincent announced his intention to seek the Republican gubernatorial nomination. The progressive Republicans rallied to his banner. Costigan predicted that even if Vincent did not win he would still be the most formidable independent factor in Republican politics in 1912. William Allen White and Senator J. L. Bristow journeyed from Kansas to further Vincent's campaign. But even Roosevelt's endorsement in person could not dislodge the Republican machine.

The campaign was launched at a convention in Colorado Springs on July 30, 1910. At its conclusion a declaration of progressive Republican principles was drawn up. Embodied in a circular written by Costigan and J. S. Temple, it summoned supporters for their insurgent movement.[2]

Returning to Denver, Costigan and his colleagues planned their battle against the county Republican machine. On September 2, 1910, following a visit by Roosevelt, they formed the Progressive Republican Club of Denver. Costigan was elected president. Despite their open commitment to direct government, the insurgents refused to participate in the selection of delegates to the Republican convention, charging that the primary was corporation controlled. Having outdrawn the Evans machine in the May municipal election, they claimed to be the real Republican Party in Denver. On September 12, with more attention to publicity than reality, Costigan announced that a Denver progressive Republican slate was going to demand recognition from the state convention.

Party regulars could not be sympathetic to the protests of a delegation that did not participate in the party primary. In addition, the convention was dominated by conservatives. The platform committee supported the Taft administration. It endorsed the controversial Payne-Aldrich tariff, which had become anathema to progressives, and it opposed the initiative and referendum. The duly elected delegates from Denver had supported the same conservative platform and candidates. In fact, Willis V. Elliot, the head of the credentials committee, was one of the delegates whose seat was being contested. Consequently, the State Central Committee voted to table the contest. They even refused a ten minute hearing to Costigan, the spokesman for the contesting Denver delegation. Costigan voiced his objections to the press. ". . . The real reason was the immovable adherence of our delegation to the square-deal doctrines of Theodore Roosevelt and the fundamental moral, economic principles of such progressives as LaFollette, Cummins, Dolliver, and Bristow, which elevate the man above money in government." The Central Committee of Denver represented not the Republican voters but the utilities, he charged. The state organization was the pliant tool of the special interests, he added; it misrepresented the Republican voters. The party must be reorganized to reflect the people's interests and not the special interests.

If the party was to be reshaped in the image of the progressives, this was not the year in which it would be done. The majority report of the resolutions committee praised Senator Guggenheim (a *bete noir* of the progressives), endorsed the Taft administration (with which the progressives were now feuding), and opposed the initiative and referendum, although it commended its submission to the electorate. Merle Vincent proposed a minority report calling for endorsement of the initiative and the referendum, a Public Utilities Commission, physical valuation of railroad property, and an Anti-Pass Law. But the convention ended with careful compromises.

The initiative and the referendum were neither condemned nor praised, and a statement was issued that the amendment was out of the hands of conventions and in the hands of the electorate. Even the gubernatorial nomination fell to a moderate as the candidate of the extreme conservatives withdrew. Vincent was overwhelmed by a vote of 931 to 36. All that the progressives salvaged from the convention was the Congressional nomination of I. N. Stevens, a shrewd politician, suspect by many insurgents, who identified himself with the progressives without ever breaking his ties with the bosses.

The "Platform Democrats"

The Democratic progressives were more successful than their Republican counterparts.

The struggle within the Democratic Party revolved around the redemption of the pledges in the 1908 party platform. In that year the liberal "Honest John" Shafroth[3] was elected Governor on a progressive platform calling for the initiative and referendum, ballots that did not identify the candidate's party affiliation, direct primary, a Public Utilities Commission, a bank guarantee bill, and a railroad commission bill. Since the 1909 legislative session enacted only the organization of the Bureau of Labor Statistics, a Factory Inspection Law, and a Campaign Expenses Law, disappointed "Platform Democrats" joined together to redeem the party pledges. Many Denver reformers were active in this group and the Republican Costigan was asked to speak at their meeting. Benjamin C. Hilliard, formerly president of the Citizen's Law Enforcement League and later to join the Progressive Party, was elected president of the "Platform Democrats." The vice-president was the former Governor, Charles S. Thomas, an active participant in the struggles of the Citizen's League for commission government and for municipal ownership of the water plant. T. M. Patterson publicized their activities in his *Rocky Mountain News* and Ben Lindsey drafted and promoted child labor legislation.

In August 1910, Governor Shafroth called a special legislative session, strategically timed so that an imminent election might make the legislature more amenable to a redemption of the pledges, but his efforts met with frustration. Except for the submission of a proposal for the initiative and the referendum to the electorate for approval, the Democratic machine and its Republican allies hampered the rest of his program. The contest over the most important issue, the direct primary, resulted in a compromise. The candidate recommended by the party convention was to receive top place on the ballot, followed by other candidates in order of their vote. Aspirants nominated by petition would come last. An inadequate Registration Bill and a disappointing Railroad Bill were enacted before adjournment.⁴

The 1910 Election

When Costigan and the Denver progressive Republicans and C. S. Thomas and the Denver "Platform Democrats" failed to obtain recognition by their respective state parties as the legitimate Denver organization, they decided to extend their victorious municipal alliance. After Costigan had suppressed an effort of the Republican machine to capture the progressive Republican meeting, the progressive Republicans, the Platform Democrats, and the Citizen's Party endorsed a unified county ticket pledged to progressive legislation.

Still, Costigan and the progressive Republicans were not ready to abandon the Republican state ticket and they endorsed the moderate Republican candidate for Governor, while their county allies supported John Shafroth. Under pressure from the machine all the Republican judicial candidates except John Garrigues rejected progressive Republican endorsement. Only those Congressional candidates who committed themselves to active opposition to Cannonism received progressive Republican endorsement.

The Citizen's Party coalition proved effective. The electorate approved the initiative and the referendum; in a year of a Democratic landslide, the only three statewide Republican candidates to win had received progressive endorsement. The Citizen's Party county ticket came in behind the Democrats, but ahead of the Republicans. The progressive Republicans had outdrawn the Denver machine in both the May and November elections.

The Eighteenth General Assembly

Mayor Speer's determination to become United States Senator made it impossible for Governor Shafroth to redeem the platform pledges despite a solid Democratic majority. The "Platform Democrats" refused to caucus on the choice of a Senator until the platform had been enacted, and a convention of Democratic editors, assembled by the Speer machine, demanded that the pledges first be fulfilled and then the most effective advocate of the platform should be chosen for the Senate. After 120 days a Democratic caucus was assembled, but Alva Adams blocked Speer. On the next day the legislature adjourned without having elected a Senator and without having considered much important legislation. The State Senate could not resolve the differences between the two bills for recall passed by the lower house and that issue remained unresolved. After much lobbying by Lindsey's aid, John Phillips, the legislature passed a Child Labor Law. In addition an Eight Hour Law, a law to force husbands to support their families, a Bank Guarantee Law and an improved Voting Registration Law were enacted.

The Progressive Republican League

Costigan and the Denver progressive Republicans were not satisfied with these limited accomplishments. They complained that the Democratic Eighteenth Assembly had been reckless in its violation of platform pledges.

Still less were they satisfied with the state of the Colorado Republican Party. The Colorado machine, they charged, no longer expressed the principles of the Republican Party. In a circular, Costigan's organization attacked violations of platform pledges, seating of candidates who had been defeated at the polls, refusal to expel a Republican state senator who openly admitted taking a bribe and, in general, bipartisan cooperation in favor of Denver public utility corporations.

While the Colorado progressive Republicans were locked in combat with the state machine, their national counterparts, determined to prevent the renomination of Taft, formed the National Progressive Republican League.[5] Separate organizations within the Republican Party were certainly not new. During the "Gilded Age" the Liberal Republicans had been formed to challenge the drift of the era. In Colorado, Costigan had been active in founding the Roosevelt League in 1907 and the Denver Progressive Republican Club in 1910. Dissidents within the state had always had relations with their counterparts elsewhere. Costigan often requested information from other insurgent organizations, notably those of Wisconsin and Illinois, while Lindsey sought funds to distribute 20,000 copies of Senator Jonathan Bourne's speech on representative government in Oregon. Even before the formation of a statewide organization of progressive Republicans, the Denver Progressive Republican Club had affiliated with the National Progressive Republican League.

The failure of the progressives within their own parties led Costigan and the Denver progressive Republicans to move in two directions. First, they participated in the organization of the Direct Legislation League of Colorado, in alliance with their allies on the western slope, in order to implement the newly enacted initiative and referendum laws by submitting progressive laws to the electorate. The Supreme Court had not yet decided whether prospective amendments had to be published in one newspaper that circulated in each of the counties or a different newspaper in each county, and the expenses of the latter interpretation, Costigan reported, would limit initiative activities.

The second effort was towards creating a statewide organization of progressive Republicans to affiliate with the National Progressive Republican League.

Merle Vincent affirmed the necessity of an effective statewide organization. He hoped that Costigan, with his unusual ability, would accept the leadership. Attempting to lighten James Causey's despair, he reminded him that while the state was corrupt it was not yet contented. He thought that Causey was too demanding to expect the average person to devote the same energy to politics that he devoted to his business. Even with limited funds, this organization could distribute literature, correspond with local leaders, and, in general, keep in contact with all parts of the state. Montrose and Delta counties, he said, were organizing and would be able to raise $1,000.[6]

The organizational banquet at Montrose, delayed to suit the convenience of the guest speaker, William Allen White, was held on September 9, 1911. In his own speech, Costigan trumpeted his progressive philosophy. "At the very least," he said, "we see in this gathering a baptism of prophecy in the Jordan waters of principle, for, whether those of us who are here are to stand as witnesses of the full noontide, or are merely to serve as heralds of the dawn, certain it is that a new morning of far greater governmental and economic justice is breaking over Colorado." This movement was national; it was "one manifestation of the ceaselessly operating law of evolution." The public utilities, he charged, had used their bipartisan machine "to elect, instruct and recall United States Senators, governors, judges, legislators and city councilors." Their motto should be: "The special interests give; the special interests take away. Blessed be the name of the special interests." In order to restore "a government responsive to the public will and guarding the public welfare" the state needed honest elections, commission government when desired, a corrupt practices law, the recall of unworthy public officials, the headless or pure Australian ballot, the short ballot, and perfected primary elections without conventions. But political demands were purely preliminary. "More fundamental yet, this movement seeks a more equal distribution of wealth through the enlargement of the bounds of human rights and opportunities." He advocated industrial accident compensation, the eight hour law for women, curbs and control of monopoly, an equalized tariff "to divide the burdens and expenses of government," and, above all, to weigh the needs and welfare of workers and consumers. The progressive movement "particularly contends that the conservation of men, women and children—their lives, their liberties and their opportunities—is the preeminent conservation policy of the world."

The national leader who best expressed these progressive principles was Senator Robert M. LaFollette of Wisconsin. As Governor he had broken the conservative state machine and had established a model of state government that the progressives of many states strove to imitate. Recognizing LaFollette's eminence, on October 16 the National Progressive Republican League endorsed him for the Presidential nomination. In his acceptance statement LaFollette affirmed that he would remain in the race until the Republican convention had made its decision. Suspecting the ambitions of Theodore Roosevelt, he declared that he would not withdraw in favor of any other candidate.

A national leader had been chosen. A statement of progressive principles had been drafted. Now the Colorado movement had to establish strength at the grass roots. They formed local Progressive Republican Clubs. Local progressives signed cards endorsing the movement and its principles, chose local officials, and supported the candidacy of Robert M. LaFollette for the Republican Presidential nomination. A solid organization was prepared to do battle in 1912.

Lindsey and the Charter Revision

While his Republican friends were preparing for the 1912 presidential nominating convention, Ben Lindsey was forced into another fight for his political life against both political machines. A charter revision consolidated the city and county of Denver and in the confusion that followed Lindsey found that his job had disappeared. Surprisingly, Mayor Speer, who had long cooperated with the Juvenile Court and was facing a tough election, appointed Lindsey to his old position, relying on a charter provision which permitted the mayor to fill vacant offices. Speer made it clear that this appointment was not an endorsement of Lindsey's charges of municipal corruption, but an effort to give the court legal standing. Lindsey had received a temporary reprieve, but a large fund had been raised to defeat the author of *The Beast,* and both major parties were expected to endorse his opponent. Despite the opposition of both political parties, despite charges that Lindsey was discrediting Denver with his articles and speeches, despite accusations that he neglected his work in favor of lecture tours, Lindsey was elected by a majority of 30,000 votes out of the 70,000 cast and the independent ticket swept the election.

Commission Government in Denver

This time Lindsey's reelection was coupled with a victory over Mayor Speer. The fight for municipal ownership of the water supply had not yet ended when Costigan and the Denver reformers undertook to destroy the political boss system and its alliance with favored business interests. By substituting a government of coequal commissioners for the relatively centralized mayoral system, Costigan and his associates hoped to prevent Boss Speer, and any future aspirants to his position, from exercising unilateral control of municipal politics.

Early in 1910 Costigan led a committee of three which examined similar experiments and drafted the necessary amendment. To effect the change the progressive coalition of 1910 united with unaffiliated citizens in a Non-Partisan Charter League. However, the Socialists blocked the reformers' effort to obtain the endorsement of the Trades and Labor Assembly. The elimination of partisan politics would not give the workers fair representation, they argued. Drawing upon their more radical and penetrating perception of power in American society, they foresaw that the machine could as easily control a commission as a mayor. The lines were drawn.

The reformers scurried through Denver, collecting 19,303 signatures. Fighting a delaying action, Speer's administration refused to accept the initiating petition, insisting that a charter convention was necessary to change the law. Nevertheless, a supervisor introduced a bill requiring a special election on the commission amendment. The city attorney unsuccessfully appealed to the Colorado Supreme Court to reverse the order of Judge Teller forcing a special election. While Costigan and a committee of lawyers tried to resolve the legal aspects of the problem, the reformers found a candidate capable of defeating Speer.

County Assessor Henry J. Arnold became the man of the hour—despite reservations the reformers might have had. When the County Commissioners reduced the assessment of the tramway and the depot, Arnold responded by refusing to impose additional real estate taxes enacted by the council, and Mayor Speer, without any legal authority, physically removed Arnold from the assessor's office. During the legal battle that ensued, the *Post,* under the editorship of George Creel, and the *News,* owned by T. M. Patterson, built Arnold into a hero and a new mayor was born.

At every meeting held by the insurgents the candidates publicly committed themselves to institute commission government if elected. Old Senator Patterson, fearing violation of the pledges once the candidates tasted office, forced Arnold to appoint a reformer as Police Commissioner. George Creel, the editor of the *Rocky Mountain News,* was chosen.

The new mayor disappointed his supporters. Unaware of the rising costs of municipal government they expected economy: the Arnold regime was even more expensive than that of Boss Speer. They expected progressive government: Arnold vetoed a minimum wage for city workers. They expected fair and reasonable administration: Arnold attempted to remove the Civil Service Commission for denying his wishes. They expected favorable treatment: Arnold refused Lindsey's requests for patronage and larger appropriations for his beloved Juvenile Court. They expected innovation: Arnold called Police Commisioner Creel's removal of clubs from the police force a criminal blunder, persistently obstructed Creel's efforts to acquire the City Farm as a hospital to rehabilitate prostitutes, and alienated his former allies by issuing an order restoring the sale of liquor in the red light district. As the reformers actively prepared for an election to secure commission government, the rift with Arnold became permanent.

The reformers themselves could not agree upon the best method to obtain commission government. While a group led by John Rush and Ben Lindsey wanted an initiated amendment, Costigan, felt that this approach was no longer valid. The Supreme Court of Colorado had declined to comment on the constitutionality of commission government until the amendment had actually passed and two members of the Court had indicated that the charter should be rewritten. A convention would be more representative, Costigan added, and would prevent a long court battle. Costigan's analysis was ignored and, as 1912 closed, initiative petitions were filed for an election on commission government. After an active campaign, hectic meetings, and exciting newspaper coverage, on February 14, 1913, the change was adopted by 5,000 votes. By this time Arnold was so thoroughly discredited that he received little support as a candidate for commissioner in the election of May 20th. His appeal, questioning the validity of the amendment, was rejected by the Supreme Court and when the Court also validated preferential voting, the victory of the reformers seemed complete.

The Fight For LaFollette

Exhilarated by the progressive climate in the state, reflected in the events in Denver and in the Democratic Party, the progressive Republicans, now affiliated with the National Progressive Republican League, strove to obtain control of the state organization and to choose a LaFollette delegation to the National Presidential Nominating Convention. The resourceful conservative Republicans responded with the formation of a Taft Republican Club and a policy statement opposing the initiative, referendum and recall. When Taft visited Denver, Costigan, despite his recorded opposition, cooly called upon Taft to disavow the conservative faction for its statement was contrary to the declared position of the Colorado Republican Party. To placate the insurgents Taft repudiated the conservative club and a new Taft Republican Club was formed. Naturally his antagonists were not mollified; they reiterated their commitment to principles, not men, and Taft, despite his personal qualities, could not win their support. They favored LaFollette. Costigan had long been an admirer of the Wisconsin leader. He was a Colorado delegate to the National Progressive Republican Convention in Chicago in October 1911 when LaFollette was chosen the progressive candidate for the Republican nomination despite Roosevelt's Secretary of the Interior, James Garfield, who wanted to endorse principles and leave the question of a candidate open. Costigan was one of the five composers of the resolutions. Upon his return, the Colorado progressive exuded confidence. Taft would not even go before the convention, he predicted. Moreover, he had been reliably informed that Teddy Roosevelt was not a candidate for the nomination, he reported, missing the import of Garfield's maneuvers.[7]

Increasingly, Costigan and the progressives committed themselves to LaFollette's candidacy. They organized a Colorado LaFollette Club, contacted sympathizers throughout the state, dispatched membership cards with the progressive platform printed on them, and requested that they recruit members and organize local clubs. In November, Costigan called upon the leader of the Taft forces to jointly request that statewide Republican primaries for Presidential electors be held. The challenge was not accepted. By December, the two factions were so thoroughly divided that Merle Vincent questioned the wisdom of participating in the Lincoln Day Dinner. Costigan reassured him that Republican State Chairman Jesse MacDonald had agreed that the dissidents would only be committed to their advocacy of Republicanism and that a national progressive speaker would be invited. To refuse to attend would open the insurgents to charges of not being Republicans. The breach between the Taft and LaFollette forces could no longer be bridged. Yet by this time the LaFollette campaign was beginning to peter out.

LaFollette and Roosevelt

While Roosevelt was despondent, LaFollette was elated as a candidacy made for principle responded to his extra-ordinary campaign and the ardor of his followers; momentum mounted through sheer fervor. Had LaFollette received Roosevelt's support as the campaign reached its peak, he might have been nominated. But, while Roosevelt praised LaFollette, he distrusted him privately and refused to endorse him. Once victory seemed possible the attitude of many insurgents changed. If there was any possibility of nominating a progressive would it not be wise to put forth their strongest candidate and thus ensure victory?

When Roosevelt completed his second term he went to Africa on a hunting trip. Despite his pique at Taft's appointments, negative reports from his correspondents, and Pinchot's documented bill of grievances against the President, Roosevelt still hoped to heal the rift in the party and restore its dominant position in the nation. Upon his return, his refusal to endorse either group left the progressives uneasy and Taft furious. Beginning in August 1910, Roosevelt campaigned through the west to reunite the party, enunciating his program of New Nationalism.

Although he discouraged their efforts, many of the most important progressive leaders had never ceased to woo the Sagamore sage. He had never publicly refused to run if called upon and his possible availability stalled the LaFollette campaign. Yet, Roosevelt had no intentions of seeking the nomination during the summer and autumn of 1911. Nor did he want LaFollette chosen. He wanted Taft to be the Republican candidate, for he was certain that 1912 would be a Democratic year. Once Taft and the conservatives had been beaten, the party would have to come to him for reorganization in a sane progressive mold. His criticism of Taft's policies became increasingly open. When anti-trust action against United States Steel specified the absorption of the Tennessee Coal and Iron Company by the steel behemoth during Roosevelt's administration (which had had Roosevelt's consent) a furious Roosevelt made a public rebuttal in the *Outlook,* advocating corporate regulation in place of trust busting. The reaction from conservatives and progressives was so favorable that by December, Roosevelt, still wary of an outright candidacy, permitted his supporters to work in his behalf. Carefully examining all of the contingencies, including the possibility that someone other than Taft could be nominated, and the chance that a loss by Taft to an able Democrat might make a victory in 1916 impossible, Roosevelt finally decided that he could win the nomination and whip any Democrat.

Increasingly, LaFollette heard reports that Roosevelt wanted desperately to be President again and was only reluctant to become a candidate against Taft. Press reports of Roosevelt's candidacy were persistent by the time the Ohio insurgents met and drew up a declaration of principles without endorsing LaFollette. Following the lead of Teddy's intimate friend, James Garfield, they declared that the progressive organization was in behalf of a movement rather than any particular candidate. By early January 1912, Gifford Pinchot, who had previously endorsed LaFollette unequivocally, openly told the Ohio Progressive Republican Convention that it would be wise to crystallize the Roosevelt sentiment so that all of the progressive support could be marshalled for the Republican Convention. Four days after these conferences Roosevelt was endorsed by the governors of Kansas, Michigan and West Virginia. Then, after arranging with six Republican governors to issue an appeal to him to seek the nomination, he became an open candidate. While many of his most fervent supporters had endorsed LaFollette and could not withdraw in good conscience, they could promote Roosevelt's candidacy. The drive for uninstructed delegates, or delegates instructed for both LaFollette and Roosevelt (in line with Pinchot's suggestion) was intensified.

Finally, a group of leading progressive financial backers requested that LaFollette withdraw from the race. Promised sufficient monetary support from other sources, LaFollette issued a statement that he had no intention of quitting. The progressive forces were split, but LaFollette was still their official candidate.

LaFollette and Roosevelt in Colorado

Although the Colorado Progressive Republicans had endorsed LaFollette, reports from local leaders indicated that Roosevelt was more popular than LaFollette even in LaFollette strongholds. From the beginning of the campaign, Costigan realized that while the insurgents might nominate a progressive Congressional delegation, at best they could obtain a divided delegation to the Republican National Convention. The state had always been pro-Roosevelt and the Colonel's friends were able to stifle the LaFollette boom while building sentiment for the Rough Rider. Facing this situation J. S. Temple wrote to Gifford Pinchot for advice. After insincerely declaring his loyalty to LaFollette, Pinchot suggested a community of interest between the LaFollette and Roosevelt forces, each electing delegates where they were strongest and combining their strength against Taft at the National Convention.

In a banquet in the Albany Hotel on January 16, 1912, Roosevelt won a major victory. Official LaFollette supporters adopted the Garfield-Pinchot line and declared both candidates to be leaders of the progressive movement. Two weeks later Costigan wrote to LaFollette's campaign manager, W. L. Houser, informing him that Colorado was pro-Roosevelt. The progressive campaign against Taft would be enhanced by supporting each of the two progressive candidates where his strength was greatest. "This must not be construed as meaning that Senator LaFollette's friends have weakened in their advocacy of his leadership," Costigan earnestly wrote, but only reflected a change in political conditions. Costigan seemed unaware that Roosevelt's friends on LaFollette's staff had helped alter the political climate.

The evening after Costigan's letter was posted, LaFollette made his ill-fated speech on improper publication pressures to the Periodical Publisher's Association at Philadelphia. Fatigued by the stress of the campaign and personal concern for his daughter who was scheduled for an operation the following day, harrassed by the desertion of his supporters, bothered by indigestion, he arrived at the banquet three hours late and delivered an interminable, dull and repetitious speech.

Roosevelt's supporters had found a way out of their dilemma. They immediately informed the newspapers that LaFollette had become incapacitated. The rumor mills once again predicted his immediate withdrawal. Erstwhile LaFollette supporters drafted a statement of withdrawal and Medill McCormick of LaFollette's staff deliberately leaked news that LaFollette would quit. LaFollette refused to sign the statement. Van Valkenberg's Philadelphia *North American,* George Record of New Jersey and Gifford Pinchot, all of whom were thought close to LaFollette, made open declarations that LaFollette was too ill to continue his candidacy and would retire from the race. The drift of LaFollette's supporters into the Roosevelt camp became a stampede.

At this time Costigan came to Washington to investigate the rumors about LaFollette. While Senator Gronna of North Dakota visited the LaFollettes to express sympathy to Mrs. LaFollette and found her husband the picture of health, Costigan, not a personal friend of the LaFollettes, spoke instead to Gilson Gardner, a supposed supporter of LaFollette, to W. L. Houser, LaFollette's campaign manager, and to John Hannan, LaFollette's secretary. They all agreed that LaFollette had had a nervous collapse, but was still, uncharacteristically, demanding personal loyalty from his followers. Progressive "loyalty must be to the cause rather than to any individual," Costigan wrote to his colleagues in an effort to explain the situation. Consequently, he had visited the Oyster Bay Squire and had been assured that Teddy would press for nomination on a progressive platform. "It has become necessary for us to avail ourselves of Colonel Roosevelt's popularity and his undoubtedly growing progressiveness in our fight on the reactionaries," he said. The Colorado Progressive Republican League endorsed Roosevelt on February 27, 1912, and the fight against Taft now revolved about the candidacy of the Sagamore Sage.

The Fight for Delegates to the Republican State Convention

Long before Roosevelt had entered the race, the progressive Republicans had realized that it would be impossible to win control of the state convention without a party primary. The state organization supported Taft. But Costigan was certain that rank and file support would be dramatized by a statewide primary, or a sufficient number of county primaries. Then standpatters could not dare to refuse the insurgent demand to include a sizeable number of progressives in the delegation to the Republican National Convention. Hopefully a progressive Congressional delegation could be chosen. But Jesse MacDonald, Chairman of the State Central Committee, would not endanger Taft's renomination by calling a statewide primary. Instead, the Colorado Republican Central Committee, one-quarter of whose members were federal officeholders, followed his lead and endorsed the President. Rebuffed in their efforts to obtain a statewide primary, the insurgents fought to force county central committees to authorize county primaries. Conservative committeemen and powerful chairmen often stood in their way. Even in counties where primaries were held obstacles were encountered. In Boulder and Jefferson precinct committeemen refused to publicize the time and place of these primaries, and in Jefferson the polls were only open from seven to nine in the evening.[8] In Denver the progressives were taught how an efficient machine could control a primary.

The composition of the Denver delegation was likely to determine domination of the state convention. Consequently, this contest was a heated and bitter one. The organization permitted only a primary election of delegates to the county convention. The progressives, who in local politics had fought for the headless ballot, demanded that the tickets be labelled as Roosevelt and Taft delegations. The stalwarts saw no reason to lend the magic of the Roosevelt name to their opponent's slate. The regular Republican candidates were more familiar to the voters and could be expected to attract more uninformed support. The dates for the county and state conventions were moved up so that the progressives would not have sufficient time to prepare a campaign. Although the progressives had an existing organization, Roosevelt was not endorsed until February 27, 1912. The county convention was held on March 25th and the state convention at Colorado Springs met later the same week. Petition forms were withheld until forty-eight hours before the filing date and in many districts Roosevelt slates could not be filed. Numerous petitions were thrown out on technicalities. The Taft supporters made lavish expenditures and invited the cooperation of the Democratic "Big Mitt" in districts where a controlled Democratic vote could aid their candidates. Thus, the hardworking, but disorganized progressives were no match for the Evans-Guggenheim machine. The Taft forces won a majority of the precinct delegates to the county convention.

At the county convention the insurgents were given an opportunity to voice their opinions, and then, without replying, Archie Stevenson recorded his majority for Taft. The Denver progressives took their hopeless case to the Republican State Convention. Costigan submitted a communique from the insurgents to chairman MacDonald, contesting the Denver delegation and claiming that the city and county parties had been usurped "by a coterie of discredited politicians in the direct employ and under the control of the public utility corporations." Their protest was ignored.

Having failed in Denver, and consequently unable to commit Colorado to Roosevelt, the best that the progressives could hope to do was to combine with the "Young Turks," who opposed the Colorado Republican leadership, to prevent the choice of A. M. Stevenson and William G. Smith. The organization dropped Smith from the slate, then, after permitting the progressives to air their grievances, the machine leaders refused a roll call vote and approved the Taft delegation, Taft resolutions and a high tariff plank. On all issues the insurgents were defeated by a vote of three to one. Indeed, the steamroller tactics of the Taft machine were so blatant that the insurgents laughed as it smoothly flattened their opposition. The success of the Roosevelt forces in carrying the majority outside Denver was insufficient to salvage anything from the convention. While Roosevelt indignantly attacked the Guggenheim-Evans machine in Colorado, the Colorado progressive Republicans contemplated their next move.

The Protest Delegation and the Republican National Convention

Costigan was vexed by the results of the state convention. The progressives should have insisted on at least a split delegation or shouted opposition to the results in and out of the convention. Roosevelt headquarters, he pointed out, wanted the progressives to contest the conservative delegation. Meantime, his confreres debated the feasibility of filing a contest until it was too late to challenge the Taft delegation. State Senator Philip Stewart of Colorado Springs, the leader of the Colorado progressive Republicans, scrupulously opposed sending a protest deputation, for a delegate to the state convention could not oppose the choice of that assembly in good faith.

On May 29, 1912, after the Citizen's Party, in coalition with the progressive Republicans, had emerged victorious from the Denver local elections Costigan issued a ringing statement to the Denver *Express,* the insurgent organ. He demanded that the Republican state chairman, Jesse MacDonald, reconvene the state convention, withdraw the delegation instructed for Taft, throw the selection of delegates before the convention once again, and (the most important part of his proposal) recognize the Progressive Republican League as the regular organization in Denver. Chicanery, he asserted, had marked the choice of the Taft delegation to the National Republican Convention. The Denver contingent, fraudulently elected through the lavish use of funds by the Evans-Guggenheim machine, had controlled the convention. If MacDonald refused his ultimatum, the progressives should protest before the Chicago National Convention. MacDonald, however, refused to recall the delegates, insisting that he lacked the authority. Merle Vincent, in a scathing open letter, denounced the State Chairman for refusing a statewide primary, for pre-selecting the Chairman of the State Convention and the delegates to the National Convention, and for ramming through an instructed delegation for Taft. Yet, even MacDonald had admitted that the state Republicans preferred Roosevelt, he charged. A protest delegation was all but inevitable.

The Roosevelt forces were contesting many Taft delegations. The President's forces in the South were firing Roosevelt supporters and hastening the state nominating conventions to prevent the organization of Roosevelt strength. Florida's choice of Taft's followers while the Roosevelt supporters nominated their own delegation precipitated Roosevelt's decision to challenge the results of all Southern conventions without reference to the merits of the case, lest any swift increase in Taft's strength swamp the Rough Rider. In the Northern states

Roosevelt pressed for presidential primaries and accepted support from all politicians, including prominent standpatters. Though at the time Colorado's Republicans met, Roosevelt's candidacy appeared hopeless, beginning in early April the colonel swept a number of primaries and conventions in bastions of Republicanism.

Under these circumstances, Costigan was able to convince his associates that a protest delegation was wise. He was chosen to lead the mission to Chicago, but since the Colorado progressives were not contesting the right of the Colorado representatives to be recognized, their only role was to offer a moral protest and they remained offstage while the main drama was performed. Beneath the carnival atmosphere created by the influx of supporters for both sides and the $50,000 brass bands that George Perkins of the House of Morgan provided for the Roosevelt forces, the Coloradans witnessed a bitter struggle for control.

The first and most important battle of the convention was fought over the 254 seats that the Roosevelt and Taft forces contested. Of these challenges, about one hundred deserved serious consideration, and between thirty and fifty were valid. Had the seventy-two Roosevelt enthusiasts whom he insisted had an unquestioned right to their seats, been certified, he would have organized the convention and obtained the nomination. Even had fifty of these been seated, the Colonel's men might still have organized the convention, or better, stampeded Taft's more reluctant delegates.

The Taft-controlled Republican National Committee had no intention of permitting Roosevelt to dominate the convention. In an open vote, Taft might have lost those of his supporters who feared the opinion of their constituents. Roosevelt could only count on eleven or twelve National Committee votes. Thus they required twenty votes for a roll call. Displaying neither fairness nor logical consistency, Roosevelt was awarded a harmless nineteen of the disputed seats.

When LaFollette blocked an effort to stampede the convention by electing Governor McGovern of Wisconsin as chairman, and the self centered Sagamore sage rejected quiet efforts by some of Taft's backers to unite on a compromise progressive candidate, the nomination of Taft on the first ballot was assured. Three hundred and forty-four Roosevelt delegates abstained from voting as the choice of Taft was registered. Assured of financial support and gambling on the nomination of a conservative Democrat, Roosevelt was about to create a new party.

The Progressive Nominating Convention

The Progressive Convention which met in early August to nominate Roosevelt, was filled with dedicated crusaders who sang stirring hymns and consecrated themselves to defeat the forces of evil and restore righteousness to the land. Roosevelt's "Declaration of Faith," his most radical speech, in which he advocated almost all of the progressive reforms enraptured the Progressives. But there were portents of future difficulties such as George Perkins outburst when the deleted anti-trust resolution was mistakingly read to the assemblage.[9]

Costigan was disturbed by Roosevelt's effort to win Southern support with a lily-white party. P. H. Troutman, who had investigated the question of the contesting Southern delegations, eased his qualms. Contests had been decided on questions of procedural merit, not color, and had the contesting delegations not been Negro the cases would have been dispatched much more quickly, he wrote. In fact, in the case of Florida, neither delegation was seated.[10]

Finally Roosevelt was unable to retain the support of the leading insurgents. Nine progressive Republican Senators and six of the seven Governors who had urged him to seek the nomination rejected the Progressive Party. Despite these handicaps the Progressive Party set forth to fight for the victory of the righteous.

The Progressive Party and the Republican Primaries

Prior to the Chicago Convention the Colorado progressive Republicans had chosen their candidates for the various positions on the Republican state ticket. Costigan had reluctantly agreed to pursue the nomination for the long-term Senate seat. Merle Vincent was to seek the short-term Senate seat, Philip Stewart the statehouse, and Attorney General Benjamin Griffith renomination. Upon returning to Chicago, Costigan led the Denver insurgents into the Progressive Party. Stewart, Vincent, Griffith, and other progressive Republicans who dominated their local Republican organizations insisted that it was possible to win Republican nominations and still deliver the electoral vote of the state to Roosevelt.

Costigan and Stewart had earlier differed about political tactics. Stewart had sought conservative support for his nomination[12] while Costigan had rejected attempts at party harmony. "An acceptable candidate to the old time control of the Republican Party must, by virtue of underlying differences in point of view, be unacceptable to the Progressive element in our state," the Denver leader had declared.[12] After the convention Costigan could not in good conscience pursue a Republican nomination. Without the Denver insurgents who had bolted from the Republican Party, Stewart could only be nominated with the consent of the Guggenheim machine. Even were Stewart to be nominated, Costigan warned, it would injure Roosevelt's candidacy. The Republican ticket included Taft electors, and, therefore, Stewart, as a Republican candidate, would attract Progressive votes for Taft. With over thirty initiated legislative proposals to consider, ballot scratching would become difficult, Costigan insisted, showing insufficient faith in the ability of the average voter.

When the Colorado Progressive Party was formed in late June 1912, with Costigan as chairman, it planned to run the earlier progressive Republican slate as the Party ticket. Stewart's decision to seek the Republican nomination presented the Progressives with a dilemma they were to face throughout the nation.

At first no difficulty arose from Stewart's actions. Costigan insisted that Stewart could pursue the Republican nomination while they systematically shaped the third party. He urged local leaders to organize the Progressive Party precinct by precinct. Since the Party had not run in the previous election, petitions for candidates were circulated, taking care that they be filed with sufficient surplus signatures to withstand conservative challenges in the courts. Though candidates would be placed on the ballot through petition, Costigan recommended that local conventions choose delegates to a state Progressive Convention so that the voice of the people could reaffirm the choice of the Progressive leaders. He was willing to accommodate the Stewart faction by delaying the Progressive Convention until the progressive Republicans had made their effort to capture the Republican Party Assembly and to commit the Colorado Republican Party to Roosevelt. But he warned his friend, Merle Vincent, that the latter's pursuit of a Republican nomination was futile and would only weaken the Progressive ticket. He reminded Vincent that the Washington office wanted a straight Progressive ticket. After all, the Progressive Party was an accomplished fact, and nothing could be gained by temporizing with the Republicans. But even after the Stewart group was rejected by the Republican Party Assembly, they continued to press for the Republican nomination.[13] Time had run out and the Progressive Party had to make up its state ticket without them.

With Philip Stewart competing for the Republican nomination, Costigan became the logical choice to head the Progressive ticket. Yet, Costigan was in a quandary. Stewart had the support of the Progressives, particularly those outside of Denver, and felt that he was only following Roosevelt's statement in his Chicago speech. Costigan accepted the nomination conditionally, pending discussion with Roosevelt. Roosevelt's stand satisfied Costigan. The Rough Rider insisted upon a straight Progressive ticket in Colorado, headed by Costigan, abstention from participation in Republican primaries, and no fusion with Republican factions. To his friend Stewart, Roosevelt wrote that his Orchestra Hall statement about taking the Republican Party into the Progressive Party had referred only to states like California where the whole Republican ticket had been absorbed, electors and all. Only in Colorado had his statement been misinterpreted. Without the Costigan faction no Colorado Progressive Party would exist. Besides, Stewart's candidacy as a Republican could carry Taft electors and Guggenheim officials. Senator Joseph Dixon of Montana suggested that the Stewart faction withdraw from the Republican primaries and accept places on the Progressive slate. Stewart balked, and the progressives nominated L. D. Catlin for the long-term Senate seat and N. S. Gandy for Attorney General.

Inevitably, the relationship between the two Progressive factions became strained for each group was draining the strength of the other. Costigan wrote to Dr. C. E. Fisher that Stewart was losing support because of his indecision, his preliminary conferences with machine men, and his suggestion of splitting electors between Roosevelt and Taft. When the Colorado Springs conference of Stewart's supporters refused to endorse the Colorado Progressive Party he attacked them as Stewart backers joined to a group of reactionaries, not a legitimate gathering of progressive Republicans. On the other side, Karl Bickel accused Ben Lindsey of using Costigan and Roosevelt to ensure a Democratic victory in Colorado. While Merle Vincent heatedly berated Progressive candidate I. N. Stevens as an opportunist who compromised with the Guggenheim machine and had been conveniently ensconced in New York when the fight for Roosevelt delegates to the 1912 National Convention was in progress. Vincent, who would support any other progressive in place of I. N. Stevens, said "For Mr. Costigan and his other associates on the Progressive ticket I entertain the greatest respect." This bickering resulted in peace making efforts by high ranking national representatives. But no one could convince Stewart to withdraw from the Republican primaries.

The controversy ended when the Republican machine, aided by the abstention of the Progressive voters, rolled over Stewart. Only Attorney General Benjamin Griffith succeeded in winning renomination. Consequently, Stewart resigned as Republican County Chairman in El Paso, and Griffith withdrew from the Republican ticket. With Merle Vincent and Clarence Phelps Dodge, publisher of the Colorado Springs *Gazette*, they joined the Progressive Party. The Progressive Party candidate for Attorney General, N. S. Gandy, thereupon withdrew to permit Griffith to seek reelection.

The reunion of the progressive forces created complications. Gandy did not mind resigning in favor of Griffith, whom he greatly respected, but because of the prestige of Philip Stewart in El Paso, three Republican judicial candidates whom Gandy thought reactionary had been endorsed by the local Progressives despite contrary assurances given to Gandy at the time of the merger. Although fusion with the Republicans on a state level had been prevented, it would prove much more difficult to prevent a merger of local tickets.

Fusion with the Republican Party

Only recently Republicans, it was natural for local Progressive leaders to want to combine their regional ticket with the Republican slate in counties where progressive candidates were nominated. In other counties where a Progressive candidacy was hopeless, many third party leaders did not want to elect Democrats by drawing votes from a regular Republican. The state leaders were in a quandary. Often they refrained from interference. Intervention, when it took place, caused a strain in relations between state and local leaders, for not all local Progressives approved of the solution.

In one such incident Judge J. B. Stuart of Jefferson County attacked Costigan for attempting to deny Progressive support to the local Republican ticket—a ticket which, Stuart claimed, had as many Roosevelt men as Taft men on it. He accused Costigan of visiting Jefferson County to prevent fusion and thus to assure the election of the Democrats. In a scathing letter to the Golden *Globe*, Costigan promptly rejected Stuart's support. "If he can prove what he says," he wrote, "I do not deserve that support. If he cannot, after such a charge, his support is inconsequential." He denied interfering and reminded the Judge that the Progressive Party was not a Republican adjunct. On the other hand, A. M. Stong of Alamosa accused the state Progressive leaders of permitting the endorsement of a conservative Republican slate, despite his urgent messages.

It is possible that Costigan could have been elected Governor if he had been willing to negotiate with the Republican Party on the state level. Yet such an outcome, he declared, while flattering, would have subordinated the cause to personal success. Costigan preferred to hazard the unfavorable odds of a Progressive candidacy.

The Campaign of 1912

The campaign in Colorado was an important one for the national party. Colorado was a state of extremes. It had a history of radicalism, had a strong progressive organization, and had been a Roosevelt stronghold. On the other hand, the state was noted for some of the most infamous machine politicians and some of the most reactionary business interests in the country. Some Progressives, enthusiastically optimistic, thought that Teddy would sweep Colorado. Even Costigan thought that the Progressives could expect a reasonable victory, but he realized that only part of the ticket could be successful after fusion had been rejected. There was a chance that Roosevelt might carry Colorado, but it would require a vigorous campaign.

Speakers with national reputations were sent into the state—Jane Addams, William Allen White, Senator Joseph Dixon, and, most important of all, Teddy Roosevelt. Roosevelt toured the state with Stewart, Vincent, and Dodge, drawing great throngs. He attacked political bosses and advocated the recall of judicial decisions. Important as the tour was, the burden of the campaign lay with Costigan and the state organization.

Though handicapped by an attack of hay fever, Costigan made an extensive automobile tour of the state, urging the necessity of an independent party in order to enact a progressive program. To R. M. McClintock, editor of the Colorado Springs *Gazette*, he wrote: "I have no doubt that Mr. Wilson, however excellent his purpose and program, will be incapable of performance through a Democratic organization." To dramatize the Progressive program, he challenged his opponents, C. C Parks and Elias Ammons, to debate the public issues and the merits of the parties, platforms and candidates. The Republican rejected his challenge. Elias Ammons accepted conditionally: the debate was limited to conservation; he felt certain that state control of public resources was a popular issue in a western state.

On October 30, 1912, City Auditorium in Denver was filled with partisans. Costigan opened the debate. The conservation of human resources and the welfare of men, women and children, not conservation of public lands, was the major issue of the campaign, he declared. He had accepted this limited debate in order to refute Senator Ammons' criticism of the Roosevelt conservation policies. He proceeded to define these policies and to give a brief history of their application. The previous practice of allowing free access to our natural resources had resulted in monopoly conditions in minerals and water power, he insisted, and in private warfare over grazing grounds. As a result, sixty percent of the commercial water power of the United States was controlled by ten corporations. In addition, these corporate interests controlled street railways in 111 towns, electric light plants in 669 towns, gas plants in 113 towns, fifty banks and fifty public service corporations. Unless government control was instituted, the future system of commercial power would be dominated by a few. He then compared the municipally owned Toronto tramway to the privately owned Denver tramway to show how municipal control benefitted the populace.

Federal reclamation policy was his next topic. Private capital for reclamation proposals was scarce, he reported, and in neighboring private and Federal projects in Colorado the former had cost three times as much per acre as had the latter. When polled about a proposed Federal plan, no resident votes were cast against it. To Ammons' contention that forest reserves cost the state taxable land, Costigan replied that twenty-five percent of the gross proceeds from the land was used for school and road purposes within the counties. A Federal policy of separating cattle and sheep grazing areas replaced open foraging in the forests and prevented the recurrence of earlier range wars. Federal leasing policy prevented the monopolization of the range by large ranchers. Once in effect, the Federal program had converted many a former opponent. The staunchest opponents of the Roosevelt conservation concepts were greedy corporations and pioneers who considered the public lands their own possession. State control, Costigan argued, had proven inadequate. The state had never supplied funds to finance reclamation. "Government conservation is necessary to protect the people from monopoly, great forest fires and the waste of resources." In conclusion, Costigan pointedly asked Ammons five questions:

1. What assurance was there that under state ownership, compensation would be provided for the use of government lands?

2. What could Ammons do as Governor to transfer title for Federal lands to Colorado?

3. Would Ammons guarantee the expenditure of $200,000 a year on conservation, or as much as the nation spent in Colorado annually for this purpose?

4. What could Ammons do as Governor to protect the people's interest in water and other resources?

5. What guarantee was there that state control would protect natural resources?

Ammons' reply showed him to be a candidate skilled in debate and well versed in his subject. First, he charged that Roosevelt's withdrawal of the public domain from sale had prevented the completion of an irrigation project that had already begun. His argument for state control was narrowly locality oriented: Colorado, he said, must use all of the water that flowed through the state in order to irrigate its land. Ignoring the claim of other states to utilize interstate rivers, he declared that other states could use the water that remained after Colorado had filled her needs. He pointed with pride to the private system of northern Colorado.

Shifting his emphasis, Ammons attacked the policy of mine leasing. By preventing the full utilization of Colorado's coal resources, county land taxes remained high and national royalties were added to farmers' fuel costs. This was a triple tax. Further, leasing discouraged risks, he argued, and, consequently, no good mineral strikes had occurred since the advent of conservation. The forest reserve policy, Ammons added, increased lumber costs fifty percent and prevented homesteaders from proving up their land. He could not guarantee $200,000 of state funds for conservation since he could not starve other institutions, but he certainly would prevent forest fires. Finally, he declared with great local pride that Colorado could guard her own reserves.

In a political rejoinder, harping on Ammons' emphasis upon contemporary use, Costigan challenged Ammons' intent to protect the state's natural endowments. His opponent would grant these resources to the first wealthy claimant, he charged. Ammons' policy was contrary to that of all the leading Democratic national leaders and avoided the prime question—the prevention of corporate control of natural resources. In conclusion, he denied that the state could benefit by adding coal lands to the holdings of companies already gorged with gain.

As the campaign progressed, Costigan's chances of victory dimmed. In order to concentrate the conservative vote, the Denver *Times,* owned by the Republican political boss, William Evans, endorsed the Democrat, Ammons. *The Rocky Mountain News,* true to its Democratic loyalties, supported Ammons although Costigan and Patterson had long worked together for Denver reform. Of the newspapers in the major city, only the Denver *Express* backed Costigan. A strong whispering campaign against wasting a Progressive vote led Costigan to assert in his last campaign speech:

"We are fighting against Privilege, against that system of government which permits one man to live from the labor of his fellow. It is your fight—you who labor and toil. Unless you believe that you will secure a greater share of liberty, a greater portion of happiness from carrying the principles which we advocate into your government, do not vote for me or our ticket.

"I am asking only that you vote your conviction and your conscience. I am asking only that your ballot express your sentiment and your will. For only that ballot is lost which is cast from motives which do not take into consideration the welfare of all the people.

"Only that ballot is lost which expresses a sentiment which is against that growing ideal of human brotherhood which civilization demands if it is to live. I am not asking that you vote for me. I am asking that you vote for yourselves and for your nation and for your state.

Only the counting of the ballots remained.

The Election Returns

On the surface the Progressive Party did very well in Colorado, as in the nation, emerging from the election with the second highest vote for its leading candidates. Yet the party strength was more apparent than real, for the only candidates to out-poll their Republican opponents were Roosevelt, Costigan, and Attorney General Benjamin Griffith. The Colorado Progressive Party failed to secure any of those essentials for future political growth, political offices. As time would show, it had relied too heavily on the excitement of the moment and the drawing power of individual candidates, particularly its leader, Teddy Roosevelt.

The Colorado Progressive Party recruited its major support from those agricultural counties which had previously been Republican, and from the commercial city of Denver. Costigan trailed Roosevelt in all counties except Denver and Ouray, and in Ouray the support of the Progressive Party was not great. The Progressives ran strongly in the truck farming and dairying counties surrounding Denver and on the fruit raising western slope where the former Republican machine was largely controlled by the Progressives. Roosevelt ran well in the agricultural counties of the northeast and east, but, ominously, the vote of the ticket fell away rapidly. With few exceptions the Progressives made little headway in the livestock sections and in the mineral and coal mining counties.

Although Costigan's vote in the industrial county of Pueblo was only twenty-one percent of the total (Pueblo was a Democratic stronghold and the Progressives could not crack it), he drew strongly in the urban center of Denver, even out-polling Roosevelt, an urban favorite. Costigan carried half of the election districts of Denver and came in second in the other half, never falling below thirty percent in any district, and trailed Ammons by only 1788 votes in a total Denver vote of 56,283. While his reputation as a reformer gave Costigan a wide base in Denver, his greatest strength was in the former Republican strongholds in the wealthy residential areas and the upper middle class districts of downtown Denver, the east side of Denver, and what were then the suburbs of Denver, as well as the multi-national working class district of the west side.

For their first campaign as a political party the Progressives had made a remarkable showing, obtaining sizeable support from all economic groups except the grazing and mining interests. Costigan now had to maintain the new party's base of strength and expand at the expense of the established parties, despite the lack of political patronage. Still, with the victory of the reform forces in Denver and the imminence of commission government, Costigan looked to the future with anticipation. He expected the Progressives to consolidate their gains in 1914 and to elect a Progressive President in 1916. Unfortunately, the progressive movement had reached its peak and the following years were to witness its decline and the eclipse of the Progressive Party.

1. The company did not accept the decision of the electorate. For most of a decade it pressed its case through the courts, up to the Supreme Court of the United States. The city of Denver expanded a million dollars in litigation costs before the matter was resolved.

2. The declaration supported the progressive policies of Roosevelt which had been endorsed by President Taft. It called for a wide range of progressive reforms a scientific tariff commission; and end to Speaker Cannon's dictorial control of Congress; confining corporations to business activities (with no effort selfishly to influence government). The elimination of a Republican machine which had become "the refuge and defender of those who have accumulated fortunes by exploiting the people"; a constitutional amendment for the initiative, referendum, and recall; an effective direct primary law; direct election of U.S. Senators; a headless ballot where each elective position was voted for individually and not as a ticket; an improved and extended Public Utilities Commission; and a corrupt practices law to limit campaign expenditures.

3. Shafroth was nicknamed "Honest John" after resigning a Congressional seat when an investigation revealed that his election was based on fraudulent returns.

4. The Railroad Law lacked an anti-pass feature, the Commission would not have had the power to initiate rate changes and the enforcement provisions were weak.

5. The League's platform called for the direct election of Senators, direct primaries for the nomination of elective officers, the direct election of delegates to national conventions, a corrupt practices act, and the amendment of state constitutions to provide for the initiative, referendum and recall.

6. Because of a rumor that the reactionaries were going to steal the name Progressive Republican the Progressive Republican Club was organized so swiftly that some counties were left out of the charter.

7. Roosevelt had stated unequivocally to LaFollette and others that he would not be a candidate, but could not openly oppose Taft.

8. Roosevelt won in Mesa, Montrose, El Paso and Weld. In Lake County proportional representation gave Roosevelt eight delegates, Taft seven.

9. In July, 1914, Amos Pinchot began a fight to remove Perkins as Chairman of the Executive Committee of the Progressive Party.

10. Unfortunately, the available evidence contradicts Troutman and indicates that political advantage in the South was the motivating factor.

11. Stewart had been willing to withhold the announcement of his candidacy until the platform had been released so that it did not appear that he was dictating to the Republican Party.

12. Karl Bickel, the editor of the Colorado Springs *Gazette* and a friend of Stewart, had refused to give to the enemies of the insurgents the progressive's platform and their strongest candidate.

13. At first Roosevelt was willing to fuse his ticket with progressive Republicans, but he soon agreed with the more radical in his organization that it was necessary to run a complete independent slate.

Lindsey accused Stewart of an agreement to stay out of the Republican State Assembly in order to win support for his campaign for the gubernatorial nomination.

Chapter IV

THE ELECTION OF 1914

The campaign of 1912 was over. Looking forward to future elections, Costigan, as leader of the Colorado Progressive Party, had to forge a permanent organization, liquidate the campaign deficit, and raise funds for current expenses.[1] Moreover, rumors of fusion had to be squelched in order to stop the drift of disappointed members back into the Republican Party.

Immediately after the election Progressive clubs were organized throughout the nation to unify their nucleus and proselytize for their cause.[2] These clubs were to be the foundation upon which a Progressive Party, dominant in the state and nation, could be built. Costigan faced the next election with confidence: Had they not run second despite the lack of organiation? Once their permanence became apparent they could enlist the remaining progressive Republicans and add progressive Democratic votes to their solid base.[3]

But the exhilaration of the campaign had led Costigan and his confreres to entertain unwarranted expectations. He seemed unaware that the hunger for position could affect his colleagues just as it affected the stalwarts. And he had no premonition of the disaster to come in 1914.

An unexpectedly acute and immediate problem was a tendency Progressives called "fusion," which was really an abandonment of the fading "Bull Moose." Third party independence was compromised wherever local Republican candidates were successful in their pursuit of Progressive support. While Costigan rejected Republican offers of "fusion," which really meant absorption of the younger organization as a unit, he could not stop the flow of members back into the Republican Party.[4]

Membership attrition began soon after the 1912 campaign. John C. Nixon, the Progressive candidate for Lieutenant Governor in 1912, supplied the rationale in a letter to Costigan. The future of their movement lay in the Republican Party, he insisted. In Weld County the Republican Party realized that its future was in innovation, he argued, and was consequently solicitous for the return of the Progressives. The time to coalesce was when the Republicans eagerly sought reunion, not when it was necessary to seek admission with apologies. The 1913 elections in the East showed that the people were not ready for the entire

Progressive program, he wrote, and, thus, the party was crumbling. Why retain a party whose organization remained incomplete despite the enthusiasm of 1912, when the Republican Party of Borah, Cummins, and LaFollette was still available as a vehicle for progressivism. While his advice was rejected, Nixon continued as an inactive member of the Progressive Party.

This was not true of other Progressive leaders. Frank Munsey, an important financial backer, issued a call for a return to the Republican Party in his magazine. Dan Hanna of Ohio preached amalgamation after victorious Democrats lowered the protective tariff. Even Karl Bickel, former editor of the *Rocky Mountain News,* joined the exodus shortly after the election.

While Costigan's decision to join the United Mine Workers' legal staff during a violent strike split the Colorado Progressives, yet other factors contributed to the decline of the Colorado Progressive Party.[5] In part, this was simply a reflection of the Party's national status. Newspaper coverage of the European war submerged domestic issues and blunted the reform impetus. Wilson's Congress enacted much of the program of the Progressive Party. Consequently, their domestic attacks on the Administration were confined to the absence of a tariff commismission to rectify the Underwood Tariff. The fervor of 1912 had represented a movement at its apex. When legislative changes failed to fulfill the utopian expectations of their proponents, the reform impulse subsided. Furthermore, the Progressive Party was rent with internal strife.

The divisive question of monopoly had momentarily appeared with the missing anti-trust plank in the platform of 1912, but the need for party unity had stifled the resentment of advocates of more restrictive legislation. Amos Pinchot, denouncing National Chairman George Perkins' connections with the Harvester and Steel combines and the House of Morgan, tried to force Perkins out of his powerful party position. Eventually, however, Roosevelt's firm support of Perkins and his policy of corporate control rather than trust busting, led Pinchot to denounce the Rough Rider himself.[6] Shortly before the 1914 campaign Pinchot's attack on Perkins leaked to the press. An effort to appease the anti-Perkins wing by reinserting the anti-monopoly plank in the platform failed, for Perkins remained second only to Roosevelt as a power in the Party.

Costigan soon became involved in the quarrel. After a conversation with him, Medill McCormick listed him as one of the Progressive leaders who doubted Perkins' ability to serve as Chairman of the National

Executive Committee at the same time as he served two great monopolies. Costigan resented the unauthorized use of his name. Like Perkins he preferred regulation to trustbusting, yet he questioned Perkins' attitude towards labor's right to organize and bargain collectively. When Perkins assured Costigan that he supported labor's rights, Costigan suggested that he inform Progressives for they had assumed that his labor philosophy was the same as that of U.S. Steel. Costigan still agreed with McCormick that Perkins should clarify his primary loyalty —was it to the Progressive Party or to Morgan interests?

A discouraged Theodore Roosevelt did much to speed the decline of the Party. He refused to repudiate an interview in September, 1913, which was widely interpreted as a desire to return to the Republican Party. He could not be induced to issue a rallying call to the Party before he left for South America in the summer of 1914. Ignoring his 1912 program, he concentrated instead on conservative issues, a demand for a protectionist tariff and a biting attack on the Democratic anti-trust program. Then he refused to run for Governor of New York and startled his followers by suggesting that they choose one of the leading candidates for the Republican nomination.

Consequently, in Indiana, Republican billboards proclaimed: "Eventually, why not now?"[7] Even without additional complications, Roosevelt had given Colorado Progressive candidates a heavy handicap.

Prohibition

In part, Progressive decline in Colorado reflected the clever exploitation of the prohibition issue by the Republican Party.

Costigan, a teetotaler, had long been a political prohibitionist and considered liquor an evil. Like gross exploitation and political manipulation it had to be eradicated to improve the condition of man. But his insistence that prohibition was a relatively minor and potentially divisive issue, a question on which the Party should not take a formal stand, alienated many for whom the consumption of alcohol was a major concern.

Throughout Costigan's career the prohibitionists had been growing in strength. While the Colorado drys were defeated by 30,000 votes in 1912, their increasing national strength improved their chances for 1914. As a noted prohibitionist, Costigan was pressed by some supporters to so commit the Progressive Party. R. M. McClintock, editor of the *Colorado Springs Gazette,* warned that voters in rural areas did not understand the industrial question and were prejudiced against Costigan's association with the mine workers. Yet, a party stand for prohibition would endorse its character and win support for Costigan's economic views. Besides, McClintock wrote, the sale of liquor was as immoral as the denial of the right of organized labor to deal with organized capital. Costigan rejected these arguments, pointing out that the Christian Temperance Union, wanting to run a non-partisan campaign, had opposed Progressive endorsement.

More important, Costigan felt, too many issues "have a tendency to defeat the most righteous cause." The primary issue of the campaign was social and industrial justice, and the liquor question would only be distracting, dividing those who should be united on the basic question. "Economic justice, logically as well as strategically precedes much moral betterment," he insisted. The Progressives could win if the campaign was limited to "the cause of the exploited men, women and children," for many considered the elimination of the sale of alcohol to be a trivial issue, no matter how seriously McClintock and he viewed the question. As a dry, Costigan stood a chance to win the prohibitionist vote in any event.

Much of the potential dry vote for Costigan, and therefore much of the progressive vote, was wooed into the Republican column by the gubernatorial nomination of prohibitionist Reverend George Carlson. Carlson's triumph in the primaries, despite the support of the Republican assembly for his opponent, surprised the Progressives. Then, much to Costigan's chagrin, the Christian Temperance Union endorsed Carlson on the claim—correct, as it turned out—that Costigan did not have a chance of being elected. Carlson made effective use of the issue in his campaign, and both he and prohibition were victorious.

The Ludlow Coal Strike

While the prohibition issue cost Costigan and the Progressive Party a sizeable vote, the coal strike tore the Progressive Party asunder. Costigan was intimately aware of conditions in the coal camps and the technique employed by the operators to control the miners and prevent unionization. Consequently, he not only supported the strikers, he acted as a special counsel for the United Mine Workers of America.

Conditions in the coal camps of southern Colorado were identical to non-union mining towns elsewhere in the country. The operators controlled the sheriff, the sheriff deputized the company employed marshal who administered civil power in the unincorporated town, and the sheriff determined the size of the majorities to be counted in the elections. Union organizers were kept out, wages down, company store prices up, and all property in the hands of the mine owners. As Costigan summed it up, the corporations exercised "the ownership of the courts, executive and legislative officials, of coroners and other juries, of the churches, of the saloons, of the schools, of the lands, of the houses upon the lands, and eventually a certain ownership of the men who toil upon the lands."[8]

Ironically, the immediate cause of the strike was the refusal of the Colorado Fuel and Iron Company to negotiate with a "lawless" body. Had the company obeyed the industrial laws of the state, the union would have had few issues. The operators ignored legislation providing for an eight hour day, a checkweighman chosen by the miners to prevent the operators from short weighing their work, the prohibition of scrip (money redeemable only in the company store), the right of miners to trade where they pleased, the semi-monthly pay day, enforcement of the safety code, and most important of all, the right to join a union and to seek jobs without being subject to a blacklist.

Strike Violence

When the strike appeared inevitable the operators recruited private detectives, experienced in strikebreaking, and stockpiled arms. The union leaders hoped to prevent violence for it would mean the loss of public opinion. But the strikers were bellicose, resenting mine guard domination, the miserable tent colonies they lived in, and the strikebreakers who threatened their livelihood. Isolated incidents resulted in a mounting death toll until the twelve hour battle of Berwind Canyon forced Governor Ammons to call out the militia. Peace now depended upon the ability of the militia to maintain an impartial truce.

But impartiality did not prevail. Governor Ammons, despite his assurances, permitted the importation of strikebreakers, and the militia commandant arbitrarily detained Ed Doyle, Secretary of the Colorado UMW, and imprisoned the colorful Mary Harris ("Mother") Jones. Most threatening to the strikers was the replacement of demobilized militiamen with mine guards.

On Greek Easter, 1914, Company B, now composed entirely of mine guards, and led by the notorious E. K. Linderfelt, attacked the Ludlow colony.[9] At 7 p.m., after a nine hour battle, the militia ignited the tents and raked the area with machine-gun fire. The colony was gripped by panic: women wih skirts aflame ran clutching their infants; a child raced from a blazing tent, but terrified by the screaming bullets, plunged back into the flames; whole families were trapped—ten children and two women died in a single pit; when the fire reached gunpowder, explosions deadened the whistling of the bullets, the roaring of the flames and the screams of the dying. A triumphant Linderfelt crushed the skull of the captive strike leader, Louis Tikas, with a rifle butt and then fired three bullets into his inert body.

The strikers responded with a series of armed attacks on coal mines culminating in the battle of Hogback Hill near Walsenburg in which Major Lester, a medical officer, was killed, and the battle of Forbes where eleven guards were slain in the streets. Only twenty lives had been lost prior to Ludlow. Forty were killed in the ten days succeeding the massacre and the strike was doomed.

Costigan telegraphed Congressman John M. Evans that the miners had confidence in Federal soldiers but not in a mine guard dominated state militia. Ammons, at last recognizing the full gravity of the crisis, requested Federal military aid. President Wilson dispatched army units and an uneasy peace reigned during which mine production gradually climbed to three-fourths normal capacity.

The President offered to mediate. While the national leaders of the United Mine Workers were amenable, the operators refused to negotiate or accept mediation. Wilson proposed a specific plan of settlement. The union acquiesced, the operators balked. Nonplussed, President Wilson appointed a commission lead by Seth Low, President of the National Civic Federation. The union international, responding to Wilson's suggestion, called off the enfeebled strike. With peace restored, the operators refused to recognize the Low Commission. All that remained of the strike were bad memories and legal entanglements.

The Strikers and Justice

Since it was difficult to single out the perpetrators of specific acts of violence, mass indictments were brought in by operator-dominated grand juries. They even indicted United Mine Workers President J. P. White, Vice-President Frank J. Hayes and Secretary-Treasurer William Green for attempting to gain a monopoly of labor and for arousing aliens to violence. The accusations were too ridiculous to be pressed, but others did not fare as well. John R. Lawson, the strike leader, was charged with nineteen specific criminal charges, ranging in severity from conspiracy in restraint of trade to murder in the first degree and including arson and assault with intent to kill. In all, over four

THE ELECTION OF 1914   61

hundred strikers were indicted, and by the time the Lawson trial began the state had decided to prosecute over one hundred and sixty defendants. The two most important trials were those of Lawson and of the defendants in the Hogback Hill case: Mike Savage, Enoch Muir, Fred Garcia and Arthur Quinn.

As the sensational Lawson trial opened, the defense lawyers, Costigan and Horace Hawkins, demanded that the presiding judge Granby Hillyer, disqualify himself as the partner of the prosecutor and a former attorney for a coal company. That motion denied, the defense tried to show that Lawson had always counselled non-violence and, in fact, was not near the scene of the death of the victim. The entire case, they asserted, rested on the testimony of two perjurers.[10] Lawson was found guilty. But during the uproar that followed, one of the jurors admitted that he had been intimidated into voting for conviction. Legal appeals, however, were unavailing. Lawson was imprisoned until 1917 when a new state administration confessed its predecessor's error in the case, whereupon the Colorado Supreme Court freed him.[11]

The second case involved four strikers accused of the murder of militia Major Lester in the battle of Hogback Hill. Costigan was the chief defense attorney. At the very beginning of the trial, he won two victories: a change of venue from Walsenburg to the neutral city of Castle Rock in agricultural Douglas County, and a writ of prohibition preventing Judge Hillyer from sitting in the case. Judge Denison of Denver presided.

After an extended trial, Costigan summed up for the defense in a masterly oration. First, Costigan had to establish that the deceased medical officer was a combatant. Major Lester, he pointed out, had violated medical non-combatant status by carrying a weapon. The entire case for the prosecution, therefore, rested on the concept that the militia must not be resisted without sufficient cause. Before examining the question of sufficient cause, Costigan shattered the prosecution's case by casting doubt upon the identity of the bearer of the fatal weapon. Presenting a map of the terrain, he showed that the position of the accused, Mike Savage, precluded his firing the shot that killed Major Lester for the bullet could not have entered at the proper angle. Since the militia was then in rout, Major Lester could well have been hit by a stray bullet. Casting further aspersions on the prosecution's case, Costigan established that a tall militiaman had threatened to kill Lester, and a militiaman answering this description had been observed shooting at the time and place of the fatality, by a prosecution witness. Besides, sufficient cause for self-defense existed,

Costigan maintained. The militia, by then composed of company guards, had come to Walsenburg from the Ludlow massacre, the scene of the murder of women, children and prisoners. The strikers had to defend their homes, the tent colony. And the witnesses for the prosecution, Costigan continued, were hired gunmen with rehearsed testimony that fell apart under cross-examination. Could they trust the testimony of men who admitted having no friend but the dollar. With an appeal to patriotism at a time the nation was about to enter a war, Costigan completed his summation: American labor must have faith in American justice if it was to contribute to national defense. Acquittal of the defendants would create such faith. The jury voted to acquit on the first ballot.

While acting as attorney for the defense, Costigan served as legal counsel for the United Mine Workers in the Congressional investigation of the strike in February 1914. Later, in December, he was a witness in the post-strike investigation of the United States Commission on Industrial Relations. In his presentation, Costigan described operator control of southern Colorado and summarized the causes of the strike—the operators, he charged, were waging private war with private armies, violating the Peonage Statute of 1867,[12] violating the Anti-Deception Laws of 1911, and utilizing an abusive militia. Finally, he offered his recommendations for preventing future conflicts of this nature:

1. The operators could not be permitted to interfere with the mails and the public right of way, he declared.

2. Congress should prohibit peonage and prevent the interstate transportation of workers who then paid for their passage with their labor.

3. Misrepresentation, fraud, or force in the interstate employment of workers should be forbidden.

4. Legislation should eliminate the interstate shipment of workers as strikebreakers.

5. Congress should bar the interstate movement of guards, gunmen and private detectives, and the private interstate shipment of munitions during, or in anticipation of a strike.

6. All persons should have due opportunity for defense before arrest, trial and conviction, or before the seizure of property. (In mining towns during strikes, it was common for individuals to be arrested without evidence and imprisoned for long periods without a trial.)

7. Congress should provide for Federal licensing of interstate corpo-

rations as a means of supervising industrial policy.[13]

8. Congress should prohibit firms with interlocking directorates and dummy directors from participation in interstate commerce; it should provide personal penalties for culpable officers in cases of corporate violations of law.

9. A Congressional law recognizing the right of labor to organize and bargain collectively with collective capital, and prohibiting discrimination against organized labor and its products, was needed.[14]

10. Compulsory Federal investigation and voluntary arbitration in labor disputes should be provided to ensure continuous service to the public. But compulsory acceptance of arbitration awards was unwise.

11. During strikes, the government should seize and operate public utilities engaging in interstate commerce, offering just terms for all concerned, relinquishing possession when the controversy was settled.[15]

"Law and Order"

After a serious struggle with dissident elements, Costigan's partisan views in favor of trade unions were incorporated into the Progressive Party's platform for the elections of 1914. The Party's industrial plank added proposals for state operated coal mining as an experiment, to be continued if successful, for stricter coal leases, protecting the rights of miners and consumers, for national legislation for old age, sickness and disability pensions, for an eight-hour day, vocational training, minimum wages, abolition of child labor and convict labor, and for state laws in these areas until the national legislature had acted. But commitment to this program was achieved only after a fight that divided the party.

For many Progressive leaders, Costigan's activity during the strike was an excuse to advocate Progressive-Republican fusion.[16] Others were so shocked by the violence that they ignored strike issues and condemned Costigan's participation. Finally, some Progressives were vehemently partial to the open shop and suspicious of organized labor.[17] Under the cry of "law and order" these three groups united against Costigan's leadership. Their greatest support was drawn from counties that were affected by the strike, either economically or because the county militia had been sent into the strike region. In Pueblo, for example, where a coal shortage had closed the steel mills, defections from the Progressive Party were so numerous that by February 1914, Josephine Roche and R. M. McClintock considered the situation to be hopeless. That March, S. A. Coston organized a Progressive faction to combat Costigan's labor policy, and to commit the party to a "law and order" program. On the progressive western slope this faction won many recruits although both Benjamin Griffith and Merle Vincent continued to support Costigan. By the end of May the Progressive Party seemed to be disintegrating over the industrial question.

Hoping to stem the tide, Costigan led a delegation to win the support of Teddy Roosevelt. James Causey and C. P. Dodge accompanied him. While waiting for Roosevelt, they plucked some flowers, and were reproved by Quentin Roosevelt. Teddy entered and smilingly chided Quentin, admonishing him to put humanity above property. The former President endorsed Costigan's position. Twenty years earlier, Roosevelt said, he would have been caught by the law and order slogan. Now he realized that law and order were only preludes to justice. He found Costigan's program admirable, especially the right to purchase or condemn coal lands not being operated in the public interest. Armed with the support of the party leader, Costigan returned to Colorado.

Meanwhile, political conditions continued to deteriorate. Preffessor Ira De Long of Boulder wrote to the National Executive Committee of the Progressive Party, extolling the virtues of "law and order" and calling for a meeting of north Colorado Progressives. Upon his return, Costigan was informed by a correspondent that about half of the Progressives of Longmont and Boulder fanatically supported the Law and Order League and intended to endorse the Republican ticket. "I still doubt very much if you Denver people appreciate the situation in the outside districts," Costigan was told. "You do not understand the rural mind with its blind conservatism and its inherent hatred of organized labor." Even J. S. Temple, Costigan's long-time associate, who had previously been sympathetic to labor, began working against Costigan after Ludlow. When Costigan rose to address the Denver Progressive Banquet at the Adams Hotel, on June 8, 1914, he noticed the absence of thirty leading Progressives.

Costigan opened with a description of his visit to Oyster Bay reporting Roosevelt's endorsement of his analysis of the industrial situation and of his proposals for its solution. Costigan affirmed his own conception of law and order. "When guns speak, justice is silent," he declared. He cited his own consistent record on obedience to the law. Some years before, when the controlling interests had openly flouted the law, he had helped to organize the Law and Order League of Huerfano (one of the coal counties) and the Law Enforcement League of Denver. "Where through those years were many of the prominent gentlemen whose names now appear on the calls for 'law and orders' mass meetings at the Brown Palace Hotel in this very city?" Costigan queried. No one had ever challenged his participation in railroad rate investigations. Why, then, question his decision to aid Horace Hawkins prepare information on the industrial conditions in southern Colorado? Why question the presentation of this material to a Congressional investigating committee for the UMWA? "I want to say to you, the members of the Progressive party," he declared, "that if any leadership of this movement involves the repudiation of the workers of this country you may retain the leadership and I, for my part, will preserve my independent judgment and conscience as a man and citizen." Law must have "fearless firm and impartial enforcement. Wrongs committed by capital, and wrongs committed by labor fall equally under the ban of law." Law and order without justice was insufficient; that type of law and order had existed under Latin-American dictatorships. Justice must be granted to all segments of society—to capital, labor, business, farmers, taxpayers and consumers. "The rights of man, to state the proposition mildly, are at least level with the rights of property."

Costigan's comprehensive answer to his critics did not still their criticism. As the applause subsided, F. D. Catlin of Montrose County rose; the former Senate candidate read an ultimatum from the thirty Progressives who were meeting separately. They demanded the adoption of resolutions that implicitly criticized the *Rocky Mountain News,* the Denver *Times,* the Denver *Express* and Judge Lindsey. No declaration for law and order could contain Costigan's addendum about social justice. And they would only join the assemblage if their terms were met. Costigan put the question to the conference without comment. His speech was adopted as the consensus of the meeting.[18] A fight for control of the Progressive Party was under way.

The split in the Progressive Party widened in direct proportion to the expansion of the Law and Order League. Edwin Miller tried to heal the breach. He informed the Denver Progressives of the conditions outside the city. At the same time he warned the "law and order" leaders that "the spirit that burned witches at stake . . . is just as dangerous a tendency to anarchy as the anarchy of union labor." But his efforts were unavailing. When the Progressive State Central Committee met, the "law and order" faction had two objectives. The Progressive Party must support the State Administration in the coal districts, and Costigan must not be the party's gubernatorial candidate.

At first, Costigan had been reluctant to withdraw as National Committeeman to seek the statehouse again. The intensive campaign would be a sacrifice. But when some of the very people who had urged that he run, now opposed his nomination, he fought vehemently for the designation. It was more than a personal reward. It now meant an endorsement of his views.

The fight against Costigan in the Central Committee suffered from poor tactical planning. J. S. Temple, who had earlier been forced to resign as Secretary because of his anti-Costigan activities, Allison Stocker, Denver County Chairman, and C. E. Fisher, a Progressive Congressional candidate, led the opposition. Their choice for an initial contest was inept. Allison Stocker attempted to prevent the seating of two Denver delegates whose credentials, he, as County Chairman, had not signed. Since they had been legitimately elected, James Causey easily defeated Stocker's motion. C. E. Fisher then called for the repudiation of State Chairman C. P. Dodge and State Treasurer James Causey for forcing Temple's resignation and demanded a reconsideration of the action. On a motion by Merle Vincent the committee voted, twenty-five to fourteen, not to reconsider the action. Costigan was victorious. Allison Stocker resigned as Denver County Chairman. But the struggle continued.

The cry of "law and order," coupled with the defection of Progressive leaders, brought many county organizations to the verge of collapse. When F. D. Catlin of Montrose County joined the opposition, Progressive leaders on the western slope found it difficult to reorganize the party. In Ouray, both the former Progressive Chairman and Secretary returned to the Republican Party. In Fremont, J. Homer Dickson called a meeting of the twenty leading Progressives to explain Costigan's position to them, only to find that P. H. Troutman and he were isolated in their support of Costigan. The others had returned to law, order and the Republican Party. Even in counties where the situation was not entirely hopeless, the "law and order" forces made significant inroads on Progressive strength. By the time that the Progressive nominating assembly met, in late July, I. N. Stevens, J. S. Temple, Allison Stocker and J. B. Stephen had joined the defectors.[19] Former Progressives now hurled charges of bossism at Costigan.

With his opponents gone, Costigan had no difficulty in winning the gubernatorial nomination. The Progressive assembly, weakened but still ardent, chanting "our Teddy and our Eddie," unanimously adopted the entire slate that had been presented for its approval. In his acceptance speech Costigan felt constrained to defend himself against charges of bossism: "The charge of dictation and bossism has always been utterly idle and false as applied to the Progressives of Colorado. Without money, without place, without power; empty handed, in fact, of all save the merit of our appeals for principle, the Progressives of Colorado from the first have made their contests. If this be bossism it is something new and not wholly undesirable in the history of politics and government."

The proponents of "law and order," demanded a respect for the law only on the part of labor. "Our years of warfare against wrong," he said, "have laid invariable emphasis on law and order as indispensable to society and absolutely fundamental in progress." Law and order was "flesh of the flesh and bone of the bone" of Progressives, for they had assailed lawbreakers, high or low, whoever or wherever they were. Those who cried for "law and order" desired "that order without law" which had been present for years in Huerfano and Las Animas, he charged. Labor strife had developed as a result of unfair actions of corporate-dominated administrations. Such conflicts could only be prevented by recognizing the role of unions and by settling industrial controversies with the impartial administration of the law. Only in that way could they enhance the conservation of human resources which was the chief concern of the Progressives, he concluded.

Fusion

The effort to prevent the nomination of Costigan had failed, but the moderates, who advocated fusion had won some concessions. While the National Executive Committee of the Progressive Party wanted completely independent slates in preparation for the coming battle of 1916, this proved impossible to achieve. After repeated factional disputes the Colorado Progressive Party maintained the compromise of 1912—there was to be no fusion on the state level, but local cooperation was permissible.

When unsatisfactory local candidates were endorsed, Party leaders repudiated these candidates. Costigan, P. H. Troutman and Merle Vincent asked Progressives to vote for the progressive Democratic Congressional candidate, Edward Keating, and not the Progressive-Republican candidate, N. N. McLean. Merle Vincent supported the progressive Democrat, Taylor, instead of the Progressive-Republican Congressional candidate, H. J. Baird. He repudiated a Progressive candidate for Congress, C. E. Fisher (Fisher had asked Teddy Roosevelt to keep out of Colorado since the Colonel's attitude on the coal strike was politically inexpedient).

How could the Colorado Progressives successfully combat the fusionists when Roosevelt, himself, had supported fusion behind Harvey Hinman in New York. To stay the crippling rumor that the Colonel was returning to the Republican Party, Costigan sent a letter to Roosevelt asking him to endorse the Colorado Progressive ticket.

The former President responded immediately with a lengthy supporting epistle, written for publication and distributed as a pamphlet. Industrial disturbances were inevitable as long as Colorado government abdicated responsibility for law and order and permitted the coal operators to import gunmen whenever the miners tried to organize, he wrote. Neither government nor the operators set an example of respect for the law, for laws safeguarding workers' rights were systematically violated. The misconduct and violence of the corporations had provoked the lawlessness of the workers, Roosevelt charged. The "law and order" group was guilty of folly for believing that it was enough to force lawbreakers on one side to comply with the law without making lawbreakers on the other side obedient. To restore order without justice, would ultimately result in revolution. Since private control had proven inadequate, Roosevelt proposed that coal mining be made a public utility. Coal fields still in the hands of the government should be leased, not sold, to secure justice to the workers and the public. If necessary to the public interest, the state should be permitted to assert compensated ownership of the mines. Unfortunately, Roosevelt's support of Costigan's program, like his endorsement of the New York Progressive ticket, came too late to undo the damage of the Hinman affair.

The Shaffer Press

As if the internal tensions were insufficient, the Colorado Progressives quarreled with John C. Shaffer, whose newspapers had been a mainstay of the Progressive Party in the Midwest. When Shaffer purchased the *Rocky Mountain News* and the *Denver Times* in 1913, the Colorado Progressives expected these papers to be a source of strength. Unfortunately, incompatability set in. The sensitive Lindsey soon complained that Shaffer's publications were treating him abusively. As relations deteriorated, national leaders of the Progressive Party were called in to heal the breach.

Like most Progressives, Shaffer was an independent who made his own decisions. Sensing Progressive efforts to dictate to him in matters of policy he reacted vehemently. When Costigan and he differed over the disposition of the Water Company, he was incensed at statements by Costigan that he felt all but read him out of the Progressive Party. In fact, it was differences over the Water Company that led to the first major clash between Shaffer and the Colorado Progressives.

Shaffer agreed with the Water Company about the price for the purchase of the water plant, joining issue with Costigan and the reformers. When the Denver Progressives accepted the support of the Denver *Post*, Shaffer accused them of submitting to dictation. At the Brown Palace Hotel he questioned Costigan's personal integrity and courage of conviction. He used the simile of Christ on the mountain to claim that Costigan had laid the world at his feet in temptation. Costigan challenged his veracity. He charged that Shaffer had summoned him to his editorial office to state that no candidate would receive his support who failed to unify the citizens of Denver.

When the mine strike broke, Shaffer's initial reaction was to side with Costigan's opponents. Clarence Phelps Dodge, Progressive State Chairman, publicly denounced Shaffer's position. As the controversy grew embittered, both sides sought aid from national Progressive leaders to bridge the gap before the Progressive Party was endangered.

Finally, Shaffer sent I. J. Duncan Clark and William Chenery to Denver to examine the situation. Both were favorably impressed by Costigan and his allies but unfavorably impressed by the staff of the *News* and *Times*. Clark corrected Shaffer's impression that the *Post* was dictating to Costigan and Lindsey. Neither liked the *Post*, they reported, but they accepted its support when offered. As a result of detailed reports on Costigan and his associates, William Chenery was was appointed editor of the *News* and for four months relations between Shaffer and the Denver Progressives improved.

During the summer of 1914, while the strike issue was splintering the Colorado Progressive Party, the Costigan Progressives and Shaffer clashed again. For a time, Shaffer joined the Progressive Party in its stand on the mine strike, but soon rumors circulated that the Shaffer press would endorse the Republican candidate. Albert Beveridge intervened as a friend of Shaffer. Since Shaffer had been personally offended by Costigan's letter to the *Post* during the Water Company controversy, he thought differences could be resolved by personal confrontation. But, in fact, not even Roosevelt could sway Shaffer. The Colonel came away from a conversation with him frustrated, certain that he had only succeeded in convincing the publisher that he himself was misguided about the Colorado situation. At the end, the breach was not healed, and Shaffer refused to support the Progressive candidates.

Despite this controversy, the *Rocky Mountain News* treated the Progressive Party fairly. The Denver *Express* and the Colorado Springs *Gazette* were two pillars of support. In general, however, Costigan felt that the most discouraging feature of the campaign was "the infamous flood of falsehood being poured out by a venal press." Undoubtedly press coverage outside of Denver weakened the effects of his whirlwind campaign.

The Campaign

Long before the convention Costigan had convinced the Progressive leaders that the campaign issues should parallel those of 1912, with somewhat greater emphasis upon economic justice as the necessary accompaniment for law and order. An effort by drys to commit the party to prohibition was rejected after a twenty-four hour debate. The convention adopted the essentials of Costigan's industrial program.

The Progressives did not limit their appeal to the industrial worker. For farmers and consumers the Progressives proposed an effective antitrust law, a state dairy commissioner for tubercular inspection of cattle, lower freight rates, the classification and disposition of all remaining lands, and a commission to eliminate the waste in marketing. They offered to solve the perennial agricultural problem of insufficient short-term credit with state farm loans from school funds at only six percent interest. Thus, the farmer's cost of borrowing would be reduced and the school fund would receive a larger return on its reserves than the banks offered. To attract more homesteaders, the Progressives offered a law preventing the destruction of homesteads by large herds of cattle. One Progressive plank would prove important to Costigan in the future—it called for a scientific tariff set by a tariff commission that would protect the consumer without injuring industry. In addition, the Progressives demanded the regulation of stock issues, federal conservation, government ownership of the telephone and telegraph, the extension of state education, the use of school buildings for the discussion of economic and social issues, and the elimination of the assembly feature of the Primary Law to ensure that no convention could influence the primaries.[20]

Meantime, long before the convention, Costigan had opened his campaign. The Republican Party and its members, he charged, had become the worshippers of property. On the other hand, the Democratic Party had permitted the special interests to use the slogans of states rights and liberty to promote the privileges of property at the expense of community welfare. "The Progressive Party, in contrast," he continued, "places the welfare of the whole public above property on the one hand, and license on the other." It endorsed the conservation of both public and human resources.

Costigan carried the campaign throughout the state. Just before the primary he traversed the western slope in an effort to counteract F. D. Catlin's defection by presenting his own industrial program to the rank and file Progressives.

After his nomination he returned to the southern coal fields as a candidate, rather than a lawyer. Defending his policies, he castigated Governor Ammons for his Peabody-like[21] policy and attacked Democratic candidate Patterson as the Governor's adviser. Returning north he aided in drafting the Progressive platform at the convention, and then organized a tour of the northern counties in a hired automobile. Benjamin Griffith and Merle Vincent, who had accompanied him in his southern tour, shared the platform in his northern swing. The speakers were introduced after screaming sirens had attracted a crowd. They worked their way through Weld, Fort Morgan and Logan Counties in a hectic trip, making eight stops a day, and emphasizing the Progressive agricultural program while attacking bossism in the major parties. In Boulder, where "law and order" had decimated the Progressive forces, Costigan returned to the campaign's primary issue: "I stand for the sort of law that is spelled L-A-W. My detractors stand for the brand of law spelled C-F-and-I." The end of October found Costigan and Troutman in the agricultural counties of the southeast, spreading the Progressive gospel. Henry J. Allen and William Allen White of Kansas and Medill McCormick of Illinois spoke in Colorado in support of Costigan. Amos Pinchot, the controversial New York Progressive, contributed both time and money. Costigan's campaign closed in Denver, with a series of street meetings and an election eve rally at the Ivy Theatre. The Progressives remained confident of rank and file support and of even more favorable election results than 1912. Unfortunately, the Progressives awoke with a sorrowful post-election headache.

Analysis of the Election Returns

For the Progressive Party the election of 1914 was a disaster. Both pro-labor candidates, Costigan and Patterson, were swamped. Costigan received less than half his 1912 vote. George Carlson, campaigning on a "law and order" and prohibition platform ran well ahead of his slate and only he and the candidate for Secretary of State were elected on the Republican ticket. Only where the Progressives retained a strong political organization did they receive any meaningful vote.

Outside of Denver it was only in the dairy counties that the Progressive vote remained higher than fifteen percent. It was highest in Arapahoe and El Paso where the Colorado Springs *Gazette* and the Denver *Express* were easily available and production was for an urban market. But the dairy counties of Douglas, Elbert and Logan, less populous and with greater per capita wealth, did not follow the pattern of the others.

The grazing and metal mining counties repeated their 1912 pattern with few Progressive votes.

In the southern coal mining counties of Las Animas and Huerfano where the operators controlled the ballots, the Progressive vote, never large, almost disappeared. Despite Costigan's activities on their behalf, labor, as expected, supported Patterson. Only in one radical coal town, Crested Butte in Gunnison County, did Costigan receive the largest vote, followed by the Socialist candidate. His activities for the union miners did, however, prepare the way for their overwhelming support for him in 1930. Where industry depended on the coal supply—in Pueblo County—the Progressive vote collapsed (declining from twenty-one percent in 1912 to three and three-tenths percent in 1914).

In Denver, Costigan's electoral percentage declined from thirty-eight and eight-tenths in 1912 to eighteen and three-tenths in 1914. He had carried half the Denver districts in 1912 and placed second in the rest. In 1914 his best showing was one second place. In upper and upper middle class central Denver, where Costigan had received an average of over forty-five percent in 1912, the "law and order" and prohibition issues provided a sweep for Carlson, and fifteen percent of the vote for Costigan. Costigan retained significant strength only outside of the central residential sections.[22]

The campaign that the Progressives had entered with such high expectations ended in bitter disappointment. Costigan still thought that a liberalized Progressive Party could hope to grow at the expense of the Democrats. A perennial optimist, he wrote that the inexorable development of events would bring ultimate victory to the progressive cause. While confident that his ideas were valid and only in advance of his times, yet he was discouraged to discover that the voters could not be taught by reason alone. "Apparently we have need of a new lesson in suffering," he wrote to Dr. Randolph Cook, "but we shall learn." To Amos Pinchot he wrote: "I have no doubt that you realize, however much the fact is to be lamented, that it is through great crises involving the wreck of lives and fortunes that the world most certainly learns its lessons." He could not have known as he wrote that another generation and the greatest economic crisis in American history would intervene before he would be called to the service of his state.

1. Progressive publications and services died, one at a time, for lack of funds.
2. Costigan rejected an offer by P. H. Troutman to name the Fremont County Progressive Club the Roosevelt-Costigan Club; it was issues, not personalities that mattered.
3. Roosevelt consciously wooed Borah, Norris, Bristow, Hadley, Kenyon and Cummins.
4. The realignment of all progressives into their party was a type of fusion the Progressives wanted, but this could not be achieved.
5. The Colorado Progressive Party lost F. D. Catlin and I. N. Steven, candidates for the Senate in 1912; J. S. Temple, State Secretary, Allison Stocker, Denver County Chairman, and such important local leaders as S. A. Coston and C. E. Fisher.
6. But not until 1916.
7. This was a highly successful campaign to effect the return of Progressives to the Republican Party by emphasizing the inevitable collapse of the third party.
8. H. M. Sammis wrote to Costigan: "I wish that you could run up here for a few days and see for yourself what a splendid little monarchy we have here, surrounded by the state of Colorado. Some place or other and on some other continent we have heard of the United States."
L. P. Barbour originally developed a prejudice against the strikers from newspaper reports. He visited the scene, talked with ranchers and farmers, and heard of feudal control by the operators, of unenforced state laws to protect miners, of mine guards who deliberately provoked violence, of a militia infiltrated with mine guards, of searches without warrants, of insults and intimidation of those who were sympathetic to the miners, and of a general violation of law by those in high places.
Cf., Fred Greenbaum, "A 'New Deal' for the Bituminous Coal Miners" (unpublished Master's thesis, University of Wisconsin, 1953), pp. 30-55, for a study of similar conditions in Harlan County, Kentucky.
9. Linderfelt was a soldier of fortune who had fought in Mexico and had become infamous among the strikers for his hatred of "wops" and "rednecks."
10. The mine guards were in a position to have fired the fatal shot.
11. James Fyler, Jr., admitted that he falsely testified against Lawson in order to be released from jail.
12. He accused the mine owners of hiring strikebreaking miners under false pretenses and keeping them at work against their will in order to pay for transportation.
13. An article was soon to appear pointing out that if the Colorado government had followed a policy of leasing coal mines instead of selling them, control would have been maintained over labor policy and the tragic events of the strike would never have occurred. Ammons' anti-conservation policy contributed to the very problems that he now had to face. "The Coal Strike and the Conservation Policy," *The Public*, May 8, 1914, p. 435, Costigan Collection.

14. By this Costigan was not necessarily advocating a closed shop. He felt that the Colorado law permitted peaceful persuasion. How much more than the use of speech this encompassed remained an unsettled question. He contended that the unorganized worker made war on the standard of living of organized workers. "The benefit of the doubt under the law, in my opinion, should be, therefore, cast in favor of morality, education and American standards of living, and if unions, as I believe, promote these, the benefit of any doubt should be given, as intimated, to organization."

15. Costigan felt that the militia had the power to take over the mines. Then the strikers could be paid to mine coal which the state could sell to the public at reasonable prices.

16. This group felt that Costigan was so biased in favor of labor that he would antagonize most of the Progressives. Thus the Progressive Party could be drawn back to the more moderate Republican Party.

17. Philip Stewart, former Progressive leader of the Arapahoe County Party and one of the leading Progressives in the state, became Republican State Chairman before "law and order" had become an issue. Allison Stocker had long toyed with local fusion. The varying opinions on organized labor of the anti-Costigan group can be gleaned from a memorandum of the meeting of the "law and order" group on June 8, 1914, Costigan Collection.

18. The group included Ira Delong, Allison Stocker, J. S. Temple, S. A. Coston, I. N. Stevens, John Grass, C. E. Fisher, W. H. Trask, B. J. Symonds, F. W. Crosley, W. D. Mier, and J. F. Coleman. They issued a statement denying any need to resort to violence when the state had initiative, referendum and recall, and felt that those who did resort to violence were not loyal or desirable citizens. The Progressive Party, they said, should pledge itself to restore order and enforce obedience to legal officers of the state and should condemn anyone, who by speeches or articles, brought contempt upon the institutions of the state or the legally organized militia. At this meeting J. S. Temple called for patriotism over partisanship and for support of the Administration despite any distaste for Governor Ammons and General Chase.

19. J. S. Temple sent a letter to the Progressive voters urging that they support the Republican ticket since the Progressive Party was not supporting "law and order." I. N. Stevens made an unsuccessful race for the Republican Senatorial nomination while Allison Stocker was successful in his quest for the Republican nomination for State Treasurer.

20. The victor in the party assembly had the advantage of the first line on the ballot and the desire of politicians to work for the apparent winner.

21. James Peabody, Governor of Colorado 1903-1905, conspired with Idaho authorities illegally to transport Charles Moyer and William Haywood of the Western Federation of Miners to Idaho to stand trial for complicity in the murder of Frank Steunenberg.

22. His best showing was among suburban small homeowners. His total reached twenty-five percent only in the easternmost and two southern districts— not quite the southernmost. He received twenty-three percent of the votes among the homeowning workers of northwest Denver. Generally, Denver followed the state pattern and former Progressive strongholds defected to Carlson; Patterson carried the normally Democratic sections.

CHAPTER V

EPILOGUE TO THE PROGRESSIVE MOVEMENT

Despite the magnitude of their defeat in 1914, the Colorado Progressives refused to abandon the struggle for economic and political reform.

Costigan explained to Governor Hiram Johnson of California that with such obstacles to overcome as the depression, the war, the economic question and prohibition, the Colorado Progressives should have been gratified that they were not annihilated. Letters from Costigan's associates did not underestimate the seriousness of the defeat, but they retained their confidence in eventual victory. More and more, Costigan found himself devoting his time to his neglected business affairs and the UMWA rather than to the Progressive Party. The satisfaction derived from the unfortunate campaign of 1914 were at best minimal, and they were limited to two indirect effects of the mine strike.

The violent events in southern Colorado had led to investigations by a Congressional committee and by the Commission on Industrial Relations. Costigan testified before both of these bodies, describing the absolute political rule of the operators, and listing their violations of state laws that were supposed to govern mining and industrial relations (some of which had been enacted before the turn of the century). He portrayed the use of private armies for private war. And he told of the violation of the Federal Peonage Statute of 1867. Rockefeller's philantrophy, he charged, obscured "the sordid practices of big business." Where Rockefeller had economic interests, Costigan asserted, he did not follow the advice of the expert advisers of his foundation but that of his company executives. Thus, his apparent benevolence served to still criticism and to delay the advent of industrial democracy and economic justice. Rockefeller's testimony before the commission, Costigan declared, "demonstrated the dangers and unreliability of charity and the inferiority of charity to economic justice." Even slavery and feudalism could boast of occasional generosity. Such testimony did not improve Rockefeller's carefully nurtured public relations.

The unfavorable impression left by the investigation of the Commission on Industrial Relations had to be erased. Yet Rockefeller had no intention of permitting any independent organization by his employees.

To meet this situation, the Rockefeller interests devised the employee-representation plan. Under this plan, employees of the Colorado Fuel and Iron Company could elect local representatives who could submit grievances against the company. Two channels were opened for such complaints: they could be forwarded through the normal chain of command up to the president, or they could be sent to special district conferences, joint committees of management and labor employees that were to be established to mediate local differences. Although the United Mine Workers and the American Federation of Labor attacked this as a pseudo-union, the newly established Colorado Industrial Commission decided that the employee-representation plan fulfilled Colorado laws. Thus it rejected a UMWA declaration of intent to strike for lack of representation. The employee-representation plan served its purpose well. It denied the reality of bothersome employee organization while granting its semblance. The very institution of the employee-representation plan was, however, a step forward from the paternalism of the Rockefeller interests.

A second consequence of the 1914 disturbance gave complete satisfaction to all those who had struggled for truly representative government in the southern coal fields. The Colorado Supreme Court upheld a challenge to Sheriff Jefferson Farr's reelection. Farr, the tool of the operators, was thrown out of office. A jubilant resident of Walsenburg wrote to Costigan: "Now they can take their wives and families to the picture shows at night without being afraid of being beating [sic] up, and insulted on the main street."

The third result of the 1914 strike was much less satisfactory to Costigan.

In an effort to prevent a repetition of the previous year's strife the Colorado legislature, in 1915, created an Industrial Commission with a dual function—that of administering the newly passed Workmen's Compensation Act and of supervising the relations between employers and employees. In its latter capacity the commission would probe labor disputes. During such inquiries the employers could not impose lockouts and the employees could not strike for a period of thirty days. Costigan had supported compulsory investigation, for he felt that an examination of the mine strike had led to the Workmen's Compensation Act and an awareness of the miners' living conditions, but he vehemently opposed a compulsory arbitration provision incorporating a no-strike period. Voluntary arbitration, he declared, could be valuable in settling a controversy, but the prohibition of the right to strike was unconstitutional—it provided for involuntary servitude. Yet he did not rest his case on the constitutionality of the law alone for the Constitution could be changed either by amendment or judicial usurpation.

The law, Costigan insisted, not only violated personal liberty, but was ineffective as well. Similar laws had failed to prevent work stoppages in Australia and Canada. Any provision to delay strikes, he asserted, would have the opposite effect. Industrial discord would result for workers would feel that they were denied equal treatment. The standard of living of American workers was inadequate, Costigan charged. The legislators had no right to deny them their one weapon to improve their standards—the right to strike. Moreover, not even the representative of capital on the United States Commission on Industrial Relations recommended the Canadian Act on which the Colorado provision had been modeled, and Professor Commons, an expert member of the Commission, labeled the Canadian legislation "unsuited to American conditions." Costigan's call for a repeal of the iniquitous law went unheeded.

The Return of Boss Speer

The frustration of Costigan and the Progressives on the state-wide level was compounded by the events in Denver. Somehow the new era of a prosperous Denver and an honest city government—confidently expected by the non-partisan coalition once the notorious Robert Speer had been removed—never came to pass. Even before the insurgents had secured commission government, the public had been treated to considerable dissension in their ranks. The fight between Creel and Arnold was open and heated. The minor disparity between Lindsey and Costigan's conception of the proper procedure for instituting commission government was greatly overpublicized. The reformers had not displayed unity in the election of the commissioners, and some of the electorate's choices disappointed veterans like Lindsey. Lindsey was much disturbed when the commissioners dismissed sympathetic city employees, including Lindsey's own brother, yet he was still confident that partisan machine politics could be eliminated.

Others were not as tolerant of the new government's shortcomings as were Costigan and Lindsey. Once the inexperienced Commission proved unable to reduce taxes while increasing services, many of the former supporters of this form of government became alienated.

When Speer returned from a trip abroad in late April, 1916, determined to return to a mayoralty with greater centralized power, he was able to rally overwhelming support. The *Rocky Mountain News,* which had caricatured the former mayor as "Rob-us, Speer-us", now, under new ownership, ardently supported him. Speer, reputedly matured and reformed, was endorsed by the Denver Trades Assembly and even a group from the old Citizen's Party. Above all, the Speer machine had never been dismantled. The reformers had fought a non-partisan struggle on a city-wide basis. They had ignored the laborious task of wresting the party machinery from the hands of Speer's local cronies. Once the reform impulse had passed, the organization was prepared for business as usual.

Opposition to Speer was weak, divided, and hopeless. Ben Lindsey was discouraged and recuperating from an operation. T. M. Patterson had aged. In addition, five of the commissioners supported amendments that called for a strong mayor. Of the press, only the Denver *Post* backed extension of the experiment, while the Denver *Express* remained neutral.

Costigan continued to oppose Speer and support commission government. The Independent Denver Citizens, of whom Costigan was a leader, declared that Speer was unfit to govern, that his election would restore wide-open gambling, public utility control, the spoils system, and additional taxation. Costigan rejected the various amendments as defective and unrepresentative, for they had not been drafted at a charter convention. The Speer Amendment, the real issue, Costigan warned, placed great power in the hands of the Mayor, who was to be Speer himself. The Mayor would choose almost all of the executive officials. Until 1919, he would even choose four members of the Council while the other five would be chosen by representative civic groups.

The issues were clearly drawn. After more than a decade of reform activity, the citizens of Denver returned Robert W. Speer to office with a thumping majority. Denver had had its reform.

Preparedness

For the focus of American attention had shifted from internal to external affairs. With the conflagration in Europe, war stories pushed domestic news off the front pages and righteous indignation was now aimed at autocratic Germany rather than at autocratic American corporations. The flow of reform legislation under the aegis of the Wilson Administration did not temper the attitude of Roosevelt and Perkins toward the new Chief Executive. Their major concern had shifted toward the preparedness of the nation for war. Although Roosevelt's initial reaction had been one of neutrality, he was not of a neutral temperament. An aggressive advocate of American nationalism, he had long attacked Wilson's Mexican policy, and was furious when Secretary of State Bryan negotiated a treaty apologizing to Colombia for our share in the Panama Revolution and proposed an indemnity of twenty-five million dollars, repudiating Roosevelt's proudest accomplishment. During the last two weeks of September 1914, Roosevelt's attitude changed from isolationism to interventionism. The warrior had replaced the crusader. The pacifists had done more harm to this country, he shrieked, than all the crooked businessmen and politicians combined.

Even Costigan, at one time, wrote that the greatest issue of the campaign of 1916 would be preparedness, and he fully expected to support the party whose stand best fulfilled this need. Nevertheless he stated that Wilson had been the man of the hour, and the President deserved the support of Americans during this crisis. But Costigan refused to commit himself until the platforms and candidates were chosen. An optimist, he still expected the weakened Progressive Party to run an independent slate, despite evidence that it was disintegrating.

Roosevelt Tries for the Republican Nomination

As Roosevelt grew more and more belligerent he withdrew from those members of his own party who opposed American involvement. As might be expected, the conservatives controlled the "patriotic" organizations. When Roosevelt met more with Frick, Gary and Belmont, and less with Beveridge, Addams and Pinchot, his progressivism became more and more submerged. After the fiasco of 1914 he was determined to hold the Progressive Party together only to ensure the Republican nomination of a preparedness candidate. The most available man was, of course, Theodore Roosevelt.

In Colorado, four years of a Democratic national administration had taught the old standpatters the advantage of running someone with mass appeal. A. M. Stevenson, who had been instrumental in securing Taft's renomination in 1912, now called for "red blooded, whole hearted Americanism, and Theodore Roosevelt." After a victory for the Colonel in the Denver County Convention, the Republican State Convention sent to the Republican National Convention an uninstructed delegation, three-fourths of whom supported Roosevelt and preparedness.

At the same time, Roosevelt retained the firm support of the Progressives. Costigan declared that the Colonel was the first, second, and third choice of the Colorado Progressives for the Presidential nomination. As if he had a premonition that this was to be last Progressive

Convention, Costigan wanted as many of the loyal legion to attend as possible, each with a half vote. When Costigan arrived in Chicago, he found the Progressive Convention pledged to Roosevelt, as expected, and heavily emphasizing the issue of armaments. Banners screamed: "T. R., Safety First;" "Roosevelt, Preparedness, America—the favorite son of the nation." The Progressives prepared to endorse Roosevelt and await the outcome of the Republican Convention.

A simultaneous meeting with the Republican Convention was chosen to facilitate discussions with the Republicans. The managers of the Progressive Convention were determined to prevent any premature nomination of Roosevelt, to avoid charges of Progressive efforts to dictate to the Republicans. Military readiness already dominated the Progressive platform and social reforms were relegated to an insignificant paragraph. No basic platform change would be necessary to make the leap into the Republican Party. But the convention was rebellious and immediate nominations were only forestalled by a letter from Roosevelt.

Efforts at unity collapsed. The Progressives suggested only Roosevelt. The Republicans would not consider him and would not negotiate seriously prior to the balloting. Roosevelt fared poorly on the first two Republican ballots. Hughes led. At the next meeting the Republicans reluctantly suggested Hughes. Discouraged, Roosevelt recommended two conservative Republican friends, but no Progressive. With the collapse of negotiations Perkins lost control of the Progressive Convention and Roosevelt was nominated three minutes after the Republicans had declared for Hughes. Confusion reigned. Roosevelt's conditional refusal of the nomination was interpreted by many delegates as provisional acceptance. Without clarification the chairman adjourned the meeting. Costigan concluded that the Progressive inner circle had dumped the movement.

The fate of the Progressive Party now rested with Roosevelt, ready to withdraw in favor of "preparedness".

The Colorado Progressives floundered as Costigan refused to comment at first. Finally, he castigated the Progressive national leadership. A group of devoted Progressives "were guided last week to an open and defenseless position, and there exposed to the merciless fire of Republican political sharpshooters," he charged. "It was a rare example of political unpreparedness and incredibly poor leadership." If the Progressive National Committee chose no ticket the Progressives would divide "according to their deep-seated conviction of paramount national issues." Some, trapped, would return to their Republican enemies. The

EPILOGUE TO THE PROGRESSIVE MOVEMENT

majority, he felt, would prefer a temporary alliance with the Democrats or a party of protest. "One thing is certain," he declared, "there will be no delivery of Progressive votes. They must be won individually. As a Progressive said at the close of the Chicago Convention: 'The Lord deliver us! But no one else shall!'" The progressive movement, he insisted, belonged to no man, but was a struggle "against invisible government and a demand for social and industrial justice, and whether captained or leaderless that movement will go on to ultimate victory." Costigan would not be delivered to Hughes.

As expected, Justice Hughes declared that he was for "Americanism and Manhood." Roosevelt endorsed him. Dutifully, the Progressive National Committee overwhelmingly endorsed the Republican nominee, C. P. Dodge voting with the majority. Costigan called Dodge's action, lacking the approval of the Colorado Progressive Party, "unwise, unjust and unfortunate." Colorado Progressives individually examined the candidates.

Costigan Endorses Wilson

Many Progressive leaders supported Hughes. He was endorsed by Roosevelt and was the candidate of their original party. Merle Vincent, thinking himself in the minority, rationalized his support for the Republican nominee. Both parties were essentially conservative, both candidates temperamentally so inclined, both were independent of and better than their parties, and both had similar platforms. While Hughes' domestic record was as good as Wilson's had been before his Presidency, he had better executive qualities and was more decisive. Wilson's domestic accomplishments were admirable, he concluded, but his extreme neutrality appeared to be indifference at a time democratic France was locked in mortal combat with autocratic Germany.

Costigan, on the other hand, delayed his own endorsement lest it be construed as an objectionable delivery of the party name. Progressives, he felt, should take individual positions. Since many Progressives were jockeying for political position in anticipation of their party's dissolution, he thought it best for the party to declare a two-year recess and make no official alliance. His silence invited constant badgering by both sides. Former Progressives, as well as regular Republicans, sought his support for Republican nominations. Wilson supporters, aware of Costigan's favorable opinion, asked him to speak for their candidate. Finally, Costigan decided to endorse the President.

Costigan had long been friendly with the Colorado Platform Democrats. Senator John Shafroth, as governor, had appointed him to a number of honorary positions.[1] Costigan had openly admired Senator C. S. Thomas, despite Thomas's low tariff convictions. With George Creel, a man of growing importance in the Wilson Administration, he had labored to reform Denver. Wilson's first term had impressed him and he was upset by the effort of the national Progressive leadership to deliver votes to the Republicans. After considerable deliberation he announced his support for the President on October 1st.

With the Progressive Party inactive in the 1916 campaign, Costigan declared, Progressives must support those candidates most likely to advance their principles. Still, they were neither converts to an old order, nor were they repudiating their past criticisms. On the contrary, if these new alliances failed to provide a government of fundamental service to the people, a new, broader, liberal movement would be formed. In 1912 the Democratic Party had seemed an unsuitable vehicle for constructive legislation. Yet subsequent events had shown these doubts to be fallacious. Wilson and his Democratic Congress had amassed a formidable record: they had instituted a non-partisan Tariff Commission, and had provided for an Income Tax, good roads, the Federal Reserve Banking Law, rural credits, military preparation, the Seamen's Act, the National Child Labor Law and a legislative declaration that labor was not a commodity. "We find a record on which the Progressive party, had it succeeded in 1912, would confidently and reasonably have based its title to reelection." Could Progressives, then, deny credit to others that they would have claimed for themselves and "turn their backs on that record for mere Republican generalities which have glittered, without fulfillment, through a generation of party ascendancy?"

To Progressive critics of Wilson's foreign policy Costigan retorted that "economic prosperity will do more to quicken essential patriotism and to make this nation self-defensively powerful than the floating of many battleships or the summoning of vast armies." He castigated politicians who, avoiding an open declaration for a warlike policy, condemned an Administration which did not take the easy road to useless conflict. Magnanimous patience was as necessary to diplomacy as unyielding firmness, he lectured, and a blind belligerence would have led us into needless strife in Europe and Mexico.

While the lines were never clearly drawn, Costigan continued, the Democratic Party had the greater portion of the plain people, despite the presence of able lieutenants of the interests, and the Republican Party had a larger portion of the beneficiaries from special privilege.

EPILOGUE TO THE PROGRESSIVE MOVEMENT

Further, he characterized the Colorado Republican candidates for Governor and the Supreme Court as reactionaries. Would a party of privilege or a party of real fraternity be more likely to meet such problems as true preparedness, eliminating private profit from war, women's suffrage, unemployment, and the "whole program of social and industrial betterment?" "Are the benefits of popular government more likely to flow from oligarchical generosity or the people's own self-preserving vigilance and wisdom?"

To be sure, he insisted, Progressives required further assurances of progressive principles before they would support the Democratic Party, and they would vote only for proven friends of popular government, those who "genuinely accept the leadership of President Wilson." "Progressives will leave their future permanent affiliation to be determined by the adherence of those they support to the fundamentals of a growingly wise, efficient, and fraternal people's government."[2] Costigan was not yet ready to join the Democratic Party.

Although Costigan refrained from campaigning in 1916, he strongly endorsed the Democratic candidate for Governor, Julius C. Gunter, while repudiating the incumbent, George Carlson. Most Progressives, he assured Gunter, were "thoroughly awake to the difference between genuine Progressivism and the ill-considered substitute offered us by Colorado's present administration." Although Carlson had masqueraded as a progressive and had emphasized prohibition, he informed former associates, Carlson had prosecuted only one side after the coal strike and had used the Commission Law "in an alarming fashion" to threaten the miners in the Leadville controversy.

The narrow victory of Wilson and Gunter in Colorado convinced Costigan that the Progressives held the balance of power in the state. Wilson's reelection, he asserted, was due to his adoption of a large portion of the Progressive platform. As the campaign ended, Costigan and pro-Gunter Progressives presented a petition to the Governor-elect. They insisted that Judge Gunter honor his promise to institute Wilson's principles in Colorado—to serve all legitimate interests. In this lengthy memorial the Progressives demanded a wide range of reforms: the extension of the powers of the Public Utilities Commission, state loans to farmers and home owners, the elimination of the thirty-day strike prohibition from the Industrial Commission Act, social welfare legislation for workers—improved workmen's compensation, minimum wages for women and minors, and the use of school attendance laws to eliminate excessive child labor in the beet fields, optional jury service for women, improved election laws—the modification of the initiative law (first, to supply pamphlets informing the electorate of both sides of the initiative question, and second, the appointment of public officials to circulate initiative petitions), the perfecting of primary laws to eliminate the assembly feature, to prohibit crossing party lines during primaries, and to extend the time between the primary and the election.

Having presented this memorial, Costigan renewed his efforts to promote progressivism.

Attempts to Continue the Progressive Party

No sooner had the campaign ended than Costigan tried to rehabilitate the Progressive Party. Within a few days of Wilson's victory Costigan issued a statement to the press declaring that, unlike the East, which was concerned with the European war, the progressive West was still thinking about domestic peace and justice and had reelected Wilson for he had embraced the Progressive platform. Progressivism was still a strong force and the Progressive Party could still be resuscitated.

As November drew to a close, Costigan sounded out key Colorado Progressives about reviving the Party. Merle Vincent, while immersed in business affairs like Costigan, saw no reason why future cooperation should be inhibited by a temporary difference on how best to advance progressive principles. Costigan found that leading national Progressives were attempting to reconstruct the party without Roosevelt or Perkins. Costigan agreed to help reorganize the Western division of the party. He asserted his determination to retain his Progressive individuality even if the rehabilitation failed. The Republican Party could not be controlled by returning Progressives, he warned his colleagues. If necessary, he preferred to ally himself with the progressive Democrats, but always remaining a Progressive.

Appointment to the Tariff Commission

After his inauguration, Governor Gunter asked Costigan to draft a list of deserving Progressives. Unfortunately, Gunter's appointment of D. C. Burns to the Industrial Commission was rejected by the Senate. Costigan was more fortunate when President Wilson appointed him to the United States Tariff Commission.

The idea of a tariff commission antedated the Progressive Era. In 1882 Congress authorized President Arthur to appoint a commission to examine the needs of industry and to draw up reasonable tariff schedules. Although composed of protectionists, the commission recommended substantial reductions. As a portend of things to come, Congress ignored its work. Nevertheless, the concept of a tariff commission did not die easily.

During the latter part of the nineteenth century and the early part of the twentieth century many thoughtful people were convinced that non-partisan, non-elective commissions could be chosen, capable of sifting the facts carefully and impartially, unaffected by political considerations, and arrive at fair, judicious, balanced decisions. After a slow start, this innovation in governmental technique expanded so rapidly that the proliferation of alphabetical agencies became a standing joke of politically-oriented comedians. In an atmosphere favorable to the development of commissions, the demand to take the tariff out of politics increased in strength.

When President Taft, showing more courage than political acumen, pressed for a tariff revision shortly after his accession to office, the entire question of the tariff was revived. The resultant Payne-Aldrich Law failed to provide a tariff commission because of obstructive opposition in the House of Representatives. However, Taft found a pretext to create a Tariff Board in a provision permitting the President to raise rates in the event that he found commercial discrimination against the United States. He appointed three Republicans and two Democrats to prepare reports comparing domestic and foreign costs of production. The commission hastily prepared useful, though incomplete reports on the wool and cotton schedules. Unfortunately, their work was ignored by the next Congress to consider tariff revision.

With the victory of the Democrats in 1910 and 1912 a strong movement for downward tariff revision began. To the Democrats the Tariff Board was a Republican device. If utilized, the work of the Board would necessarily delay the enactment of a tariff, possibly until the electorate had changed the composition of Congress. Consequently the Democrats emphasized the flaws and ignored the positive aspects of the preliminary report of the Board. They killed the Tariff Board by refusing to appropriate funds for its continuance. The examination of tariff schedules was relegated to a new cost-of-production study division of the Department of Commerce.

Yet the demand for a tariff commission would not be stilled. With the advent of the war the Administration realized that the world economy would be dislocated and began to listen sympathetically to demands for an impartial commission. Support came from such diverse groups and persons as the National Grange, the Farmers' National Congress, the American Federation of Labor, the editor of the American Agriculturist, the Massachusetts Board of Trade, the Merchant Association of New York, the investment banker, Herbert Lehman, the Republican Mayor of Philadelphia, Rudolph Blankenburg, and the future Democratic candidate for President, James Cox. Under pressure from the Administration, Congress created the Tariff Commission. Its function was not to fix duties or recommend rates for tariff schedules, but to compile tariff information. The commission was to investigate the effects of the customs law, the relation between the rates on raw materials and finished articles, the effect of rates on industry and labor, the volume of imports in comparison with the volume of domestic production, the conditions of international competition including comparative cost of production, tariff relations with other countries, and the effect of preferential provisions, economic alliances, export bounties and preferential transport rates on international trade. In addition, it was expected to recommend non-partisan legislation to eliminate overlapping and obscure customs statutes. The customs laws were long overdue for an overhaul.

Wilson staffed the Commission with men of an independent turn of mind. Under the law the terms of the Commissioners were staggered to ensure continuity and to limit the influence of any single administration. The chairman, appointed to a full twelve-year term, was Frank W. Taussig of Harvard, the nation's leading tariff authority and a political independent. The ten-year term went to Daniel Roper, the Democratic Assistant Postmaster-General. The only other Democrat on the original Commission was a Congressman of independent inclination, David J. Lewis of Maryland, who was appointed for eight years. The only Republican, Congressman William Culbertson of Kansas, proved to be a thorn in the side of high tariff Republican Administrations in the twenties. The six-year term was given to a former Republican, the pro-Wilson Progressive Congressman from California, William Kent.

Costigan received firm support for his appointment from the two Democratic Senators from Colorado with whom he had long been friends.[3] Although he was appointed to the position with the least prestige, the two-year term, it was the best position from the point of view of tenure. Wilson would still be in office when his term expired and Costigan was sure to receive an additional twelve-year term. Costigan left his home with some reluctance. He was not certain that the responsibilities and salary of the new position were sufficient to leave a flourishing legal practice and a familiar environment for new, albeit exciting duties. Except for a short interval in the late twenties, Costigan spent the rest of his career in Washington.

EPILOGUE TO THE PROGRESSIVE MOVEMENT

Postscript to the Progressive Movement

While Costigan toiled in Washington, the legislative accomplishments of Colorado insurgents were under constant attack from conservatives. As early as 1917 progressives were on the defensive against legislative endeavors to make the initiative and referendum meaningless. Attempts to emasculate the primaries were repeatedly beaten back. Although these laws remained in force, they never fulfilled the hopes that the progressives had placed in them. Writing in 1930, Lee Taylor Casey summed up the effect of direct legislation: In sixteen years not a single referred measure had been adopted. Since 1922 no referred amendment had appeared on the ballot. Since 1922 only three initiated measures had been placed on the ballot and only one of these had been adopted. The power of recall had never been resorted to in reference to any statewide office. The primary had been weakened and its elimination narrowly averted. Only the headless ballot had added to the political independence of the voter.

In the decade after the progressive movement, while Costigan was secure in his administrative post, Progressives fared poorly in the pursuit of both office and legislation. Many former Progressives who returned to the Republican Party had sought political office, but none were elected to a major position. Even Ben Lindsey was removed from the Juvenile Court. In Washington, Edward Costigan and his wife Mabel unsuccessfully attempted to secure Constitutional amendments to provide minimum wages and to eliminate child labor in industries engaged in interstate commerce. The progressive movement had fallen victim to fraternal strife, untimely division, misleadership, partisan politics, the distractions of war and the failure of their success. The temper of the nineteen-twenties was not conducive to its revival.

1. Shafroth had appointed Costigan to the American Society for Judicial Settlement of International Disputes, the Commission to Investigate Coinage of Money and Issuance of Currency in the United States, and to the American Academy of Political and Social Science.
2. The *Rocky Mountain News* attacked Costigan for supporting Wilson. If Progressives endorsed Roosevelt they should follow his endorsement of Hughes, who was making the campaign Teddy would have made. If Progressives were right in supporting TR in June, they must be wrong in supporting Wilson now. The burden of the opposition of the *News* towards Wilson rested on the issue of preparedness. The state must support the Republicans and become "more closely associated with the Greater Americanism that is sweeping the country."
3. George Creel recommended Costigan for appointment as Attorney-General.

CHAPTER VI

THE TARIFF COMMISSION

The effort to take the tariff out of politics by the creation of a Tariff Commission met the fate of so many progressive hopes in the climate of post war America. In fact, it was almost immediately subject to attack. Although the Act of 1916 restricted the Commission to an investigatory role, by 1918 Congress was reluctant to grant enough money. Chairman Taussig and William Kent employed economists from their own salaries until hard lobbying by Costigan and Kent produced Congressional financing. Having parried a threat from the Democrats, the Commission faced a newly elected Republican majority. Only a brilliant speech by LaFollette prevented an effort by the Senate Committee on Appropriations to eliminate all funds for the Commission. The Tariff Commission had been spared the fate of its predescessor.

Despite this apparent victory for the advocates of a scientific tariff postwar America was not receptive to reasonable tariff rates. The adequacy of the Underwood Tariff had never been tested, for it was in effect only during the dislocations of a world at war and a world recovering from combat. The conflagration had altered the American economy. A domestic chemical and dye industry had been encouraged when hostilities cut off the normal source of supply, and, on the advice of the Tariff Commission, the duties on dyestuffs had been increased. Farm production had expanded beyond any ordinary national needs in order to meet the requirements of battle-torn Europe, and farmers had finally been convinced of the efficacy of tariff protection. Despite Wilson's opposition, an Emergency Agricultural Tariff was passed. Once the farmers had been placated there was no major resistance to thorough upward revision of the schedules. The resultant Fordney-McCumber Tariff raised rates on manufactured goods twenty-five percent above the controversial Payne-Aldrich Law. High duties were also imposed on farm products. Yet ardent protectionists were not satisfied. They were determined that the impost should be used to prevent European imports, not just to enable American producers to compete effectively.

Commissioner Culbertson, with the aid of Senator Smoot, was able to deflect some of these protectionist demands with a provision that permitted flexibility. The President could raise or lower schedules fifty percent upon the recommendation of the Tariff Commission, and he could even substitute American valuation for European valuation if it was deemed necessary.[1] Unfortunately, the faith of Costigan and Culbertson in the flexible provision of the tariff was soon to be frustrated.

The Tariff Issue

While Costigan had long supported objectivity and reasonableness in establishing import duties, he had never been an advocate of free trade. Indeed, before completing college he had endorsed protection, and as late as 1908, in a letter to Congressman Robert W. Bonynge, he had pointed out the importance and advantages of setting a levy on souvenir post cards: "A careful investigation of the business mentioned convinces me that a Republican Congress has, in this manufacturing line, a splendid opportunity to demonstrate publicly the advantages of the protective tariff from the point of view of home manufacture and home labor. Indeed, I doubt whether any illustration comparable to this one has arisen in this country since the phenomenal development of the tinplate industry."

Within a year the Payne-Aldrich Tariff had become an issue and progressives had begun to echo Albert Beveridge's demand for a commission that would remove the tariff from politics and determine scientific schedules that were adequate without being burdensome. They wanted schedules based on comparative costs of production.

Opponents of the comparative cost of production principle registered vigorous objections to its flaws. There was, for example, no single cost of production for any item. Expenses varied from section to section, from company to company, from factory to factory, and from time to time. Within the same productive unit it was difficult to determine costs. What percentage of sheep raising should be attributed to the production of wool and what percentage to meat? How then was the cost to be determined? Was the tariff to be set high enough to protect the borderline producer? If so, who was to be the marginal firm? No matter what the level of the tariff there would always be a marginal producer, fabricating his goods at a cost roughly equal to the domestic price. If the tariff were raised it would permit less efficient firms to enter the market. If it were lowered the less efficient would be forced out of business; but the marginal producer would still exist, albeit higher in the scale of efficiency. With a sufficient tariff, it was argued, grapes could be grown in Maine hothouses and the new wine industry would demand a tariff equal to the difference in cost of production between Maine wine and Algerian wine.

Progressives denied any intention of protecting inefficient concerns. They wanted a tariff to protect an American standard of wages and competence, not to protect inept management or items that were not suitable for American manufacture. Efficiency could create high wages with a low cost of labor. Where wages were low, legislation would enable workers to fight for their share of tariff benefits. But progressives could not explain how unprotected businesses could pay higher wages than protected industries. Did a tariff tend to make firms lax and reduce their incentive to produce more effectively and thus reduce the real wages that they paid? Since cost of production was considered a trade secret, how would foreign manufacturers be persuaded to allow the examination of their books? The progressive Republicans, like the standpatters, were still committed to a protective tariff. Unlike the conservatives, the progressives no longer felt that domestic competition would reduce prices to the lowest reasonable level. Trusts had interfered with the mechanism of a free market.

Costigan fully accepted the progressive Republican approach to the tariff and included this solution in the campaign platforms that he helped to draft during the progressive era. As a result of his trip through Europe towards the end of World War I, he recognized that rigid schedules would not be desirable in the postwar world. Many nations were preparing policies that would create self-sufficient economies. Some of the Allies had proposed a common market in opposition to the enemy states—Costigan had branded this proposal as an attempt "to erect the temple of permanent peace on the shifting sands of economic war." During Christmas of 1917, Costigan had proposed that Congress grant the President the right to raise or lower rates on a comprehensive scale so that the United States could be placed in an effective bargaining position. An expert commission, he thought, could advise the President as to the wisest course in revising tariff schedules. The major purpose of such a law would be to eliminate rate discrimination:

"Treaty and tariff policies should aim at the extermination, not the promotion of discrimination. Economic alliances, except in extremity, should be studiously shunned, because of their tendency towards compulsion and hostility. Our object should be liberated, not shackled, commerce; our means, friendly; our spirit, international, inviting the beneficent give and take of cooperative right action, in an orderly, united, and self-governing world."

The Fordney-McCumber Tariff and Flexibility

Despite the highly protective nature of the Fordney-McCumber Tariff, it had one positive feature from Costigan's point of view; through the influence of William Culbertson the flexible provision was revised to conform more closely to Costigan's 1917 proposal. The Commission, as originally created, lacked administrative functions. It was to aid Congress in drawing up tariff schedules. Under its original mandate the Commission prepared a report that revamped the administrative structure of the tariff, brought its construction and phrasing up to date, and overhauled the customs law to eliminate redundancies and useless vestiges of a past age. Although Congress discovered the contents of this draft almost by accident, its features were incorporated in the Fordney-McCumber Act and thus the new law was more carefully written than its predecessors. More important for the Commission, the new mandate brought it much closer to a tariff-making role. It was ordered to investigate the plausibility of changing schedules (taking into account the difference between domestic and foreign costs of production) and to report its findings to the President. The law enabled the Chief Executive to adjust rates by as much as fifty percent.

Costigan considered the flexible provisions of the new statute to be a marked advantage over the "old fashioned log-rolling method in tariff making." He felt it would "lessen the dissatisfaction which always grows up under long-continued, rigid tariff laws." The readjustment of particular rates could be undertaken, after a comparison of costs of production, without the disturbances which attended general revision.[2] He recognized the difficulty in applying this principle, since each producer's expenses differed, yet the investigation should prove very useful, he said. It would indicate the efficiency of American labor and show whether high-cost industries were being supported through tariff duties for the national interest or for private ends. It would also determine whether monopolistic industries had used this protection to raise domestic prices unnecessarily. Such knowledge would aid in determining scientific commercial policies.

Unfortunately, Costigan left out an important factor in his portrayal of a bright future for the Tariff Commission—its changing membership.

The Members of the Tariff Commission

The original members of the Tariff Commission, the Wilson appointees, had been dedicated to a scientific tariff. Thomas Page, Wilson's replacement for Daniel Roper, felt that the Tariff Commission should be limited to an investigation of fact while Congress should retain the decisive voice on schedules. Consequently, he resigned soon after the enactment of the Fordney-McCumber Act. The Harding and Coolidge appointments were to change the nature of the Commission. With one exception (Alfred Dennis) their appointees were ardent protectionists determined to reduce imports to a minimum. Chairman Thomas O. Marvin, the faction's leader was an active member of the protectionist Home Market Club of Boston. William Burgess had previously been a lobbyist for the pottery manufacturers. E. B. Brossard, an agricultural economist whose chief concern was with the highly protected sugar beet industry, helped to prepare the minority report dissenting from a recommendation to reduce the sugar schedule. Henry H. Glassie, a lawyer whose wife's family had large holdings in a Louisiana sugar company, refused to disqualify himself during the sugar hearings. Baldwin regularly voted with the chairman. With the gradual elimination of the Wilson appointees, the flexible provision became flexible only for schedule raises.

In the first years of the Fordney-McCumber Act the Wilson appointees clashed repeatedly with Harding's choices about the functions of the Commission. Could it initiate investigations? How were reasonable rates to be computed?[3] What was the purpose of the tariff? Commissioner Culbertson, a Republican nominated by Wilson who wanted schedules based on comparative cost of production even if it led to reduction, reported that Chairman Marvin regarded the importation of any goods as ceding a portion of the national domain. If this was a fair appraisal of Chairman Marvin's attitude it would explain why he and his followers were concerned only with increasing rates and never reducing them.

Costigan and his allies wanted the Commission to examine all of the tariff schedules, on its own initiative, and amend them as revision became necessary. Marvin, Burgess and Glassie preferred a narrower scope for the Commission. They wanted to investigate only a few items at the request of the President, preferably only those that concerned applications for rate increases. President Harding, accepting Chairman Marvin's more restrictive conception, decided that the Commission should investigate only the necessity for specific changes and

THE TARIFF COMMISSION 93

not prepare a general and scientific revision. The Commission was to conduct preliminary examination of complaints and formal investigations requested by the President. Even within these limitations, basic differences caused the Commission to be rent by factional strife.

The Sugar Tariff

Of all the intra-Commission struggles, the investigation into the sugar duties was probably the most important and certainly the most controversial. In March 1923, President Harding asked the Commission to examine the reasons for the rise in sugar prices in the preceding months. Costigan supported the majority report that factors other than the tariff had caused the fluctuation, but added that the duty was one cause of higher sugar prices.

At the end of 1923 the sugar schedule itself came under the scrutiny of the Tariff Commission. In the following year it became a major political issue. The first skirmish arose when Costigan challenged Glassie's participation in the sugar schedule hearings. Mrs. Glassie's admitted sizeable interest in a family-owned Louisiana sugar corporation constituted a conflict of interest, Costigan insisted with the support of Commissioners Culbertson and Lewis. Since the Tariff Commission was not a judicial body, Glassie responded, his wife's interests should not affect his role as a fact-finder. Chairman Marvin and Commissioner Burgess concurred. The preliminary investigation had indicated a reduction in the duty. In the absence of Commissioner Glassie the Wilson men would have had a majority of the Commission and a recommendation for a reduction would have been likely. When President Coolidge refused to interfere and allowed Glassie to use his own discretion, Costigan's Congressional allies amended the Independent Office Appropriations Bill to prevent payment of the salary of a Tariff Commissioner who participated in cases in which he had a pecuniary interest. Glassie thereupon excused himself from the hearings.

Glassie's neutralization did not still the controversy. The sugar interests began to apply pressure on both the Administration and the Tariff Commission.

William Culbertson, generally considered to be the leader of the scientific tariff faction was known to desire a diplomatic appointment. Just before the sugar hearings began, Culbertson was offered a position on the more prestigious Federal Trade Commission. Since Glassie had not yet withdrawn from participation, Culbertson's removal would have placed the high tariff advocates in command. Culbertson remained on the Tariff Commission. After the hearings had been in progress for some months and Costigan had moved for the preparation of a sugar report, Culbertson was again approached. Senator Smoot called Culbertson into his office to meet with Congressmen from the sugar beet states and representatives of the sugar lobby. They proposed costs of production on the basis of a given year rather than the average of several years. At the very least, the sugar lobby hoped to delay the report on the sugar schedule until after the November elections, when it could be pigeon-holed by the President.

Throughout June and July, Culbertson and Costigan resisted outside pressure for postponement. Meanwhile, Commissioners Marvin and Burgess instituted delaying tactics. On July 9th, Chairman Marvin reported that the President wanted the Commission to examine the duty on butter and drop all other work, but Culbertson, who had been in constant communication with the President, challenged this interpretation of the President's position while Costigan formally objected to dispensing with work on the sugar report.

In early July, Culbertson was called to the White House to justify a series of paid lectures delivered at Georgetown University. The act creating the Tariff Commission forbade outside gainful employment. Costigan had rejected an invitation to give the Georgetown series himself as ethically questionable. But no Commissioner had objected to Culbertson's acceptance of the offer and he had been delivering discourses as a member of the Tariff Commission for years. He felt that these talks were legal, tended to clarify the role of the Tariff Commission, and did not conflict with his role as a Commissioner. After Attorney General Harlan Stone was consulted by the President, it was rumored that a brief favorable to Culbertson had been replaced with an unfavorable report. Commissioners Costigan and Lewis were rushed through the Attorney General's office when they tried to file a brief in support of Commissioner Culbertson.

Finally, Culbertson was called to the White House on July 25th, and told that while committing no moral error, he had technically violated the law. He was ordered to drop the Georgetown course, but incongruously, was permitted to deliver a summer series at Williamstown, Massachusetts. The President asked Culbertson to see that the sugar report be delayed a few months, at least until after the Williamstown assignment. Fed up, Costigan informed Progressive Presidential candidate, Robert M. LaFollette, of the history of the sugar investigation. Sensing a campaign issue, external pressure to delay the report ended.

Frustrated, the sugar lobby tried a new approach. If a high tariff Democrat could be appointed to replace David J. Lewis, the majority of the Commission would be protectionist. To achieve this goal, the National Tariff Council, led by former Colorado Governor Jesse MacDonald, set out to raise $100,000. When Costigan learned of this plan, he attacked his old enemy, MacDonald, in a letter to the *Denver Post*. Lewis had been an impartial judge on tariff matters, he said, and although a Democrat, had joined the Commission in recommending increases on those items that he thought necessary—wheat, sodium nitrate, and barium dioxide. Although Lewis was endorsed by an advisor, Culbertson, and by both the Republican and Democratic members of the House Ways and Means Committee, Coolidge would not commit himself on the appointment. Lewis' term expired on September 7, 1924. On the following day he was first informed by a sympathetic Culbertson that the President would reappoint him only if he would submit an undated letter of resignation. Lewis indignantly refused. That afternoon Lewis was ushered into the President's office. President Coolidge, while signing the commission for a recess appointment, asked if Lewis had brought the letter with him. Lewis' negative reply obviously disappointed Coolidge, but he declined an offer by Lewis to forget that the commission had been signed. He had no intention of using the note, he said, and only wanted it if it were necessary. Lewis would serve at the President's will in any event. When Congress returned after the election, Lewis' recess appointment expired and Coolidge replaced him with Alfred Dennis.

After all this maneuvering, even the expert staff on the Commission divided and two separate reports were filed⁴ Joshua Bernhardt, the head of the sugar division of the Tariff Commission, had been officially placed in charge the investigation. Although he made every effort to prevent social contacts with the Commissioners, in order to remain above the controversy, both Burgess and Marvin attempted to influence his work. He employed the same measuring unit that had been used in the wheat study—a weighted average cost of production based on a given period of years. With the aid of twenty-five accountants and consulting the staff experts on specific matters, Bernhardt drew up a report on which Culbertson, Lewis and Costigan based their recommendation for a lowering of the duty. By this time the antagonism between the two factions had become so great that the report had to be sent through the Secretary of the Commission, Chairman Marvin having refused to forward it to the President.

A separate minority report was prepared by the agricultural economist, Dr. Brossard. He had been appointed to aid Dr. Bernhardt, and used this opportunity to prepare a dissent. Dr. Brossard, an expert on sugar beets, was as determined as Commissioners Marvin and Burgess that the sugar duty should not be lowered. His report was based on a single year, chosen to supply figures favorable to maintaining the existing tariff level. For this study the cost of land was determined, not by its market value, but by capitalizing the rate of profit per acre. By this means he found the average cost of land to be $200 per acre, or four times the value of equivalent farm land. His report, then, was the basis for the recommendation by Commissioners Marvin and Burgess that the sugar duty be retained.

The two documents reached President Coolidge in the middle of an election campaign. He requested further information, then shelved them to avoid political repercussions.

Costigan's Tariff Brickbat

The sugar report was the last victory for the advocates of a scientific tariff. Lewis was denied reappointment, Culbertson was made minister to Rumania, and Costigan remained as the only Wilson appointee on the Commission. Since Alfred P. Dennis, who had replaced Lewis, began his term with an effort to cooperate with the chairman, for a while Costigan was the only nonconformist on the Commission. Soon, however, Costigan and Dennis formed a permanent dissenting minority. Frustrated, Costigan despaired of any scientific use of the flexible provisions of the Fordney-McCumber Tariff as long as a protectionist majority controlled the Commission.

Costigan was not the only progressive to be discouraged by the activities of the regulatory Commissions. In May 1926, supplied with information by Costigan and others, Senator Norris attacked the Administration for packing these commissions with members catering to the businesses they were chosen to regulate. He called for the abolition of the Interstate Commerce Commission, the Federal Trade Commission and the Tariff Commission. Costigan wrote to him, agreeing that the Tariff Commission had been undermined by protectionist appointments, and they searched for alternative methods to combat the packing of the Tariff Commission. They could suspend appropriations for the Commission; they could abolish it; they could withhold approval of Presidential nominations; or they could amend the existing laws. Nevertheless, they took no immediate action.

On December 29, 1925, the American Economic Association dis-

THE TARIFF COMMISSION 97

cussed the Tariff Commission in one of the sessions of its annual meeting in New York. Frank Taussig, first chairman of the Tariff Commission was the major speaker and Costigan was a commentator. The Commission had become partisan, Taussig charged, therefore, permanent rates would be preferable to the flexible provisions. The cost of production was difficult to determine, he asserted, and consequently the difficulties of the Tariff Commission were due to its power to recommend rate changes.

Costigan strongly challenged Taussig. He declared that the decisions of international courts were difficult to obtain without bias, yet such decisions had been, and were being made in the World Court. The Commission, he said, could pursue its duties "with common sense, disinterestedness, and efficiency." The limitations on the number of its members and the length of individual service should make it possible for it to function as a non-partisan group. Yet within the last year it had "ceased to represent disinterested and non-partisan independence." One possible ameliorative, he suggested, was to give the public access to important Commission reports. More important, a Congressional investigation was a necessary forerunner to corrective legislation. Until the investigation, the Senate should refuse to confirm the nominations of Brossard and Baldwin, and Congress should refuse to appropriate funds until it had "adequate assurances that the membership of the Tariff Commission will be safeguarded by law and will conform to the standards of disinterested public service."

Jacob Viner, an acquaintance of Costigan, was sitting next to the *New York Times* reporter and alerted him to the importance of the paper. The *Times* featured Costigan's statement on the front page and the nation was electrified. Editorially the *Times* called for a Congressional investigation. The *Denver Express* headlined an editorial: "Found: A Federal official who recommends his own separation from the Federal payroll!" The *Express* commended Costigan for his proposal. Commissioner Dennis, supporting Costigan, declared that the unsatisfactory conditions on the Commission were actually understated.

Investigation of the Tariff Commission

In early March, Senate Democratic Minority Leader Joseph Robinson joined Senator Norris in a demand for an investigation. High tariff partisans echoed their call. Commissioner Glassie welcomed an inquiry as an opportunity to clear his name, and Senator Smoot helped drive through a motion to create a select committee.

During the hearing's first uneventful days, former Commissioners Taussig and Page explained the Commission's operations prior to enactment of the Fordney-McCumber Act and protested against its flexible provisions. The testimony of Chairman Marvin, presenting the position of the protectionist majority, was followed with interest. It was highlighted by Senator Robinson's accusation that he had attempted to discredit Dr. Bernhardt's work in the sugar report.

With the testimony of Commissioner Dennis the hearings began to generate excitement. Dennis arraigned Commissioners Marvin, Glassie, Brossard and Baldwin for undermining the Fordney-McCumber flexible tariff provisions and destroying the nation's faith in their administration. These provisions had become flexible only in an upward direction, he charged. Of seven cases considered in 1925, the five cases that had indicated a higher duty had been completed and sent to the President, while the two cases that had pointed towards a lower duty had languished. Despite his scathing indictment of the majority of the Tariff Commission, all of whom were appointed by Republican Presidents, the Democratic Dennis absolved Coolidge of any responsibility for packing the Commission or of pressuring Commissioner Lewis. (The President was a personal friend of the Commissioner.)

The testimony of Commissioner Costigan was eagerly awaited. It was his commentary that had brought about the investigation. He was the only current member of the original Tariff Commission. He had helped to direct the investigation of the Tariff Commission and had participated in the preparation of questions that were asked the Commissioners. When he finally emerged into the spotlight, the public was not disappointed. The early members of the Commission had regarded their roles as judicial ones, he declared, and had tried to promote the science of government and the supremacy of the law. They had revised the customs administrative laws for the first time since 1799. It had been expected that the flexible provisions of the Fordney-McCumber Tariff would be used primarily to lower rates, and both President Harding and Senator Smoot had declared rate reduction to be its major purpose. Hence, the Commission was not doing its job— it must be reformed. (The alternative of its abolition, he added, would only cause a return to tariff legislation by logrolling.) The Colorado Progressive reviewed the hearings on the sugar schedule, including the difficulties with Glassie and the harassment of Culbertson and Lewis by the Administration. He revealed that the division within the Commission between the advocates of disinterested scientific standards and the champions of the special interests had spread to its staff. They had become completely demoralized. To rectify the situation the Tariff Commission and the laws governing it had to be revamped. It should become a permanent, independent, judicial and nonpartisan fact-finding and rate-reducing body, with rate-making powers similar to those of the Interstate Commerce Commission. The findings of the Commission should be published and open to public perusal. He suggested clearer legislation setting the bounds of this body. This law should have an emergency provision allowing Congress or the Commission to act immediately when long investigation was impractical. The President, as the party chief, he asserted, could not be a good tariff judge. If all else failed, the Tariff Commission would have to be eliminated.

Commissioner Glassie, who followed Costigan to the stand, denied that the Tariff Commission was a judicial body, and thus contravened Costigan's charges about his role in the sugar hearing. He challenged Dennis' charge that it was impossible to get the Tariff Commission to recommend a reduction in the tariff. He claimed, with little credibility, that the items decreased under the flexible tariff provisions had more importance than items increased in terms of the effect of these changes on the volume of imports and exports. Although he contradicted Costigan's and Dennis' interpretation of the proceedings of the commission, his testimony did not arouse much interest. It was the testimony of the next witness that stirred the greatest excitement generated by the hearings.

In the eyes of the public William Culbertson had long been the chief proponent of a scientific tariff. Both Norris and Costigan had based their accusations on notes Culbertson had given to Costigan while still a member of the Commission. When the contents of his memoranda were released by Costigan, Culbertson was deeply shocked by what he considered a breach of confidence. He soon felt that Costigan had betrayed their friendship for political advantage. But Costigan's loyalties were to causes, not personalities, and he was then trying to salvage the concept of a scientific tariff. The Senate Select Committee soon summoned the Minister to Rumania to testify. Culbertson was furious when the State Department granted him leave. In desperation he cabled Senator Curtis to give the President an opportunity to assign him to some special duty that would preclude his return and prevent his political destruction. His cable unavailing, he reluctantly prepared to sail, warning his friends not to meet him publicly lest they jeopardize their careers. Then, at the last moment, William Allen White wired him to cancel his voyage. The influential editor was seeking an administrative subterfuge to prevent the minister's return. White's mission failed and Culbertson embarked with misgiving.

In a press release upon his landing and in the testimony that followed, he attacked his former friend, Costigan, for releasing his memoranda and letters without requesting permission. Although he clearly supported Costigan's statements about the protective tariff group in the Commission, he contradicted his ertswhile friend's statement about the role of the Administration. The Administration, he said, had never applied any pressure to change his position in the sugar case and could not be held responsible for the actions of Chairman Marvin and his supporters. Unfortunately, the statements of Minister Culbertson contradicted the statements of Commissioner Culbertson. Costigan informed the press that Culbertson had never denied the validity of the incriminating memoranda, despite his complaints about their use.

Then, during Culbertson's testimony, Senator LaFollette confronted the Minister with a devastating letter. Soon after he had assumed his duties in Bucharest, Culbertson had sent a note about Brossard that had been forgotten by all until Costigan had received Culbertson's press release; a copy was found in Costigan's files. "It's not much of a compliment to see that Brossard is selected to fill my place," Culbertson had written. If this appointment was a revelation of the President's policy, then it was fortunate that he had left the Commission before he was forced to break with the Administration and the Republican Party. "I didn't suppose that Coolidge would do the thing so rawly if he did it at all," he had declared. "Evidently our suspicions were correct and Brossard had been playing with the sugar lobby and now he has his reward." [5]

After the hearing Culbertson sat dejectedly with his head in his hands. In reply to a question from Thurston of the New York *World*, he said: "What could I do? I was damned if I did and damned if I didn't." He could not attack the Administration and hope to realize his life-long ambition—to remain in the Foreign Service. But when he tried to protect the Administration he was overwhelmed by his own careful documentation.

D. J. Lewis, following Culbertson to the stand, supported Costigan's statements in every particular, and thus repudiated part of Culbertson's deposition. Finally, the Committee heard the testimony of Commissioner Brossard, who claimed to have only a small role in the sugar investigation as an agricultural expert. On June 30th, the Committee adjourned.

When the Committee resumed its investigation on January 10, 1927, it examined Brossard's role in the sugar investigation more carefully. A. M. Fox, a member of the Commission staff, reluctantly contradicted Brossard. He testified that Brossard had not only worked on the report but had discussed with him what should be said about Brossard's own role during the sugar hearings.

Commissioner Burgess, the next witness, attacked those who had made up the majority report recommending a reduction in the sugar tariff as free trade theorists. He castigated Culbertson. Culbertson's attitude, he said, was the result of his personal animus toward Chairman Marvin, contracted when Culbertson was not appointed chairman. Culbertson's figure for an increase in the wheat schedule had been picked out of a hat, he charged. In addition, Culbertson had used the staff for personal purposes—the Georgetown lectures. During the sugar investigation, he declared, Costigan, Culbertson and Lewis had created an artificial majority by forcing Glassie to be disqualified. They had used their majority to do as they pleased, neglecting all other work, infringing the rules of the Commission, and using arbitrary methods. He insisted that the advisory council had been by-passed by the Wilson appointees and all information had been supplied by Joshua Bernhardt.

The testimony of Burgess and Brossard was swiftly punctured by Senators LaFollette and Robinson, Commissioners Lewis and Costigan, and Dr. Bernhardt. Senator Robinson brought in the night records of the War Department building where the Tariff Commission had its offices. These showed that Dr. Brossard had worked diligently on the minority report, contravening the testimony of Burgess and himself. LaFollette revealed that copies of the majority sugar report had been supplied to the advisory board, contrary to Burgess' intimation.

Joshua Bernhardt was most effective in rebuttal. He reviewed the investigatory methods of the Commission to prove that ordinary procedure had been followed in the sugar report. He detailed the aid that he had received from more than twenty-five members of the staff in his investigation of the sugar industry. Point by point he contradicted Burgess's testimony on the progress of the sugar report, describing the delays. He documented Brossard's role in drafting the minority report and, in general, left his opponents' testimony with little credibility.

Costigan and Lewis completed the job that Bernhardt had undertaken. Lewis indicated specific flaws in the Brossard minority report—the over-valuation of farm land and the pretension that little Mexican labor was being used in the beet fields. He discounted Burgess' complaint that the Chairman had been by-passed in sending the report to the President, merely stating that the Chairman had refused to forward the report. Costigan challenged Burgess' claim that there had been no effort to stall the sugar investigation. He disclosed that Burgess had admitted visiting President Harding in order to convince him that a sugar investigation would be unsettling for business. In addition, Burgess and the non-judicial attitude of the Commission had ruined the faith of foreign nations in their impartiality he charged. Foreign nations would not trust them with necessary information on production for fear that it would be leaked to their American competitors.[6]

A thoroughly discredited Commission returned to work.

Costigan Resigns From the Commission

The investigation did not terminate the struggle between the two factions. Marvin, Brossard and Lowell remained, as it were, a high tariff wall that made scientific tariff-making impossible. In January of 1928, Costigan wrote to Senator Robinson insisting that legislation to give the Commission new powers could not accomplish anything so long as the composition of the Commission remained unchanged. He did not think that Congressional selection of the Commissioners would be an ideal solution, but it was one way out of a tragic solution. With the Commission functioning as it was, Costigan soon found his position unbearable.

On March 14, 1928, Costigan's patience ran out. After a decade of struggling for a scientific tariff, he decided against any further effort on his part. He sent a letter to Senator Robinson, announcing his resignation. The flexible provisions of the Fordney-McCumber Act had not reduced the tariff, he said. The provision to permit the mutual reduction of tariffs after bilateral or multilateral negotiations had been ignored. The Commission had made thirty-two reports. The President had acted on twenty-three of these, raising eighteen and lowering five schedules—and the five duties that were reduced were on minor items. The President had refused to act where the evidence showed the need for lowering a duty, as in the sugar, linseed oil and halibut investigations. The Commission had never been given the power to initiate their own investigations—the Senate, the President, or private interests had determined what investigations were to be concluded. The Colorado Progressive detailed charges that the Commission had been packed with high tariff advocates, that there had been attempts to influence the Commission during the sugar hearings, and that he himself had eventually been isolated as the sole advocate of judicial procedure on the Commission. The Commission had been used to convert the farmers to a mistaken notion that their problems could be solved by the tariff rather than by permanent agricultural remedies. He attacked the rationale of protectionists—that a tariff was necessary to maintain American standards. After all, the unprotected boot and shoe industry paid higher wages than the highly protected woolen and worsted industry. And the automobile industry, which had asked for removal of the tariff since it did not fear world competition, paid higher wages than the highly protected potters and meat packers.

Upon his resignation from the Commission he returned to Denver to practice law and soon become the general counsel for Josephine Roche's Rocky Mountain Fuel Company. Without a political office and without membership in an active political party, Costigan's political career appeared to be at an end.

Costigan continued to advise his Senate friends on tariff questions. In 1929 he helped Senator LaFollette challenge an effort to put through a new tariff, and his former aid, Dr. Simpson, worked to improve the more reprehensible features of the Act. He complained to LaFollette that the tariff had had an adverse effect on our foreign relations. American tariff policies were doing much "to alienate foreign sympathy, understanding, and trade relations; and no one who has traced the intimate connection betwen commercial policies and war can view this aspect of the problem without grave apprehensions over America's international future."

In October 1929, he condemned the effects of the tariff. He charged that the prizes involved in tariff-making made the Teapot Dome scandal insignificant. It raised the cost of living, sowed the seeds of international hostility and war, and gave little protection to American standards. Three-fourths of agricultural prices were fixed by the world market, he declared, and agriculture could not be put on a par with manufacture by agricultural tariffs. American productivity, not the tariff, assured high wages. The use of child labor in the protected sugar beet fields, he asserted indignantly, was one proof of the falseness of the protectionist argument. The only positive virtue of the new bill, he reported, was a provision that would have the Commission report to Congress instead of to the President so that the schedule would be subject to open debate.

Soon the growing economic depression replaced the tariff as a political and economic concern.

1. American valuation would change the rate base from European to American wholesale prices, greatly increasing the actual tariff while eliminating a loophole

that importers employed of undervaluing a cargo in order to pay a lower duty.

The bill, including the flexible tariff provision, had much opposition, but not from groups that had to be placated. Senator Underwood attacked the flexible tariff provisions as giving the President unlimited power. Sir Robert Horne, British Chancellor of the Exchequer, declared that the tariff would make it more difficult to pay international debts. But only two Republican Senators, Borah and LaFollette, voted against the bill.

2. Opponents of flexibility felt any changes between general revisions would cause business uncertainty; almost any tariff rate, they felt, would be better than indetermination. Since comparative costs fluctuated, they saw no end to constant adjustments.

3. Marvin, Glassie and Burgess hoped to raise the effective tariff by increasing the cost-base on which rates were computed. The effects of American valuation have been discussed in a previous footnote. Another technique suggested to raise the rate base was a bulk line cost. This was determined by charting the cost of production of the various concerns in the industry. Where the gap between the cost of production of firms became too great, the line was broken and the companies with higher costs were considered to be sub-marginal. This, then, is the cost of production to the marginal producers — a cost which is in practice roughly equivalent to the wholesale price. The bulk line cost is considerably above the weighted average cost of production: those concerns which command a larger share of the market are usually more efficient than the smaller houses and the weight of their efficient production reduces the average cost of production in direct proportion to the percentage of the market that they command. On the other hand, Commissioners Culbertson, Lewis and Costigan desired to establish rates, based on comparative costs of production, that would protect American industry from unfair competition and, at the same time, permit no undue profit.

4. Apparently Weber's anonymous bureaucrats who make only administrative decisions regardless of the political framework in which they are asked to work can be found only in the ideal bureaucracy. Real bureaucracies are made up of men with very definite ideas.

5. William S. Culbertson to EPC, July 27, 1925; both Thurston of the New York *World* and Ross of the St. Louis *Post-Dispatch* told Costigan that Culbertson was contradicting everything that he had told the press for years. Dr. Page and Dr. Wallace told Costigan that Batchelder had convinced Culbertson to present the Administration's point of view.

6. Gilbert Hirsch, a member of the Tariff Commission's overseas staff had complained that Europeans were suspicious of Burgess, for they felt the Commissioner had given French ceramics secrets to American competitors. The French government, as a result, was hindering efforts to obtain information in the plate glass investigation. Finally in despair of being able to accomplish his job under such a handicap, Hirsch resigned. Upon his return from a lengthy trip to Europe, Costigan challenged Marvin's statement that Europe was satisfied with the American tariff. On the contrary, he said, Europeans accused the U. S. of using the promise of lowering the tariff to acquire commercial information which was used to American commercial advantage. Many countries, he declared, would no longer cooperate with the Commission.

Chapter VII

THE ELECTION OF 1930

1929 was a great year for stock market speculation. By September the New York *Times* industrial index rose from 331 to 449, with most of the increase coming in the three summer months. While Radio Corporation of America had never paid a dividend, it had risen in 1928 from 85 to 420 and reached a high point of 505 in September of 1929; General Electric went from 268 to 396, United States Steel from 165 to 262. Shares traded on the New York Stock Exchange in 1928 had shattered all previous records and the volume continued to rise. The demand for stocks exceeded the availability of shares in producing companies. Fortunately, investment trusts arose to fill the gap. These were firms whose only asset was a portfolio of stocks which were manipulated to make a profit for their founders and investors—in that order. By autumn of 1929 the total capitalization of investment trusts was eight billion dollars, an eleven-fold increase over 1927, and these companies supplied the much needed additional shares for speculation.

Stock market euphoria carried over into other aspects of economic life. Injudicious loans were made, particularly to South American dictatorships. Installment purchases led to living on next year's income, and with a sizeable unemployment rate, next year's income was not always forthcoming.

Despite a significant increase in the real income of manufacturing workers, industrial productivity increased twice as rapidly as real income. With the farmers suffering from a relative depression throughout most of the decade, this led to a marked imbalance in distribution of earnings. Five percent of the population with the highest remuneration received one-third of all personal income. The economy then depended on their expenditures for luxuries and venture capital. Yet as the decade advanced, productive investment, as distinguished from speculation and replacement of physical equipment, fell off markedly. In 1924 financing that resulted in additions to physical equipment was seventy-six percent of new financing, in 1929 only thirty-five percent. Capital formation in 1924 was $3,460,000,000, in the larger economy of 1929 only $3,186,000,000. By 1928 two chief catalysts of the economy, automobile production, and public and private construction, had leveled off. To add to the economic problems the corporations were inundated with promoters, grafters, swindlers, frauds, and imposters. Excessive holding companies and investment trusts created an economy dependent on high dividends for its survival.

But our economic problems were not only domestic. The United States, as a result of World War I, had become a creditor nation, but a creditor nation which exported more than it imported. The Fordney-McCumber Tariff intensified this problem. How then were other nations to pay for our exports? To some extent this problem was solved temporarily with private short-term loans. But by the end of 1928 call loans on the New York stock market were bringing twelve percent interest—and this was considered risk free. Why go through the bother of investing corporate funds in increased production? When the world money markets became aware of these rates, capital poured in from all over the world—intensifying the imbalance in the international flow of capital and goods. The scene was set for Thursday, October 24, 1929.

Black Thursday marked the collapse of the business-oriented society of the nineteen-twenties. As the depression continued through the winter, Colorado's Republican Senator Lawrence Cole Phipps, a wealthy former mill hand whose life mirrored the capitalist folklore that had dominated the previous decade, decided that sixty-seven was a good age to retire. His successor was to be Costigan, a progressive reformer who was more suited to the decade to come.[1]

While no Colorado Democrat had been elected Senator for eighteen years, 1930 was destined to be a Democratic year. The stock market crash had cost the nation thirty billion dollars—twice the national debt and a sum almost as great as the entire cost to the United States of its participation in the World War. One of every four factory workers had been laid off and street corner apple vendors had become a common sight. The power elite was so little aware of the severity of the crisis that a poll of the upper-crust National Economic League placed unemployment eighteenth on the list of problems for 1930. In such circumstances the party in power could not avoid a serious defeat.

Yet the progressive Democrats lacked an adequate candidate. The times called for a man of bold ideas, a man willing to carve out new paths in legislation—unprecedented paths if need be—in order to cope with a depression of unprecedented magnitude. Costigan seemed such a candidate to many liberal Democrats. He had never feared to advocate political experiments, yet he had not succumbed to the delusion that all the ailments of mankind could be cured with one bold stroke of the legislative pen. At first, his nomination seemed remote. For fourteen years he had been politically inactive and, although he had often voted for Democratic candidates, he had never joined the Democratic Party. He was still "a Progressive of Republican antecedents and Democratic consequences."

Oscar Chapman

It was Oscar Chapman who first suggested to Costigan that the Democratic nomination might be secured. Chapman, a young law student who had been the Chief Probation Officer in Judge Ben Lindsey's court, had become Costigan's law clerk in June 1928 when Lindsey's denunciation of the Ku Klux Klan had cost him his judgeship, and Lindsey had chosen to depart for California.[2]

In an effort to obtain Lindsey's reinstatement, Chapman had increased his poltical activity, becoming the Secretary of the Denver Democratic Party. By 1930, Chapman had become Costigan's junior partner. A liberal with a keen relish for politics, he preferred campaign management to campaigning for office.

When Chapman first broached the idea of the Senatorial nomination to Costigan in January of 1930, the latter declined, protesting that he had long been politically independent and really had no party. But, Chapman reminded him, the Democrats had no candidate. With the rash confidence of youth, he assured his senior partner that he could even win the support of the three Democratic captains whom Costigan had helped to jail during the Progressive era. Costigan protested that he lacked campaign funds. Chapman assured him that he could win on speeches alone in an independent state like Colorado. Besides, the time was ripe to elect someone of his caliber. For a time the senior partner refused to take the idea seriously.

But Chapman was not to be denied. Mabel Costigan and Josephine Roche joined the conspiracy to convince Costigan that he should run. Knowing Costigan's sympathy towards labor, Chapman persuaded labor leaders to urge his candidacy. They intensified their activity after Costigan's speech to the Colorado Labor Convention in April 1930.

Although Costigan resisted a formal declaration, his availability was repeatedly mentioned and he began to act like a reluctant suitor. In the middle of April he used the setting of a Jefferson Day dinner in Southern Colorado to bridge the gap between his independent background and the party regularity of the local Democrats. The progressive struggles which he had fought were in the Jeffersonian tradition, he assured the diners. In the near future, he predicted, the greatest sundering of party lines since 1893 (when Republicans left the party en masse) would take place. In this way he dismissed the importance of party regularity without ever mentioning it. Although he delayed an announcement, by the end of May Costigan was an open candidate for the nomination.[3]

On May 23, 1930, in a lengthy reply to Dr. Ben Beshoar, Chairman of the Las Animas County Democratic Committee (a county from which he expected strong support), he explained his views on the Senate. The peace and prosperity of the entire world depended on the leadership of the United States, he wrote. Thus Senators should be chosen for views that would promote the general welfare. He reiterated his heartfelt political dedication: "Our personal fortunes are unimportant; the welfare and happiness of mankind should be the final tests governing our support." He outlined the objectives that national leadership must have in the crisis. The Republican Senators represented special privilege, he charged, and not equal opportunity. While the Hoover panic had been brewed by false assurances that the country was sound at a time when stock speculation should have been curbed, still the Republicans remained inactive in the face of disaster. They seemed to think that the jobless could be returned to work by the occasional lavish expenditure of money to carry elections, he mocked.

Meanwhile the Administration, using the facade of an industrial conference, obstructed the passage of Senator Wagner's proposal to create new jobs. Colorado's Senators were silent, he declared, when they should have demanded accurate information on unemployment, the creation of government employment agencies, public works, further immigration restriction, the prohibition of child labor, and old age and unemployment benefits. Industrial unemployment was not an isolated problem, he continued. The value of farm lands had declined by twenty-one billion dollars; yet Republican administrations had killed the export debenture plan and the Farm Loan Board had proved ineffective. The Republicans could only offer the same tired economic program—higher tariffs. Unfortunately, the tariff raised farmers' costs much more than it raised the price of their products; it provoked retaliation and indignant nations closed their markets to the surplus from American farms. Increased trade, without injury to industry, required a scientific tariff. The citizen's faith in the nation would be restored when the government was free from falsehood and manipulators. Once again he sought to campaign on issues, not personalities.

On June 4th, in a letter to the Chairman of the Democratic State Central Committee, Thomas Annear, he announced his decision to run

THE ELECTION OF 1930

for the Senatorial nomination. Referring to his earlier letter to Dr. Beshoar, he took issue with a decade of Republican policies, outlining an activist program on unemployment, farm relief and international cooperation through a world court and liberalized trade. Industrial relations could be improved by legislation that recognized the dignity and rights of labor and by eliminating judicial abuse of injection and contempt procedures. He called for the protection of Muscle Shoals and Boulder Dam from private exploitation. While demanding enforcement of the law (including the Eighteenth Amendment), and governmental economy (subject to the needs of public welfare), he contended that the invasion of public rights by private privilege must be resisted.

The Primary Contest

Costigan had been convinced to campaign for the Senate. He still had to win the nomination and he had few Democratic allies. To compete in the primary elections he needed the support of at least twenty percent of the delegates to the Democratic Assembly scheduled to meet in Colorado Springs on July 28, 1930. How were these votes to be obtained for the new Democrat?

To solve this problem the Democratic Volunteers was formed by a group of young Denverites, including Oscar Chapman, John M. Keating, John A. Carroll, Charles Brannan, and an old labor friend of Costigan's, J. O. Stevic; its sole purpose, to secure Costigan's nomination and election to the United States Senate. They soon laid plans to steal the Denver delegation from the machine of Mayor Stapleton. Delegates to the Denver county convention were nominated by precinct cliques. Since the machine worked quietly and efficiently, no more than three or four people attended each meeting. The volunteers packed the precinct caucuses and sent their own representatives to the county convention. With a plurality of the Denver delegation to the Colorado Democratic Assembly, the Costigan candidacy built sufficient impetus to win a designation. Chapman's successful amateurs, most of whom had never attended a convention, found no old, respected professional to place Costigan's name before the Assembly. John M. Keating, who was at least the nephew of a former Democratic Congressman, made the nominating speech.

At first, newspapers had speculated that Costigan would be unopposed for the nomination. Morrison Shafroth, son of the liberal Democratic Senator, John Shafroth, ended these rumors by declaring his candidacy four days before Costigan's announcement. James A. Marsh entered the race soon thereafter. Shafroth, with greater organizational support outside of Denver, won the highest designation from the Democratic Assembly — trumpeting to his followers that he had overcome Costigan's large expenditures and support by the Denver machine.[4]

The designating assembly was only a prelude to the primary. Costigan was an inspiration to those who worked with him, but he had never established a Democratic political image and he was not an adept politician. Chapman ran his campaign, supplementing the candidate's personal assets with practical political knowledge. Chapman's exertions for Lindsey had introduced him to most of the Democratic politicians in the state. In addition, he was an unusually astute politician. Despite limited funds, he converted the fervor of young amateurs and the efforts of the labor movement into an effective campaign.

Although the $4,587 that the Costigan forces spent on the primary was twice the expenditure of his Democratic opponents, they still lacked funds. Chapman, true to his promise, ran the campaign on a shoestring. He raised $14,000, mortgaging his home and even pawning jewels. In contrast, the Republican victor in the primaries, George Shaw, spent about $50,000 in the primaries alone.[5]

During the primary campaign Costigan concentrated his fire upon the Republicans. In a manifesto the Volunteers assailed the Republican candidates for auctioning the nomination and trying to make the United States Senate "a private office for the agents of industrial autocracy." They solicited the services of Colorado Democrats to enlist one hundred Democratic Volunteers for every paid Republican worker. Their appeal ended with a quotation from Costigan: "Self-governing intelligence alone can save the citizens of our country."

Costigan's limited funds were supplemented by fervent volunteer aid from organized labor. The International Brotherhood of Electrical Workers sent laudatory letters to their local Colorado chapters. In June the Colorado State Labor Political Convention endorsed his fighting opposition to special privilege. His strongest labor support came from the Railroad Brotherhoods; they sent two special editions of their newspaper, the *Labor Advocate* (edited by Costigan's good friend, former Congressman Edward Keating), strongly urging his election. Through rural free delivery and personal distribution by their members, they made certain that the newspaper reached all Colorado voters.

Although the campaign for the nomination was fought largely on Costigan's terms — a discussion of national problems and the Administration's importance — personal charges and innuendoes did enter into the battle. Morrison Shafroth accused Costigan of heavy campaign expenditures, and, in the final week, called for a public report. Costigan retorted that Shafroth's statement was politically inspired. No unsupervised disclosure could be of value so close to the primary. He had helped to draft the Primary Law, he assured Shafroth, and did not intend to violate the $5,000 limit. No one could monopolize honesty, Costigan chided. Indeed, he had invited a Congressional committee into Colorado to investigate campaign expenditures and he had proffered his full cooperation.[6]

His opponents not only exaggerated his expenditures, but they emphasized that he was a recent recruit to Democratic ranks. John Barnett, an extremely conservative Democrat, introduced Costigan to the Democratic Assembly as a man who, having been expelled from the Republican Party, came to his first Democratic convention soliciting the Democratic designation for the Senatorial nomination. Costigan replied with a story General Pershing had told him in France during the war. As a second lieutenant on his first assignment, Pershing had noticed that the privates muttered under their breath whenever they saluted him. The young officer asked a sergeant what they were saying. When the embarrassed sergeant enlightened him about the feelings of enlisted men towards second lieutenants, Pershing decided to take action. The next time a saluting private grumbled inaudibly, Pershing, returning his salute, said coldly "And the same to you!" Whereupon Costigan turned to Barnett, saluted him, and exclaimed: "The same to you."

In the last week of the primary campaign, Shafroth's campaign manager questioned Costigan's political antecedents. Costigan replied that a number of national Democratic leaders supported his bid, and that his democracy was attested to by Woodrow Wilson. Former Republicans, like Senator Henry Teller, Governor Elias Ammons, Congressman Edward Taylor, and Morrison Shafroth's father, Senator John F. Shafroth, had all been welcomed by the Democratic Party. It could not now be made an exclusive preserve.

While Costigan found it necessary to parry personal attacks by his opponents, he was mainly concerned with projecting his ideas on methods to cope with the depression. His major problem was to reach a maximum audience with minimum funds. After Chapman resigned as Secretary of the Denver Democratic Central Committee in order to devote his entire time to the campaign, they intensified the use of radio. His final radio address before the primaries summed up the issues that had been stressed throughout the campaign. The special interests, he told his audience, must be frustrated and the government restored to the people of the country. The farmers needed price stabilization, reduced freight rates, an enlarged overseas market through an export debenture plan, and a bounty for continental sugar producers. A non-partisan reduction of the tariff, he added, would aid farmers through diminished costs. It would improve business, increase production, raise the purchasing power of the dollar, discourage monopoly, suppress unfair trade practices and liberalize commerce. The national unemployment problem could be mitigated by Federal employment agencies, through necessary public construction, with reduced immigration, by restricting child labor, and through old age and unemployment insurance. He called for legislation to establish harmonious industrial relations and to end the judicial abuse of organized labor. Public investment must be guarded against the usurpations of the private power interests. Hence, he advocated government ownership and operation of Muscle Shoals and Boulder Dam. Echoing his letter to Annear, he insisted upon law enforcement and upon government efficiency and economy so far as these were consistent with public welfare. To end this final address, he quoted a letter attacking the lavish Republican campaign expenditures and he reminded the voters that the Senate would deny membership to anyone elected with a slush fund.

The Results of the Primary

Costigan won a smashing victory in the primary, polling more than the combined vote of his opponents. He had solid urban support. He carried nine of ten counties in which manufacturing was important, and twenty-one of Denver's twenty-two districts, losing only one upper middle class suburb. His support among the coal miners was amazing. Huerfano gave him eighty-one percent of the vote, Las Animas seventy-two percent; the coal mining areas of Boulder returned eighty-five percent and Gunnison seventy-six percent. The sugar beet farmers seemed impressed by the bounty. Costigan swept fourteen of the sixteen counties in which the production of sugar beets was important. He carried a majority of the wheat and corn counties, but by lesser margins. He was victorious in all four fruit-growing counties. Despite the absence of any clear parallels to the progressive era, Costigan retained his Progressive strongholds and added the support of coal mining and manufacturing areas. He continued to be less effective in the metal mining and the tariff-conscious grazing counties of the Rocky Mountain region and the southwest.

Having won the nomination, Costigan prepared for the campaign. First, he anointed wounds with a declaration that he had hoped that one of his distinguished opponents could have won so that he could have been released from service for a short while. He immediately sounded the note of the campaign—the special interests versus the people's government—and promised to continue the "partnership" for better government and human rights until these ends were attained. To drive monopoly and self seekers out of government, he affirmed, the people of Colorado must reject a slush fund candidate, for the special interests expected a thousand-fold return for each dollar invested.

As the campaign moved into its second phase, the depression continued to deepen. Successive Republican administrations had painted a picture of a prosperous nation protected by a tariff. The former Tariff Commissioner knew the portrait was fraudulent. He had observed the tariff-abetted imbalance in international trade and he was cognizant of the depressed areas in the American economy. Prosperity during the nineteen twenties, he declared, had bypassed farmers, textile workers, and coal producers. Unemployment had grown throughout that decade. It had risen by 16.80 percent from 1920 - 1923, by an additional 8.80 percent from 1923 - 1925 and another 7.30 percent from 1925 - 1927. Despite rising unemployment, self-seeking employers had imported a million Mexican farm laborers. In the meantime, five million American farmers abandoned the land and swelled the ranks of the unemployed. Despite the wealth of the United States, he declared, Republican policies had caused our government to be "loaned to monopolies, and thousands of millionaires have been created in the very period in which 80 million of our 120 million people have been left to die propertyless." Costigan emphasized the inequities in the distribution of wealth. Even while Herbert Hoover, campaigning for the Presidency, had promised the elimination of poverty, one percent of the population owned fifty-nine percent of the wealth while thirteen percent of the population possessed ninety percent of the national substance; yet two-thirds of the nation lived below minimum standards of health and decency. Despite such unsound foundations to the economy, the executive branch neglected to warn the nation of the dangers ahead, and the Federal Reserve Board disregarded the stock speculation that eventuated in the panic of 1929. He castigated the Administration for obstructing those who sought to ameliorate the depression—particularly for thwarting the legislative efforts of Senator Robert F. Wagner of New York. And he taunted the Republicans for reacting to the challenge of a depression by raising tariffs in order to swell the profits of manufacturers.

Rather than deny the existence of a depression, the Colorado Republicans echoed Hoover's plea for confidence, and attacked Costigan for his gloomy view of conditions, for his lack of faith in America. But hardly had the Republican State Chairman challenged his pessimism, Costigan noted, than the Republican President had made an equally somber speech.

The Republicans concentrated their attack on a proposal for a sugar bounty in place of the sugar tariff. His opponent, George Shaw, called it a "will o' the wisp." Shaw advanced the sugar tariff as the main campaign issue, for not only were Colorado farmers dependent on sugar beets, but Colorado livestock interests used the beets as cattle feed. Shaw's campaign manager charged that Costigan's interest in sugar beets was suspiciously recent: he had voted for a tariff reduction at a time when he had no plans for a bounty. The Colorado Springs *Gazette* accused Costigan of being a free-trader in a necessarily protectionist state. The sugar bounty was "a cheap vote-getting device," they declared. Congress would not pass it. If enacted, it would prove impractical.

Costigan's arguments against the tariff were carefully articulated. The tariff could not benefit the farmer: "The new tariff law breaks faith not only with democratic standards but also with Republican leadership and traditions. It is heedless alike of unemployed workers and of farmers who face bankruptcy. It is a prohibitive and profiteering statute without democratic purpose, devoid of the spirit of reciprocity; and calculated to fasten monopolies more firmly on America. It is intended to guarantee larger future dividends to manufacturers, who are already prosperous, and, except in minor respects, it condemns American agriculture to harder and harder experience. By inviting retaliation, it is already closing foreign markets to our great surplus crops; and it is loading farmers, like the rest of us, with increased living costs through unnecessary taxes imposed on practically all goods consumers must buy." A tariff on hides and shoes, he expounded, might increase a farmer's income from hides by two dollars, but at the same time it would increase his expenditures for shoes by seven dollars and fifty cents. The tariff on sugar beets, though produced wholly for domestic consumption, did not benefit the farmer. It only increased sugar production in the Philippines, Puerto Rico and the Hawaiian Islands. Costigan warned that the price of sugar beets would be lowered a dollar a ton, despite the rise in the tariff, because of an anticipated increase in island production.

The solution to this problem, he continued, was two-fold: a scientific

THE ELECTION OF 1930

tariff to rectify differences in the cost of production, and a bounty of one and one-half cents a pound to continental producers, amounting to three dollars and ninety cents a ton. A scientific reduction in the tariff would save the consumer far more than the cost of the bounty. A lower tariff would decrease island production, hence reduce the sugar surplus, and thus raise prices. The idea of a bounty was not a radical one, he insisted. Great Britain was the most recent of the many nations that had adopted it. The high priest of protection, William McKinley, he noted, had approved the use of a sugar bounty, and even Alexander Hamilton, in his *Report on Manufactures,* had made a similar proposal. Furthermore, Costigan disclosed, O. H. Webb and W. D. Hoover, two leaders of the beet sugar farmers, supported the bounty proposal as the only feasible solution to the problem.[7] Twenty-two Senators had supported a proposal by Senator Howell of Nebraska for a sugar bounty payable in customs warrants. A sugar bounty was both a conservative and a viable solution to a difficult problem, he insisted.

Costigan discarded other solutions. In a reply to a written series of questions he rejected ending Philippine competition through independence or sugar import restriction. The Philippine right to self-government and independence rested on American promises, he declared, not economic advantages.[8] He spurned an increased sugar tariff, and warned against an elimination of the Cuban differential.[9] Both moves would only increase Philippine production and would place Cuba outside the American sphere of influence and open it to other imperial ambitions. Both military and humane considerations supported the retention of the lower impost on Cuban sugar. He cautioned his correspondent against trying to determine international policy solely from the domestic view of beet sugar.

His Republican opponent could not speak about the problems of sugar beet farmers, Costigan charged, because he did not understand agricultural problems at all. He reminded everyone of Shaw's assertion that wheat farmers could make a profit if wheat fell to fifty cents a bushel, a figure that farmers considered to be disastrous. Shaw's blunder and Costigan's sugar bounty proposal helped the Democrat to cut deeply into normally Republican agricultural areas.

Not only was the bounty called a radical innovation, but Costigan's entire program and his independent career were subject to charges of radicalism. He countered these accusations in a brilliant radio address from Loveland in agricultural Larimer County on October 28th. Some people were too conservative to enjoy the new moon, he quipped. Radicals, too, could be ridiculous, but he himself was a gradualist progressive, or a Jeffersonian-Wilsonian Democrat. Calamitous radical change would come, he contended, if the arch-conservatives dammed progress long enough for the repressed waters to burst through. By this reasoning, the true radicals of America were the Republicans, whose policy of drift had allowed agriculture, the backbone of the country, to corrode. The true conservatives, then, were those who proposed constructive remedies to prevent the deterioration of the economy; those who wished to open the markets of the world, to eliminate unfair and discriminatory taxes, and to obtain lower freight, light, and power rates; those who wished to defer farm foreclosures, to supply long-term farm credit at reduced interest charges, to eliminate excessive unemployment, and to obtain industrial relief. The archaic Republicans were the destructive radicals, the Democrats the constructive conservatives.

These issues earned enthusiastic support for Costigan. Fortuitously, Costigan became the beneficiary of a primary schism. William Hodges, a former attorney for the Public Service Corporation, had accused his primary opponent, George Shaw, counsel and trouble-shooter for the same organization, of excessive campaign expenditures: the company had supplied a thousand employees to support Shaw's campaign, he railed. A Senatorial committee came into Colorado for a preliminary investigation. After the contest the committee substantiated Hodges's indictment. While the Democrats made political capital of these charges, the animosity generated by the internecine dispute undermined the effectiveness of Shaw's campaign, particularly in Hodges's stronghold, Denver.

Costigan repeatedly denounced excessive campaign expenditures. The special interests, he contended, expected substantial profits on their investment. The power companies sought control of the government. They wanted a Senator who would support their attempts to secure ownership of Muscle Shoals and Boulder Dam. Such a huge expenditure by the Public Service Corporation, protested Costigan, "implies excessive earnings, unlawful purposes, or both." Excessive imposts of power companies permitted returns of two thousand percent on their investment. Using Canadian power plants and Muscle Shoals as a yardstick, the charge for electricity in Colorado should be two cents, he asserted, not seven cents per kilowatt.

He envisioned enormous possibilities for the government-built plants of Muscle Shoals and Boulder Dam. With little further cost, "our streams and rivers can be easily coined into human happiness by government, as surely as they can be transformed into gold by monopoly." These dams, he affirmed, were America's opportunity "to take our choice between the evils of private monopoly and the benefits of public welfare." Used as competitive regulators in the power industry and as a measuring rod for rates, they could keep prices from becoming unreasonable. Since trusts made large expenditures to influence public education and public agencies, government retention of these dams was necessary to protect public liberties. To Costigan, whether the people's representatives or private monopoly controlled this future source of power was the most momentous issue of the campaign.

The depression, public indignation with the Republican Party, and repeated broadcasts of pertinent issues led to a smashing victory.[10] Costigan carried fifty-three of the sixty-two counties with fifty-five percent of the total vote. He succeeded in separating the farmers from the Republican Party, losing only Prowers of all the agricultural counties. He swept the manufacturing and commercial centers. Coal mining centers gave him overwhelming support, invariably returning larger margins than the rest of the county. Shaw received his maximum support from grazing and metal-mining counties, and even there Costigan won more counties than he lost.

The commercial entrepot of Denver remained his stronghold. He emerged victorious in all of the working class and lower middle class districts except the Negro, Republican District V. He failed to capture the upper and upper middle class of west and west central Denver, the traditional Republican strongholds where he had run well in 1912. By joining the Democratic Party, he had shifted some of the basis of his political support in the metropolis, but he was supported in both campaigns by the multi-national southeast Denver and east Denver—an area in which his support had fallen away sharply in the election of 1914. Despite strong support from former Progressives, the Denver election results reveal no clear relationship between the two periods.

Costigan had finally won a significant victory on his own terms. Without compromising his principles, he had engaged in a successful campaign based on the economic and moral issues of the day. It remained for him to try to implement his ideas in the highest legislative body in the country.

1. As early as 1923, in a letter to Governor William Sweet, Costigan had had hinted that he was available for a Senatorial appointment.
2. Because of Lindsey's opposition to the Klan and what it stood for, the Klan actively opposed his reelection in 1924. As a result of Klan opposition and Lindsey's support for LaFollette, Lindsey's normally overwhelming majority was reduced to 300 votes. This made it possible for Lindsey's opponent to win a court contest over the results.

3. Costigan still had no final impression of the likelihood of his nomination for he feared that the conservatives would organize to prevent a progressive from becoming the nominee.

4. The *Rocky Mountain News* expressed surprise that Shafroth had received the highest number of votes in the Democratic Assembly. Costigan was a close second.

5. The Colorado *Labor Advocate* reported that Shaw spent $54,000. Since Shaw's campaign headquarters alone spent $35,000 this estimate seems reasonable, for other groups of supporters made additional expenditures.

6. Costigan told Senator Nye that charges of excessive expenditures in the Republican primary were premature, but that he was studying the situation carefully and would notify Senator Nye if the situation required investigation. Costigan postponed a potent issue since he was not yet certain of its validity.

7. W. D. Hoover wrote numerous letters of advice to Costigan. An old progressive friend, Albert Dakan, supplied the candidate with much material on the sugar beet problem. In one letter he pointed out that on the basis of the 1923 crop, The Great Western Sugar Company, sugar processors, made a profit equal to ten dollars for every acre planted in sugar beets, while the farmers, with a greater overall investment, and hiring five times as much labor, realized an average profit of sixteen dollars per acre. Joshua Bernhardt, the former sugar expert of the Tariff Commission, was important in Costigan's formulation of the bounty concept and in the later Jones-Costigan sugar bill.

8. Costigan had advocated Philippine independence since 1899.

9. Under the Reciprocity Treaty of 1903, Cuba paid a lower duty on sugar than other nations exporting sugar to the United States.

10. The extent of Costigan's accomplishment in defeating Shaw can be measured by the unofficial betting odds. After the primaries Shaw was a two-to-one favorite. As late as the Sunday before the election Shaw was still a five-to-four favorite. By the day before the election Costigan was favored to win.

Chapter VIII

RELIEF FOR THE UNEMPLOYED

At first the depression of 1929 seemed no worse than the depression of 1920. Not even those closest to the scene—the social workers—foresaw the bleak future. Yet, while the country had recuperated by 1922, by 1931 conditions were still deteriorating. The nation was mired in an interminable bog. Unemployment swelled from four million in March of 1930 to eight million in March of 1931—and still conditions worsened. Many of the jobless suffered the desolation of the unwillingly and hopelessly idle, for they had not earned a paycheck in more than a year. They stared at their hungry offspring with despair, their gaunt little bodies huddled together in bed to keep warm, knowing that they could not even attend heated schools for lack of clothing and carfare—and the ranks of the jobless continued to expand. By December of 1931, American labor had already lost eleven billion dollars in wages, Unemployment was not to reach its peak of thirteen million until 1932, and even then the end was not yet in sight. Although huge sums were raised to aid the unemployed, in areas where more than one of every three bread-winners met rebuffs at the hiring gates, relief standards sank below minimum sustenance requirements. Funds were not available for anything but the most essential food supplies. Finally, in cities like Philadelphia, even this meager subsidy ceased as resources dwindled. One pregnant woman, with a family of young children, borrowed fifty cents, purchased stale bread for three and a half cents a loaf, and fed her family on this for eleven days until more public funds were made available. At the same time the price of apples declined to less than the cost of picking and transporting them; thereafter apples rotted on the trees while children went hungry. Farmers were no more content than unemployed industrial workers. After a decade of inadequate income the market for foodstuffs collapsed: prices declined to from one-half to one-fifth pre-depression levels. Nevertheless, the National Administration resisted demands for immediate action, issuing optimistic statements that not even they believed. "Individual initiative and rugged individualism, long advertised by President Hoover," Costigan charged, "developed in practice the weakness of their strength, and since 1929 our nation has been sitting in the ashes of repentance weeping the bitter tears of remorse and regret."

By 1931 community reserves had reached the point of exhaustion. A thoroughly depleted Chicago had not paid its teachers in over a year. The teachers had been forced to borrow on their insurance and place themselves at the mercy of loan sharks. Philadelphia twice had to discontinue aid. Houston refused all Negro and Mexican applicants. And some Colorado counties suspended all assistance for lack of funds. Yet the President rejected any Federal action that might infringe upon the sacred principles of individual initiative, voluntary contributions, and community responsibility. The director of the Presidential Organization on Unemployment Relief, Walter B. Gifford, without surveying the extent of unemployment, the need for succor, or the funds available pontificated that in his considered judgment, localities, with the aid of counties and states, were fully capable of meeting their relief needs. Gifford's government commission had been created to stimulate voluntary activities (people were advised to give a job of lawn-mowing to one of the unemployed rather than doing it themselves) and to induce personal donations by advertising in free newspaper space and on free radio time. A typical advertisement read:

"TO-NIGHT SAY THIS TO YOUR WIFE, THEN LOOK INTO HER EYES.

"I gave a lot more than we had planned. Are you angry?

"If you should tell her that you merely contributed—that you gave no more than you really felt obliged to—her eyes will tell you nothing. But deep down in her woman's heart she will feel a little disappointed, a tiny bit ashamed.

"But to-night confess to her that you have dug into the very bottom of your pocket; that you gave perhaps a little more than you could afford; that you opened not just your purse but your heart as well.

"In her eyes you'll see neither reproach nor anger. Trust her to understand. Trust her to appreciate the generous spirit, the good fellowship and manly sympathy which prompted you to help give unhappy people the courage to face the coming months with their heads held high with faith and hope.

"It is true the world respects the man who lives within his income. But the world adores the man who gives beyond his income.

"No; when you tell her that you have given somewhat more than you had planned you will see no censure in her eyes. But love!"

The Progressive Conference

While the Administration relied on individualism, a "lame duck" Congress, elected in a year of prosperity, ignored the pleas of New York's Senator Robert Wagner for a program of public works and unemployment insurance in order to alleviate the distress of the needy. (Costigan was the first Senator to demand federal aid to state relief programs.) In an effort to help the Administration during this crisis, the Democratic hierarchy—James Cox, John Davis, Alfred Smith, Joseph Robinson, John Nance Garner, John Raskob and Jouett Shouse—called for cooperation with the President.

Costigan replied for many liberals in the *Atlantic Monthly*. Opposition for opposition's sake was not advisable. Yet, he warned that "conciliation must not degenerate into surrender of principle." He decried "policies dictated by incapacity or by hostility to necessary human-welfare." In 1930 the voters had withdrawn confidence from Hoover, he reminded his readers, and public opinion could no longer be stilled in order to coddle business. The policies of three successive Republican Chief Executives had accelerated "the unfortunate economic tendencies which finally culminated in our present chaos." Until they confessed to this indictment and instituted a program of constructive legislation, he decided, "no compromise with the Administration can have more than trivial significance."

In March, Costigan joined Republican Senators Norris, LaFollette and Cutting and Democratic Senator Wheeler in a call for a conference of progressive leaders of both parties to outline constructive legislation for the new Congress. Progressives of all shades from all parts of the country flowed through the staid halls of the Carlton in Washington. Old progressives and socialists mingled—Harold Ickes, Sidney Hillman, Donald Richberg, Charles Beard, Florence Kelley, Lillian Wald, Robert P. Scripps of the Scripps-Howard press—with new liberals like Mayor Frank Murphy of Detroit. John Dewey was barred for advocating a third party. William Green of the AFL spoke to an unfriendly audience. Borah denounced the capitalists for concentration and speculation. Everybody castigated Hoover. Norris warned against over-optimism and predicted constructive legislation only after another Roosevelt became President—to loud applause. An unusually cheerful Lincoln Steffens told Leo Wolman: "I've been waiting for this moment for years— to see all you fellows together, up against a blank wall and not knowing what to do about it!" In an effort to achieve results the conference was divided into subcommittees to discuss the combination of wealth, trusts, tariff, the depression and unemployment. Introductory speeches were followed by a roundtable discussion. Costigan, as the chairman of the subcommittee on tariff, blamed the high rates for a decline in trade, championed reduced schedules, recommended the addition of people's counsel to the Tariff Commission, and suggested that the Commission should report to Congress and not to the President. After the subcommittee chairmen spoke, the Conference called for emergency relief, the reciprocal reduction of tariffs to lower the cost of living and to widen world markets, and aid in marketing surplus crops abroad. They requested scientific efforts to give labor the same security given to investment capital — the world owed the able-bodied man a living. Business and employment stabilization, they asserted, could be achieved through legislation and national planning agencies. They demanded that public utilities be closely regulated and competitive public ownership be instituted when necessary. The reform of legislative machinery was necessary: the Administration should be represented on the floor of Congress and a permanent Congressional committee should continue to act in the absence of Congress. Finally, the Conference resolved to terminate the existence of a lame duck Congress and to abolish the Electoral College.

Enter Social Workers, Stage Left

The Progressive Conference disbanded. Although the economic clouds continued to darken, the executive branch and the "lame duck" Congress ignored their resolutions and the new Congress was not to meet until after a drab Christmas. While Costigan sought a solution for the most pressing and immediate problem of the day, relief for the totally impoverished, the Social Work Conference on Federal Action in Unemployment was constituted on October 13. In late October, Costigan probed for reliable information on the needs of the nation, local resources, and state efforts to cope with their responsibilities. He queried the New York and New Jersey relief boards as to efficacy of the new laws that they were administering. He asked Walter Gifford for federal information on the nation's needs and the capacity of existing organizations — only to find, to his dismay, that such information was not available. Finally, a letter to Prentice Murphy, Director of the Philadelphia Children's Bureau, on October 26th began a contact with social workers that was to lead eventually to the New Deal relief legislation.[1]

On November 7, 1931, some important social workers had breakfast with Costigan. Later, they met in his office with Senator Robert M. LaFollette, Jr. and Congressman David J. Lewis. The meeting was chaired by J. Prentice Murphy. In opening, he remarked that while accurate information on the extent of the relief needs of the nation was lacking, still the group gathered in that office was as well informed as anyone. The social workers gave a clear account of the situation. First, William Hodson of the New York Welfare Council reported that $80,000,000 were being lost in wages every month in New York City alone, yet relief expenditures amounted to only $3,500,000 a month. Having lost these wages, the unemployed drained savings and bank accounts, borrowed, or just suffered. Normally, he continued, contrary to common belief, seventy percent of assistance funds came from public treasuries and only thirty percent from private sources. To sustain life, therefore, public funds must be increased. Allen T. Burns, Executive Director of the Community Chest and Councils of Social Agencies, followed. Since the second winter of the depression had been worse than the first, the third winter could only be worse than the second, he warned, inasmuch as more of the unemployed would have exhausted all of their personal resources. In a discussion that followed Burns' statement the experts revealed that unemployment had grown by 800 percent, relief by 300 percent. Relief needs were likely to grow at a much faster pace than any foreseeable rise in available funds. Fund raisers had consistently underestimated the problem. Social workers had been forced to spread the sum, and thus support had been administered at below-minimum standards. In addition, social workers' case loads had increased four-fold, from twenty-five to one hundred cases per worker — an increase that made effective case work almost impossible. Conditions were terrible and they were likely to get worse unless aid was forthcoming.

The social workers' program was outlined by Joanna Colcord of the Russell Sage Foundation. Community responsibility should be retained, they felt. Thus, the Federal government should deal with no unit smaller than a state or territory. The county or city should continue to be charged with responsibility for family welfare. A federal grant-in-aid program advantageously fulfilled these goals, Miss Colcord suggested. It preserved local administration of local affairs. Federal inspection could bring the benefits of central knowledge without infringing on local autonomy. A requirement to match central funds with state funds would preserve the initiative of the state and its sense of responsibility. If administrative discretion were permitted as to the manner and amount of matching funds, they could compensate for the difference in the wealth of the states. In addition, by taking the distribution of funds out of political hands, such a system could prevent pork barrel. After a state application indicating either insufficient funds or constitutional limitations which prevented borrowing for relief purposes, the Federal government would make a grant. Competent personnel should be used to administer the funds even if residence requirements had to be waived. In the near future, she suggested, public welfare standards could be raised by a newly-created national department. In conclusion, Miss Colcord admitted that social workers were undecided whether direct payment, work relief, or a combination of both was most efficacious.

The three legislators listened intently and prepared to act. LaFollette was called away that afternoon to participate in a personal drama. His wife was in labor; what should have been a joyful occasion became a moment of sorrow for the infant girl lived but a few hours. After a period of bereavement, LaFollette drafted a bill incorporating many of the suggestions of the social workers. Costigan, while awaiting the opening of Congress, continued to gather information. Leagues of municipalities were interrogated about conditions and the need for Federal help. Jacob Billikopf of the Federation of Jewish Philanthropies aided him in further inquiries to social workers and economists. Still probing, he held another conference with social workers in New York on November 30th. Finally, when the Seventy-second Congress opened in early December of that dreadful winter of 1931, Costigan and Congressman Lewis introduced identical bills. Although originally referred to the Senate Commerce Committee, Costigan's bill was transferred to LaFollette's Committee on Manufactures to be considered jointly with LaFollette's proposal.

The two bills were very similar. Both incorporated grants-in-aid to the states. Both provided for the dispensation of welfare through state agencies with national supervision (Costigan preferred the Children's Bureau and LaFollette suggested the creation of a Federal Emergency Relief Board). Both furnished additional funds to states if the original grant was insufficient. Costigan apportioned forty percent of the appropriation to the states in proportion to their population, on a matching basis. The balance of funds was for administration and for further allocations to the states on the basis of need — a practical approach which was adopted in the joint bill.

During the cheerless Christmas recess, when innumerable children awoke to a cold, giftless house, the committee held its hearings. Even if unemployment had not been widening, the need for funds would have continued to grow, for the jobless were exhausting their own resources. Witness after witness catalogued increasing idleness, depletion of resources, debasement of subsistence standards as funds dwindled. The outlook was almost hopeless. The anticipated local resources could meet only a portion of the anticipated needs. Each winter of the depression disclosed an intensified crisis. With one voice, those closest to the scene — the social workers — cried out for federal aid to states and localities. Witnesses for the opposition were right-wing fringe groups — the Sentinels of the Republic and the Woman Patriot Publishing Company, both of whom opposed national aid — and Walter Gifford, who insisted that local relief assets were adequate and that Federal participation would only eliminate a sense of local responsibility.

The testimony completed, the Costigan-LaFollette Relief Bill was favorably reported and brought to the floor of the Senate. LaFollette opened the debate. Costigan followed with his first major oration, a speech that the Washington columnist, Robert G. Allen, called "one of the most beautiful and telling I have ever heard." With his deep voice, his soft, precise, conversational manner of speaking, he informed the Senate and the nation that:

"The Webster-Hayne debate on the true boundaries between State and Federal authority, the lightning-charged controversies over secession and reconstruction, the stirring encounters over the wartime powers of government, the constitutional rights of individuals were secondary in essential and fundamental importance to the pending measure . . . It involves nothing less than the inalienable right of American citizens to life."

If a timid Senate permitted citizens to perish for lack of federal aid while billions in doles were being given to bankers, railroad executives, and financial institutions, "a new and black chapter of American history will open," he warned. Federal assistance during times of disaster had ample precedent: the California earthquake of 1906, supplies to Poland, Austria-Hungary, and the Balkans in 1919, Russian relief in 1921, help for victims of the Japanese earthquake of 1924, and support during the Mississippi flood of 1927. Could they then ignore the disaster that began in 1929? Major municipalities desperately needed subsidies while little was known about further needs of small cities and rural communities. Eighty percent of welfare costs were already supplied through public funds. The opposition was really saying "that it is all right to give county relief, municipal relief, State relief, but the moment we pass to Federal cooperation with the States, to Federal aid . . . then, by some curious alchemy, we have established a dole." Costigan emphasized his far-flung efforts to gather information on the depth of American hunger. The bill had been drawn up according to the recommendations of experts in the field. Consequently, this bill was best suited to most national subsistence problems.

Despite these efforts, even fellow-Democrats with liberal inclinations withheld their support. The proposal, they claimed, would violate state sovereignty. Besides, they warned, the President would veto a grant-in-aid relief bill. Senator Black rejected any central agency that would tell Alabama how to dispense charity. Senators Black, Walsh, and Bulkley resolved, instead, to lend money to the states. The Senate Democratic leader, Joseph Robinson, supported the substitute measure: it proposed to supply funds only after the exhaustion of state and private resources and the Governor's formal request for aid.

Costigan defended his own product. The bill for rural sanitation had been passed without drawing any such fine distinctions, he informed the Senate, although it provided that the Public Health Service in Washington determine the amount of state participation. Referring to Senator Wheeler's statement that roads were built with state-matched federal aid, he argued that only by national supervision could "pork-barrel" politics be prevented. The safeguard of national standards had already been proven on highway bills. Besides, the constitutions of thirty-four states prohibited extending their credit in aid of individuals, associations or corporations, and prevented their borrowing funds from the federal government for public assistance purposes — they would be ineligible for aid under the substitute bill. It was an effective defense of his measure — but nevertheless the Costigan-LaFollette Bill was defeated. The debate made Costigan a national figure. The *St. Louis Post-Dispatch* commented: "Edward P. Costigan of Colorado has held a seat in the United States Senate scarcely two months and yet his name is better known throughout the country as a sincere worker for the people than a dozen Senators who have been in office ten years."

Costigan and LaFollette were not to be thwarted easily. They promptly introduced similar legislation. To no one's surprise the subcommittee found that conditions had continued to deteriorate while the nation's legislators dawdled. Toledo, Ohio, had reduced its daily individual subsistence allotment to little more than two cents per meal. Birmingham had discontinued all subsidies in rural sections of the county. New Orleans had rejected all new applicants while counties in Colorado had been forced to abandon their programs. For eleven days Philadelphia had dispensed no relief, while the constitutionality of a state appropriation was being tested in the courts. Philadelphia's future looked particularly bleak, for the state constitution prohibited an income tax, and all other revenue sources seemed exhausted. Yet despite the overwhelming evidence, the Senate refused to pass the grant-in-aid.

While Congress pondered the question, Costigan and Senator Otis Glenn of Illinois debated over a national network. Senator Glenn had contended that localities were capable of dealing with relief problems. Absence of gubernatorial requests for aid, he asserted, was sufficient proof of financial ability. Costigan retorted that 8,300,000 were totally unemployed and 6,000,000 partially unemployed. Forty percent of the Chicago work force was jobless. Relief needs had grown two hundred percent while Community Chest funds had increased only fifty-nine percent. One to two million homeless workers, for whom no locality admitted responsibility, were "drifting in fluctuating tides across America." Welfare funds had always come from public treasuries, he reminded the country, and Federal funds had already been used to feed foreign citizens in need. No constitutional question had been raised for all the years that Federal grants had been used to promote road building, agricultural extension work, and sanitation. While billions of dollars in national funds were being used to support business, "who will now deny millions for our stricken people?" "The dikes are broken, the ocean of need is pouring through," he declared. "Federal action must no longer be blocked."

And national action was no longer blocked. The efforts of Costigan and LaFollette were not in vain. The Congressional and radio debates had awakened the nation. By a vote of seventy-two to eight, Congress enacted a compromise measure, sponsored by Senators Wagner, Robinson, Pittman and Bulkley. It permitted the Reconstruction Finance Corporation to make five percent loans to states in proportion to their population, and to inform the state governors of the availability of the funds. The loans were to be repaid by deductions from future grants-in-aid for the construction of highways.

There were many objections to the bill. Senator Reed pointed out correctly that the loan was a facade, since appropriations would be increased to cover the deductions. Senators Couzens and Borah charged that crucial funds would be tied up and held for states, even if they did not apply. Senator Davis of Pennsylvania complained that, according to her attorney general, Pennsylvania could not borrow money for public assistance. LaFollette, faced with a similar Wisconsin prohibition, proposed an amendment that the Reconstruction Finance Corporation advance funds regardless of constitutional prohibitions. Costigan itemized the bill's inadequacies. It lacked both central guidance and a provision to use welfare agencies. Its allocation according to population provided no reserve fund which could be used for transients and areas without resources. Senator Reed feared that, since central control was lacking, a governor might handle the funds in a scandalous way. Senator McKellar assuaged this fear, in part, with an amendment that empowered the governor to use existing state boards to control the distribution of funds. Although the enactment fell far short of perfection, Costigan had awakened the nation to Federal responsibility for community sustenance.

Loans to the Unemployed

Costigan soon sought other methods to alleviate the distress caused by the depression. He realized that Federal aid to the states could sustain the welfare machinery but it could be no solution to the problems of the depression. Somehow the machinery of industry had to be set back in motion. The Administration proposed arming the Reconstruction Finance Corporation with two billion dollars to make loans to great financial and railroad institutions in order to check deflation and ultimately to restore production. Although he saw the need, Costigan hesitated to support the measure because it was being pressed by business interests "some of which have declared before, and doubtless will again in opposition to what they like to term 'Government in business'; except in their business and for their own substantial private profit." Ironically, he remarked, they had opposed doles in the form of relief while accepting a two billion dollar dole for themselves. At least the directors of the R.F.C. should not make loans to corporations in which they or their family had an interest. But his amendment was defeated and relief to corporations easily passed.[2] When the R.F.C., with all its efficiency, succeeded only in making some large companies more solvent, it was obvious that another approach would be necessary.

At this time progressive attorney Donald Richberg proposed a plan to conquer the depression. The obvious remedy for unemployment was to put men to work; if sufficient demand for industrial products could be created it would stimulate industry and create reemployment. A simple way to increase purchasing power, and thus employment, Richberg suggested, was for the federal government to loan the unemployed three to five hundred dollars. After Costigan inquired of leading economists about the merits of the proposed legislation, he found that while some thought the measure useless, most of those queried supported it as at least a partial solution. Therefore, he joined Congressman Fiorello

RELIEF FOR THE UNEMPLOYED 129

LaGuardia of New York in sponsoring such a bill. Despite these relatively favorable opinions, and the overwhelming support of organized labor, the measure was never seriously considered.

Cutting the Salaries of Federal Employees

While Costigan was trying to increase the national purchasing power with loans to the unemployed and aid to state relief programs, Hoover took the oposite tack. He tried to balance the budget by reducing Federal salaries. Costigan vehemently objected. It would diminish purchasing power and it particularly affected a group whose real wages had lagged behind price increases. But he did agree with Senator Norris that if economies were necessary, there should be graduated wage reductions while the lower salaried government employees retained their full income. He decried the example of the government reducing compensation at a time of distress.

The End of the Session

Costigan continued to fight for new legislation despite his colleague's desire to depart. In July, when Congress tried to escape the oppressive heat and humidity of a Washington summer and to prepare for the Presidential Nominating Conventions, Costigan resisted adjournment "while present farm, industrial, and business distress continues unabated." He attacked a proposal to widen the R.F.C. in order to expedite a public works program. It was totally inadequate, he declared, and had been suggested solely to terminate the session. Not a dogmatic thinker, he offered to support any measure that might aid the nation, but he opposed leaving until credit had been provided for consumers and grants-in-aid for relief offered to communities.

Despite inadequate measures to meet the crisis Congress had adjourned, Costigan asserted. Administration measures had failed to meet the problems of the depression because of over-cautiousness and big-business bias, he charged. The nation had a reponsibility to help its residents to live and find work. Much had been said about doles, but the nation could not refuse aid to loyal citizens while big business was bolstered through the R. F. C. He conceded that Congress had reluctantly passed some positive laws. It had grudgingly permitted the Red Cross to distribute wheat held by the Grain Stabilization Corporation. Although it had acted timidly and without safeguards, Congress had provided public works and had offered relief funds camouflaged as loans to the states. It had created the useful, though inadequate, Reconstruction Finance Corporation—which unfortunately bolstered large, favored firms while refusing succor to smaller banks. And no loans had been extended to the unemployed.

But prosperity could not be created, Costigan warned, by aiding financial leaders. Adequate markets and increased employment were necessary. Farmers had received little reinforcement, yet the principle of a moratorium on farm mortgages had been espoused, seed loans had been authorized, and the Federal Land Bank was safeguarded against mortgage losses. The Lame-Duck Amendment to the Constitution would make the national legislature more responsive to changes in the national temper. Congress had adopted the Income Tax Amendment, defeated a sales tax proposal, and created the principle that federal revenue was to be based on ability to pay. In addition, an effort had been made toward currency and credit expansion. Costigan reluctantly opposed one proposal to aid some citizens—a veterans' bonus—because, as he pointed out, the costs of the last war in interest, buildings, and veterans' expenses were greater than the civil expenses of the government. At a time when millions were unemployed it would be improper to give federal funds to persons who had other means of support and thereby make it necessary to deny help to the many needy. These limited efforts of Congress were insufficient for the scope of the task. The depression, Costigan concluded, was a disaster worse than war. Thus it was a federal responsibility. Private industry lacked the resources and the unity for the task.

Franklin Delano Roosevelt

When the central stage in Washington closed down the focus of national attention shifted to a drama being enacted in Chicago—the choice of the Democratic contender for the starring role in the District of Columbia.

The leading candidate for the Democratic nomination was the urbane, witty, and glamorous Governor of New York, Franklin Delano Roosevelt. He was a proven vote-getter—he had carried New York in 1928 against a Hoover landslide and in 1930 by three-quarters of a million votes. He was a proven administrator—New York was one of the best run states in the Union (it had been since Smith's residency in the State House). He was a proven progressive—as the Governor of the Empire State he had amassed a commendable record on public power, unemployment relief, labor legislation and conservation; as a candidate he espoused the cause of the forgotten man at the bottom of the economic pyramid, and had called for "bold, persistent experimentation."

At first the magnetic Roosevelt seemed to have a tight grip on the nomination. He was victorious in all the early contests in 1932—Alaska, Washington, North Dakota, Georgia, Iowa, Maine, Wisconsin, Nebraska, Michigan and Kentucky. But Farley and Flynn had not accounted for every contingency. The arch-reactionary, former Republican John J. Raskob, was still national chairman, due largely to the use of his own funds to keep the national organization solvent. He represented the business-high tariff wing of the party and was determined to prevent the nomination of the candidate of the liberals.

Raskob's activities, and the ambition of leading Democrats in a favorable year, led to efforts to prevent Roosevelt's nomination. Favorite son candidates started to sprout. "Alfalfa Bill" Murray was chosen by his native Oklahoma, but his defeat by Roosevelt in North Dakota brought him back to earth. Missouri pledged itself to its isolationist Senator James Reed, Illinois to populistic Senator J. Hamilton Lewis, Maryland to its eloquent Governor, Albert Ritchie (who was a serious candidate). Al Smith, incensed at Roosevelt's independence, decided to make the race again, and, together with Tammany, prevented FDR from asserting complete control over his own delegation. John Nance Garner of Texas had decided to accept the support of William Randolph Hearst and seek the nomination. Finally, in the event of a deadlock, Newton D. Baker and Owen Young were widely spoken of as possibilities. While Roosevelt had trounced Smith in New Hampshire, where Roosevelt had organization support, he was swamped in Massachusetts by a margin of three to one as James Curley had run a poor campaign and had raised up factional struggles that pitted the machine against F. D. R. Two days later Smith ran surprisingly well in Pennsylvania and prevented Roosevelt from sweeping the delegation. Finally, the support of Hearst, McAdoo, and the Texas Society of California carried that crucial state for Garner. The Roosevelt steamroller was stalled.

Colorado had not yet committed itself.

Costigan and Roosevelt had long been acquainted and the Senator was an early advocate of the debonaire New Yorker's bid for the Presidential nomination. Both had been important members of the Wilson Administration—Roosevelt as Assistant Secretary of the Navy and Costigan as a Tariff Commissioner—and during those exciting days they began an association that continued through the years. When Roosevelt was mentioned as a Presidential candidate, Costigan showed signs of approval without publicly committing himself. Although Costigan had been mentioned as a possible running mate for Owen D. Young, he never doubted his own preference. As early as June 1931 he wrote FDR about the growing friendliness of the Mountain States towards his candidacy.[3] The admiration and respect with which Costigan held the New York Governor was returned in full measure. Roosevelt appreciated Costigan's style and borrowed a sentence from Costigan's *Atlantic Monthly* article for a speech: "the demand is for a people's not a profiteer's sovereignty."

Costigan delayed his endorsement of Roosevelt in order to use his influence to assure consideration of the economic issues in the Democratic platform. But he soon realized that postponing Colorado's endorsement would aid those who wished to prevent Roosevelt's nomination. When the Colorado Presidential Nominating Convention met, Costigan sent a message:

"It is my judgment that by all odds the most available Democratic candidate who by any stretch of the imagination may be termed progressive . . . is Franklin Delano Roosevelt. . . The character of the unyielding opposition he faces endorses his sincerity. Governor Roosevelt . . . has become the candidate of the overwhelming progressive sentiment of the West and South."

The liberals did not have much trouble capturing the Colorado delegation, for even conservatives had long been ready to join the Roosevelt bandwagon in the West. With little dissent the Colorado Democrats chose representatives instructed to vote as a unit for Roosevelt so long as his name remained before the convention. Although Costigan declined to lead the slate, he worked effectively for Roosevelt, using Oscar Chapman as his floor manager.

Roosevelt went to Chicago with almost a majority of the delegates, but not the requisite two-thirds. He was uncertain how long his lines would hold and James Farley, his campaign manager, worked feverishly to sway the convention. After the third ballot John Nance Garner of Texas decided to withdraw and released his Texas and California delegations in favor of F. D. R. On the fourth ballot William Gibbs McAdoo answered the call for California; amid the boos of the pro-Smith galleries he announced the vote that cast all the old leaders of the party into the background.

With unemployment mounting to fifteen million, with rumors of a banking system teetering on the edge of disaster, with an opponent who had earned the reputation of inertia in the face of crisis, nomination appeared to be election and many professionals advised Roosevelt to sit out the campaign, making only a few carefully staged speeches in the East. Roosevelt chose to contrast his energy to Hoover's apathy. He looked beyond the election to the confidence that must be created in his administration. With conflicting advice from low tariff and high tariff advocates, New Nationalists and followers of Brandeis, orthodox economists and advocates of economic planning, Roosevelt's speeches incorporated all points of view and embraced none, creating an image of activity, while allowing the future President the utmost flexibility. The composition of his cabinet and his refusal to take any joint action with the discredited engineer permitted him to take office committed to no one course.

The New Deal and Relief

It was in this atmosphere that the Second Session of the 72nd Congress opened. Costigan and LaFollette immediately renewed their appeal for Federal grants-in-aid to state relief programs for the need was still overwhelming. R. F. C. loans had made it possible for many cities to continue disbursements. Nevertheless, the R. F. C. was the wrong body to dispense this money for as Costigan charged, it was run by bankers, not workers trained in welfare techniques. Many communities had reached their debt limit. Borrowing for public assistance was destroying their credit rating. Some states could not apply because of the loan provision, while others hesitated since they had to declare poverty before doing so. As a result, while people went hungry and the states' resources were depleted, the R. F. C. still had unexpended designated assets. Communities that had participated in the R. F. C. program found the available assistance was inadequate, and necessary long-range planning was precluded by the short-run nature of the R. F. C. loans.

Once again Costigan's efforts were frustrated. Wagner proposed to continue R. F. C. supervision, anticipating a less security-minded, more relief-oriented body under a new administration. The larger appropriation, he felt, would improve standards. He defended his substitute as the best legislation that could be passed. The substitute replaced the Costigan-LaFollette Bill.

LaFollette and Costigan, dissatisfied with the result, telegraphed President-elect Roosevelt, requesting his opposition to Wagner's proposal. Wagner had offered the compromise measure as acceptable to Hoover. They were confident that a special session would be receptive to a more adequate bill. They suggested that he confer with his Relief

Administrator, Harry Hopkins, who fully understood the situation and the importance of grants-in-aid.

Roosevelt had long been aware of Costigan's efforts. As Governor he had cooperated with the Senator's attempts to gather information on the state relief needs and activities. In return, the Coloradan had sent the subcommittee records to the Governor. During the 1932 public assistance controversy Roosevelt had unsuccessfully tried to influence Senator Wagner, and his effort, in 1933, to honor Costigan's request met the same fate.

But, during the hundred days, Roosevelt wrote the script. While he rejected the last-minute plea of Costigan and LaFollette to create a truly national banking system—as well as more radical suggestions, and was mesmerized by Lewis Douglas and the economy bill, the progressives still played the major roles. Typical was his treatment of the second Bonus Expeditionary Force. While he opposed the bonus, he fed them, housed them, conferred with their leaders, sent the Navy Band and Eleanor to cheer them, and then recruited most of them for the Civilian Conservation Corps. An air of change swept over Washington and in this atmosphere the Costigan-LaFollette Bill breathed a new life. Harry Hopkins, and William Hodson convinced Secretary of Labor Frances Perkins of its efficacy. After a conference with the President, Hopkins and Perkins joined Senators Costigan, LaFollette and Wagner to draft the Administration measure. On March 21st, Roosevelt made his request to Congress, on March 30th it passed the Senate, and on May 12th it sat, signed, on the President's desk. After numerous disappointments, Costigan had triumphed; in recognition of his role, Hopkins sent the first allocation, for $302,645, to Colorado.

Public Works

During this Special Session, Costigan introduced a bill for LaFollette, Bronson Cutting of New Mexico, and himself which authorized the federally administered expenditure of six billion dollars for public works, with loans and grants to states or their subdivisions to further local construction. On such projects the thirty-hour week was to be enforced. When Senator Wagner brought up his new public works proposal (a program administered through the R.F.C.), Costigan successfully offered an amendment to permit urban water systems and rural irrigation systems to be constructed out of this allotment.

As time passed, Costigan tried to assure the maintenance of welfare standards and a broad definition of public works. In early 1934 he joined with Senators Wagner, LaFollette and Copeland to prevent a conservative sponsored reduction of the white collar force of the Civil Works Authority. In fact, he feared that the entire program was in danger. When the Administration's emphasis shifted to work relief, Costigan sought to protect self-liquidating projects already in progress that might not be so considered. One undertaking for transmountain water diversion, of particular importance to the people of Colorado, was not, he thought, covered in the language of the act. The Senate accepted appropriate amendments.

The Gubernatorial Campaign of 1934

Yet the fight for public assistance did not take place in a political vacuum. Relief legislation, and the administration of the program, became intricately intertwined with the struggle for power between the conservatives and progressives in the Colorado Democratic Party.

Not only had the Costigan forces committed the Colorado delegation to Roosevelt's candidacy in 1932, they apparently had won another important fight, the choice of a second Senator from Colorado. The two candidates for the nomination were John T. Barnett, an extremely conservative Democrat and Alva Adams, a member of Colorado's powerful Democratic family. Adams had earned a liberal reputation during a short Senate term to which he had been appointed by the progressive Democratic Governor Sweet and he had aided Senator Walsh in his disclosure of the Teapot Dome scandal. The liberals were so firmly committed to Adams (Costigan even endorsed his candidacy!) that Oscar Chapman managed his campaign. With Adams' victory, they seemed to dominate Colorado politics. Political prognosticators failed to reckon with two new developments—the surprisingly moderate path chosen by Alva Adams and the political skill and popularity of the conservative Edwin Johnson.

Even before Adams had been sworn in as Senator, Costigan proposed that the two Senators obtain the advice of Colorado Democratic leaders so that they could submit a list of five persons for each important position the new President had to fill. But because of the divergent philosophies held by the two Senators, efforts at mutual accommodation were not entirely successful. Although Adams would support much of the New Deal, his political tendencies were more conservative than the Administration's, while Costigan tended to move in advance of the President. The Costigan forces became increasingly suspicious of

Adams and the political cooperation that the progressives had desired never materialized.

In the meantime a very definite threat to the Colorado liberals had emerged in Denver. When Lieutenant Governor Johnson had announced that he was going to seek the 1932 gubernatorial nomination, Governor Billy Adams, the uncle of the Senate candidate, had reluctantly decided not to oppose him and Johnson obtained the nomination by default.

Ed Johnson was always a competent, honest administrator, but his point of view was different from that of the National Administration, and decidedly opposed to the ideas of the senior Senator. Where Costigan had always thought of the American economy in terms of the world economy and had advocated flexible tariffs, Johnson wanted a self-contained America which would preserve the American market for American producers. To achieve this he supported high tariffs and opposed any action that would permit additional foreign products to enter this country. Where Costigan was an ardent supporter of Roosevelt's economic policies and shaped New Deal legislation on relief and sugar, Johnson disliked the price the Administration tried to exact for a subsidy to agriculture—the curtailment of production. Where Costigan made every effort to use government agencies to raise wages, Johnson opposed the prevailing wage amendment to the Emergency Relief Act. Where Costigan preferred an income tax to meet increased costs, Johnson pressed for a sales tax. Many progressive Democrats considered Johnson to be practically a Republican. He received ardent support from the anti-New Deal, anti-Costigan Denver *Post*. Johnson represented a point of view that Costigan had spent a lifetime combatting; a clash between the two was inevitable.

After Johnson became Governor he strengthened his political machine. A man who never ceased to campaign, on even an unofficial trip he would stop at every wide spot on the road, shake hands with some supporters, whom he always knew by name, and ask about the children.

Soon it was rumored that Johnson intended to contest Costigan's renomination in 1936.[4] No one believed Johnson's disclaimer in September of 1933 that he would not be a candidate against Costigan, even though Johnson had declared that Costigan was an able Senator with a great record, that he was working in complete harmony with the Administration, and that he had the President's confidence. In fact, Costigan was told that Johnson had been eliminating his followers who had held state offices, even those under civil service, and was claiming credit for all national relief accomplishments in Colorado, while berating the national administration anytime someone had to be dropped from the rolls. Some of Costigan's supporters were so convinced of Johnson's candidacy that they were tempted to vote against sound measures when these bills seemed intended to strengthen a machine that would eventually advance Johnson to the Senate in 1936.

Because of this fear, and because of Johnson's conservatism, the progressives decided that it was essential to enter a nominee against Johnson in 1934. The logical candidate was Assistant Secretary of the Interior Oscar Chapman, and the *Rocky Mountain News* called upon him to enter the contest. But Chapman, with national commitments, had little interest in the state house. Indeed, he had never been enthusiastic about running for any political office. Without Chapman, the race might be hopeless, but the progressive Democrats were determined to contest the nomination. Since the Costigan forces in Colorado could not agree on a candidate, Josephine Roche, Assistant Secretary of the Treasury, decided that if there was no one else to oppose Johnson, she would. When the liberals in Colorado were informed that Miss Roche would run, they were distraught. They had not been consulted in the choice, and John Carroll felt that they could not run a successful campaign with a feminine candidate. Costigan informed Carroll that they could not allow Johnson's forces to gather their strength and that the race must be made. Carroll, despite his reluctance, became campaign manager. Somehow he was expected to convince the large groups of patriarchal immigrants who had voted for Costigan that they should support a woman for the gubernatorial office.

As opposition to his renomination became apparent, Johnson attacked Costigan, Josephine Roche, and Dan Burns for their failure to obtain more funds for Colorado from the Public Works Authority. (They were members of the Authority Advisory Board.) Johnson tried to undermine the progressive identification with the New Deal. Since Oscar Chapman was in the Department of Interior, he charged, the only explanation for the lack of funds was that Costigan was alienated from the Administration because of adverse votes for almost all New Deal measures. Instead of fighting to obtain federal funds for Colorado projects, Johnson continued, Costigan was on a junket involving a Saint Lawrence Seaway that would bring Cuban sugar to Chicago to compete with Colorado beet sugar. His own administration, he declared, was on good terms with Roosevelt and received more than its share of relief funds. But Costigan appointees were on the State Public Works Authority Board and the state received few funds for public works. (In his charges, Johnson ignored Costigan's activities for the Casper-Alcova Dam, the Caddoa Dam, the Grand Lake Diversionary Project, the Uncompahgre Project, and the transferrence of the Air Corps Technical School to Colorado—among other projects—and he neglected to mention that he sought Costigan's aid whenever he came to Washington to try to influence Roosevelt's policy).

Finally, in the heat of the campaign, he accused the self-effacing senior Senator of a desire to become state dictator, and he declared that Merle Vincent, Josephine Roche, and Costigan had only become Democrats to obtain jobs.

Just as the race seemed to be polarizing, former Governor Billy Adams declared his intention to seek the nomination. Although Senator Alva Adams intimated earlier that he did not wish Governor Adams to run, when the former Governor made his announcement the junior Senator endorsed him. No one knew from whom Billy Adams would draw votes.

The problem of obtaining a designation by the Democratic Assembly, so that Miss Roche might run in the primary, was cleared with ease. With the overwhelming support of Denver and many officials who had been recommended for their positions by Chapman and Costigan, Josephine Roche came in second, behind Governor Johnson but ahead of the once peerless vote-getter, Billy Adams. Faced with the prospect of ignominious defeat, Adams withdrew and threw his support to Ed Johnson.

With the Adams family supporting Johnson, the progressives faced the insuperable task of defeating the combined machines of Johnson and Adams with a female candidate. Still, Josephine Roche had the support of organized labor as well as the Costigan forces. Costigan himself came to Colorado and strongly endorsed his close friend, eulogizing her abilities.

The liberal campaign was based on the contention that Colorado needed a governor who would identify with the New Deal. While Josephine Roche declared that the New Deal was fundamentally conservative, being an effort to recapture the American tradition, Costigan said that Roosevelt was leading the nation to a renewal of its vital forces by returning flexibility to governmental machinery and by guaranteeing equality of opportunity for all. He declared that Colorado had endosed the New Deal—a combination of the Square Deal and the New Freedom—before Roosevelt's candidacy, that Roosevelt was willing to use the resources of the nation to win the peace and not reserve the nation's heroism only for war. The progressives, he said, were at home in a new Administration where the programs that they had advocated for twenty years were being enacted. He emphasized Josephine Roche's familiarity with the problems to be solved and her wisdom in counsel. He praised her qualities of mind, heart, and education, and her self-sacrifice during the struggle. In seven and one-half years as a coal mine operator, he declared, she succeeded where her competitors failed, "primarily because she loves justice and practices it." She was as close to the problems of the farmers, he told his rural audience, as to those of the industrial workers. "She has been in the vanguard of liberal causes, because she is the devoted friend of all men, women and children." He parried the charges of radicalism by the Denver *Post* by listing all of the accomplishments of noted progressives who had been pilloried by the press. He charged, moreover, that as long as Johnson openly accepted the endorsement of that paper, he was not deserving of popular support.

Sugar beet growers, upset by crop restrictions and not yet the beneficiaries of bounty checks, voted against Miss Roche despite their earlier support for Costigan. Ignoring her fine record as a mine owner, the first and second generation coal miners in the former Costigan strongholds of Las Animas and Huerfano did not support her, but coal miners did supply the margin of her victory in Gunnison and supported her in the northern fields. Johnson carried industrial Pueblo (the Adams stronghold), the grazing northwest and southwest, the farming northeast, east central and southeast, the mountain region and the western slope. The progressives were able to maintain their margins only in Denver and its environs. Despite Miss Roche's gallant race, Johnson was easily renominated.

Johnson versus Costigan

Although Johnson had personalized policy differences with Costigan earlier, his attacks on the senior Senator began in earnest in 1934, as a reaction to the decision to contest his renomination. He had blamed Colorado's Senators, particularly Costigan, for the federal policy that caused additional taxation in Colorado. He chose to press for a sales tax rather than an income tax to solve this dilemma. Before the primary campaign of 1934, Costigan had been warned by a correspondent that Johnson had designs upon his Senate seat and to this end had been eliminating his followers.

Following the bitter primary fight the victorious Johnson forced a reluctant Harry Hopkins to discharge the Colorado Relief Administrator, Captain Shawver. Shawver, who had been appointed with the support of Costigan, was charged with hostility to state self-help projects and with using his position to aid the candidacy of Roche. Though Shawver denied both charges, Johnson secured his removal and the appointment of a more acceptable administrator.[5] Having tasted victory again, Johnson kept Costigan on the defensive by lashing out at him during the prevailing wage controversy.

The Emergency Relief Appropriation Act of 1935 marked the triumph of work relief over direct assistance, the Works Progress Administration replacing the Federal Emergency Relief Administration. The bill was greeted with considerable controversy. Conservatives were appalled at the shift of focus from state to national responsibility. Progressives considered the appropriation inadequate. Social workers regretted the abandonment of the unemployables to local poor relief. The bill, as it came to the floor of Congress, provided for a security wage, higher than direct welfare payments but lower than wages in private employment. In this way relief workers could be lured into private industry. The American Federation of Labor feared that the security wage would destroy wage standards. Pat McCarran, the Nevada conservative, for motives of which progressives were suspicious, proposed to pay W.P.A. workers the hourly wage prevailing in the area. At the same time, the number of hours per month would be limited, thus providing incentive for a return to private industry where the total monthly wage would be higher. Costigan, joined by junior Senator Alva Adams in his alignment with the liberals, voted for the Prevailing Wage Amendment and against the Administration. The amendment passed. But in the end, after much delay, the security wage was adopted by the threat of a Presidential veto.

Johnson pounced upon an opportunity to weaken the alliance between the supporters of the Administration and the Colorado progressives. Without mentioning the vote of Alva Adams, he asserted that Costigan's vote on the Prevailing Wage Amendment had defeated the public works program. Costigan retorted angrily: "Governor Johnson of Colorado with characteristic recklessness has rushed in where angels should fear to tread. Instead of laboring as some of us are doing to work out in this case as in many another solution of a public program with a full sense of official responsibility and with fairness to the entire country, he is raising a cloud of dust to create a misleading impression of his undying devotion to the President."

Roosevelt had always enjoyed his support, he affirmed, without the encouragement of Governor Johnson. The Governor should at least have waited for the resolution of the legislative situation before "hurling himself into a national situation of which he knows nothing." Costigan, obviously concerned, wrote to the President assuring him of his readiness to endorse any adequate public works program that met Roosevelt's approval. But though Howe acknowledged Costigan's message, the Administration sent a letter of appreciation to Ed Johnson for his support in the fight over the Prevailing Wage Amendment. Continuing his offensive, Johnson sponsored a resolution in the Colorado Senate to rebuke the senior Senator for voting for the Prevailing Wage Amendment. It was tabled and thus disposed of. Not to be denied the initiative, Johnson deprecated his antagonist by congratulating Joseph O'Mahoney of Wyoming for changing his vote and thus contributing to the Administration victory over the McCarran Amendment.

But Johnson lost the next round. He failed to prevent the appointment of Paul Shriver as Works Progress Administrator. The dynamic young redhead, a close friend of Oscar Chapman, was one of the original Democratic Volunteers, the backbone of the Costigan campaign in 1930. In 1933, through the influence of Chapman and Costigan, Shriver joined the flood of young intellectuals who staffed the new agencies. He received a position with the Public Works Authority. After two exciting years in Washington, establishing a fine administrative record, he was Hopkin's choice for Colorado Relief Administrator. Governor Johnson immediately attacked the appointment. Its purpose was to build a political machine for Costigan, he charged. A politician like Shriver was not qualified to spend millions of dollars.[6]

Shriver's supporters rallied to his defense. Hopkins declared that the choice was a personal one, based on Shriver's administrative record, and truthfully declared that he had not been recommended by either of Colorado's Senators (Chapman had recommended him). In a ringing statement Costigan defended Shriver, contending that support for him reflected support for the New Deal against the special interests.[7] Johnson was only able to delay Shriver's confirmation. When Senator Adams approved the appointment, it became impossible to prevent the young administrator from remaining in the office.

Shriver had not held his position very long before he was engaged in his first clash with Johnson. The issue was relief for aliens. Back in April, Johnson had claimed that as the result of a drought, Mexicans were inundating Colorado to obtain relief when there was not enough available for citizens. He threatened to call out the National Guard and deport all aliens from the state. In the middle of May, Johnson repelled Mexicans at the the state line. Secretary of State Hull became furious.

But a crisis was averted when the Mexican Government announced that it would grant one hundred acres of land to Mexican citizens who returned home to work them. Hardly had Shriver been confirmed when Johnson demanded that he deny aliens work on projects. Shriver indignantly refused. "If the President is in error in not limiting employment opportunities to citizens," he said, "I prefer to stand with the President and err on the side to humanity." Nevertheless, he told Johnson, he would forward the request to Hopkins, but he reminded him that if aliens were not employed they would become charges of the counties. If the Governor really wanted aliens deported, he should raise the issue with the immigration authorities. Johnson professed disappointment in Shriver's decision to employ interlopers whom the state government was prepared to aid with transportation. "You have made your position clear and the responsibility for keeping aliens on jobs that rightfully belong to American citizens is yours and yours alone," he admonished, "and Colorado is again blocked in her efforts to return these people to their own homelands."

Finally, while Colorado newspapers were predicting a formidable challenge by Governor Johnson to Costigan's renomination, Costigan endorsed an amendment by Senator Cutting that could not have endeared him to Colorado's conservatives and moderates—that strikers should be granted relief. Costigan and his allies fought to supply sustenance to all in need.

1. Senator Robert F. Wagner of New York was in touch with social workers as well, but he still had faith in a public works program.
2. A loan of $92 million to the Dawes Bank of Chicago caused a storm, for Charles Dawes had been the first director of the R. F. C.
3. Costigan feared that the question of repeal of Prohibition might split the Democrats and advised that Roosevelt refrain from discussing this issue when he spoke in Denver lest he antagonize the powerful dry faction. He suggested that Roosevelt speak about his experiences as Governor in the fields of electric power and agriculture. Chapman thought that Costigan favored Roosevelt at least from the time of his election to the Senate.
4. Ed Johnson had denied that he had any intention of opposing Costigan, that the rumor was based on unauthorized statements by his supporters—some former Costigan supporters now believe this to be the case.
5. After the primaries, Costigan received reports that supporters of Josephine Roche were being forced out of administrative positions.
6. The Fort Collins *Leader* editorially suggested that Governor Johnson apply the same standards to the head of the state highway department.
7. In a letter to A. C. Shumaker, Costigan recommended that his son submit his qualifications to Shriver for he would make no recommendations since Roosevelt wanted to keep politics out of the Works Progress Administration.

CHAPTER IX

THE JONES-COSTIGAN BILL

Senator Costigan did not expect aid to state relief programs to do more than mitigate the effects of the depression for those who were most desperate. From the beginning of the crisis he had called for a multifaceted program. An early advocate of public works to take up part of the slack in employment, he cooperated with Senator Wagner in such efforts. He was instrumental in the Progressive Conference demand for a scientific reduction in the tariff to increase international trade and thereby to stimulate production. Employment exchanges and unemployment insurance had been among his proposals. He had sought to stabilize business and employment through legislation and national planning agencies. In addition, he had called for the close regulation of public utilities, and, when necessary, for competitive public ownership.

When the New Deal attempted to organize industry under the National Industrial Recovery Act, Costigan applauded its efforts. Yet, he was not satisfied that industry was honoring its bargain. Gerard Swope of General Electric had implied that if the anti-trust laws were suspended, with no restrictions on profits, trade associations would be willing to guarantee adequate minimum wages, old-age pensions and other benefits to employees. From the bill's inception, Costigan wanted assurances that the public would benefit. He fought alongside George Norris to reword Section 7 of the N.I.R.A. to prevent the use of company unions to evade the real collective bargaining intended by the provision. He offered an amendment protecting the regulatory powers of the Federal Trade Commission. To protect the interests of toilers and customers he demanded industrial, consumer and worker analysis of all codes in which price fixing in any form had been implemented. He endorsed the recommendations of the Consumer Advisory Board and the Labor Advisory Board to plan utilization of resources so as to increase consumption, to eliminate only harmful competition and to promote the public interests (not to increase profits at the expense of the consumer). If monopolies failed to function in the public interest, they suggested it might be necessary to revoke monopoly-creating patents, to remove protective tariffs, to tax profits, or to create public competition. In addition, the Labor Advisory Board emphasized the absence of adequate representation for workers on code authorities and the infrequency of real collective bargaining. They demanded that a labor board be created with sufficient power to force industries to adopt acceptable employee codes. While the NRA had not been wholly satisfactory, upon its collapse Costigan proposed a constitutional amendment permitting Congress to establish maximum hours, minimum wages and to supervise conditions of employment. Thereupon, Congress could regulate production, industry, business, trade and commerce in order to prevent unfair practices and methods. Government, he insisted, must have the power to deal with the problems of the modern economic system.

Similar principles should apply to financial institutions. If an uncontrolled securities market had precipitated the crisis, then the market must be investigated. The stock exchange must be controlled to prevent a repetition of the panic of 1929. If people with limited resources had lost their savings as a result of bank failures, a Federal Deposit Insurance Corporation must be formed to secure the funds of small depositors. If the central government was to guarantee deposits, it must establish minimum standards. If banks failed because of speculative management, then it was necessary to examine the role excessive salaries played in the shortage of funds.

Long an advocate of public power and the yardstick concept, Costigan quickly endorsed the Tennessee Valley Authority. When it appeared that President Hoover wanted to sell Muscle Shoals, Costigan protested: "Our streams and rivers can easily be coined into human happiness by government, as surely as they can be transformed into gold by monopoly." Since private power companies could increase prices and profits by increasing their debt structure and concealing real costs through holding companies, Muscle Shoals and Boulder Dam could help determine reasonable rates based on prudent investments. With this in mind he submitted a resolution to the Senate requiring that the Federal Power Commission report on the relative costs of electrical generation, transmission, and distribution.

He cried out against children laboring for a pittance while their parents could find no employment: "The child is really the state, for he is the torchbearer who stamps the future with the folly or wisdom of the present." The aged as well as the young needed protection. Not only did New Deal social security legislation meet with Costigan's firm approval, but he proposed low value annuity bond insurance for those omitted from its coverage.

To raise the funds for an active government he suggested revenues based on the ability to pay, increasing the income and corporate assessments, not the regressive excise on sales, and amending the Constitution to permit imposts on tax exempt securities. He supported LaFollette's unsuccessful fight for income tax publicity and championed a successful compromise that released income tax data to state officials. Finally, he supported the social purposes of the levy on wealth, the dispersion of concentrated fortunes and the forced release of idle surpluses for investment.

All of these measures, Costigan felt, were essential to combat the depression, yet for legislative purposes it was necessary to concentrate his efforts. One such area of emphasis was measures to aid the farmer.

Costigan was well aware that agriculture had been excluded from the prosperity of the twenties and that the farmer's economic position had continued to deteriorate in the thirties. He had endorsed the farm-bloc export-debenture plan. Repudiating the Republican claim that the tariff could protect the farmer, during the campaign of 1930 he had proposed a bounty to aid sugar beet growers. In 1932, cognizant of Presidential opposition, he postponed his introduction of a bill incorporating the bounty features pending the outcome of a motion to enact the export-debenture plan. When this well-known plan died, Costigan decided to delay the introduction of his bill until a more suitable time.

The New Deal took the first effective steps to aid the farmer, although it failed to solve the farm problem. The Agricultural Adjustment Act instituted a system of domestic allotment and price stabilization similar to a plan proposed by the Farmers Union, the more radical of the farmers' organizations. However, the New Deal measure tried to limit production rather than export the surplus crops at the world price, the world market being glutted, and did not base prices on the elusive cost of production. Costigan supported the Administration. In his eyes, the major flaw of this plan was that it did not include sugar beets and sugar cane.

Costigan did his utmost to have these items included in the Agricultural Adjustment Act until a bounty of one dollar a ton could be enacted. Sugar was a basic commodity, he emphasized. Beet sugar was produced in seventeen states and sugar cane in two. He reiterated that the tariff had failed sugar producers. It had only stimulated island production. In fact, sugar beet prices had been higher under a one-cent tariff in 1914 than they were under a two-cent tariff in 1932.

Even some supporters of the Act opposed Costigan's proposal. When Smith of South Carolina protested that the United States grew insufficient sugar for its own needs and its inclusion in the legislation would only increase production—contrary to the general aim of the bill—Costigan retorted that Smith had not similarly objected when Southern-produced peanuts were declared a basic commodity. Senator Robinson of Arkansas wished to exclude any new products. Aside from Costigan, he revealed, only opponents of the bill wanted to add items. Nevertheless, the Costigan Amendment passed the Senate on April 19, 1933, only to be rejected by the House-Senate Conference Committee. The admission of sugar, they warned, would open the gates for other articles. Costigan considered such an argument fallacious for no other amendments were likely to be introduced at that point. He rejected as inadequate an interpretation that, as a competitor of corn, sugar beets were already in the Agricultural Adjustment Act. If sugar had been incorporated, he argued, why not name it specifically?

Sugar Stabilization Agreement

Although sugar was not an item in the Agricultural Adjustment Act, the Agriculture Department tried to help this chaotic industry. Representatives were called together to devise a stabilization agreement under the provisions of the National Recovery Act. While the negotiations were still in a tentative stage, Costigan expressed discontent with the proposed draft. He could understand the sugar representatives' reluctance to agree to a quota system which did not provide a bounty or adequate prices. He still felt that sugar should have been part of the Agricultural Adjustment Act.

Costigan reservations were strengthened by a letter from a correspondent. Katherine Lenroot was uneasy about the proposed agreement for it lacked provisions to protect the agricultural laborer. Employment of children was still prevalent, she wrote. A picker's pay was only twelve dollars an acre and his income had been insufficient in 1920 when he had been paid two and a half times as much. Yet some laborers had been forced below the inadequate contract wages. Now, a new type of contract provided for payment only after the crop had been sold and the employee often failed to receive all of his earnings. The farmers developed another dodge. They called the local relief office for workers. Once toil had begun, they would slash the agreed rate. If the employee balked they threatened to have him removed from the relief rolls for unwillingness to work. The pickers' income was so low, she reported, that many were forced on welfare despite their employment in the beet fields, and relief funds were thus being used to subsidize the farmers.

Nevertheless, the agreement was approved by most of the parties concerned. All the producing areas signed. It was accepted by Secretary of State Hull, who was concerned with Cuba's interests, Secretary of Interior Ickes, who was responsible for Puerto Rico and Hawaii, Secretary of War Dern, who represented the Philippine Islands and by the Co-administrators of the Agricultural Adjustment Administration, George Peek and Charles Brand. Still there was no word from the Secretary of Agriculture Henry Wallace.[1]

By October 5, 1933, most industries had already endorsed National Recovery Administration Codes. But on that day, Wallace's assistant, Paul Appleby, and A.A.A. General Counsel Jerome Frank, informed Costigan's office that Secretary Wallace could not sign the agreement. It did not guarantee augmented returns to domestic producers, they objected. Under its provisions only a rise in the price of sugar could increase income and higher costs would injure the non-sugar producing farmers. The excess would be stored and the processor could borrow four dollars from the R.F.C. for each ton stored. While this protected the refiners' margins, similar pegs had failed to support wheat and cotton prices, or to reestablish prewar parity. Limiting imports from the Philippines and Cuba would not prevent its disposal on the world market. And such sales would drive down the London quotation and demoralize the world sugar industry. As an alternative to the stabilization proposal, Secretary Wallace had decided to sponsor Costigan's plan for a bounty to growers within the A.A.A. A fuller explanation was offered in a department memorandum early in January 1934.[2]

Long before Wallace's criticism of the agreement was made known, the Depatment's objections had been outlined in a note to the President. As an alternative, Wallace offered a bounty to American farmers financed through a processing tax. At the same time, the tariff would be reduced to the difference in the cost of production between American and Cuban producers. This would aid the Cubans without injuring the Americans.

When the Secretary of Agriculture rejected the agreement, Congressman Fred Cummings of Colorado toured the Western states to rouse beet growers' support for it. And the governors of California, Colorado, Idaho, Montana, Nebraska, Utah and Wyoming pressured President Roosevelt to approve it. The Administration and advocates of the Sugar Stabilization Agreement held conferences to iron out their differences while the President and the Secretary of Agriculture sought a workable plan.

Drafting the Sugar Amendment

During this period Costigan was being pressed by Mr. Kearney and Congressman Cummings of Colorado, mainstays of the stabilization accord, to by-pass Secretary Wallace and go directly to the President. Cummings warned that Wallace's refusal to sign the agreement would mean the loss of Democratic seats in sugar beet states in the next election. Meanwhile, Joshua Bernhardt, a former economic advisor to the Tariff Commission, was assigned the task of drafting a bill incorporating Costigan's proposed bounty. Cummings and Kearney, categorizing the proposed bounty as ridiculous, joined Governor Blood of Utah and others in protesting the choice of Bernhardt to draft a parity program for sugar. Bernhardt, they charged, had participated in the Tariff Commission's effort to lower the sugar schedule and was thus unsuited for the task. The promoters of the bounty plan were forewarned that they could expect serious opposition to their program.

On January 9, 1934, the Denver *Post* reported an imminent break between Costigan and his Democratic colleagues from the mountain states over the Wallace program.[3] Nevertheless, Costigan informed the Secretary of Agriculture that he was introducing a bill to include sugar beets and sugar cane in the A.A.A. He inferred from a speech that Wallace had predicted the inclusion of beef cattle and sugar in the Agricultural Adjustment Act and he asked confirmation. Wallace replied that Costigan had properly evaluated the Department's intentions. The Secretary forwarded the Senator's letter to the legal department and invited Costigan to a conference about the form of the amendment.

At the end of January, while the emendation was being drafted, Congressman Cummings called the diehard proponents of the sugar stabilization agreement into a meeting. Wallace was out of town. Costigan suggested to the White House that it might head off trouble by advising this group, in a confidential memorandum, that the government intended to include sugar in the A.A.A. Roosevelt approved. The industry remained silent for a while. By February 5th a draft of the bill was ready and on February 12, 1934 the Administration measure was introduced by Costigan and Representative Marvin Jones of Texas.

This proposal was ingeniously drawn so as to afford a higher income to tillers without raising the retail cost to the consumer. The tariff on sugar was to be reduced by one-half cent a pound while an identical processing tax was simultaneously imposed. The proceeds from this impost would finance a bounty to sugar beet and cane farmers, who

THE JONES-COSTIGAN BILL

would then restrict output. The national quota would be determined by the Secretary of Agriculture on the basis of a three-year average of annual domestic production and each planter would be assigned his share. In consideration for the right to sell stated amounts of sugar in the American market, Hawaii, Cuba, Puerto Rico and the Philippines would have to agree to production quotas. The world market would no longer be glutted. To stifle domestic opposition the President threatened to accept a Tariff Commission recommendation to reduce the schedule by one-half cent a pound, without any compensatory actions.

The House Agriculture Committee Hearing

Tension filled the hearings of the Jones subcommittee of the House Agriculture Committee. A valid rumor had circulated that the Administration had considered eliminating national beet sugar production. The representatives from sugar beet states lay in wait for the government witnesses.[4] Representative Clifford Hope of Kansas tried to force the first government witness to admit that the Administration wanted to destroy the industry. Weaver, Chief of the Sugar and Price Division of the A.A.A., was elusive; the President was trying to stop the expansion of protected high cost pursuits, he replied. Representative Hope attacked:

Hope: "Then, in other words, the whole purpose of this measure is to gradually eliminate domestic sugar production; is that it?"

Weaver: "Of course, it could be done drastically and at the cost of a great shock to the sugar producing population."

Hope: "Then are we safe or justified, rather in assuming that it is the policy of the administration to ultimately eliminate the domestic producer and American production?"

Weaver evaded the question, pointing out that emergency legislation was involved. Representative Cummings joined the inquisition. Finally, Chairman Jones had to bail Weaver out by asking him if the primary purpose of the bill was to eliminate the industry. To this question, Weaver could honestly answer "No!"

Weaver's testimony caused a storm of protest from the sugar beet interests. They remonstrated against any attempt to prevent the expansion of production. Costigan issued a statement declaring that Weaver's testimony was either innocent or hostile, but in either case foolish. The Jones-Costigan Act would no more injure sugar than corn or wheat had been injured by the A.A.A. The Act, he insisted, was meant to stabilize the industry and to improve the income of sugar farmers without penalizing the consumer.

The next day Rexford Guy Tugwell, Assistant Secretary of Agriculture, came to the hearing to try to improve the situation. The Administration had not yet decided on a permanent beet sugar policy, he testified. The bill was only an emergency stopgap, and no long range plan could be worked out until the effects of this legislation had been examined. The proposal was a compromise between various interests, Tugwell reported, and if all received their requested quotas, the market could not absorb the production. He parried Representative Hope's effort to extract an admission that the limitation of output was the first step to the elimination of the industry; Tugwell cut him short and affirmed that the only purpose of the bill was to give the farmer a parity he had not had for years. The Administration's intention, he declared, was to mold an efficient activity that could support itself without a tariff or bounties. No pursuit should be supported by a duty, he asserted. Yet, the industry was then irreplaceable, despite its high costs. The quota did not curtail sugar output, he insisted, it only prevented its increase. Nevertheless, Tugwell's testimony did not quiet opposition.

Opposition to the Bill

Costigan spoke to a nationwide radio audience on March 6, 1934 to rally support for the sugar bill. Like gold, he said, sugar makes men lose their sense of proportion; it was "not so much a food as an explosive." It had made fortunes for the few, for the speculators who "seem to hold that their advantages can only be preserved by slander and the use of an occasional newspaper to throw the dust of falsehood into the eyes of the unsuspecting." Despite assertions to the contrary, the bill, by making sugar a basic commodity and creating a more moderate tariff, would yield farmers a parity income without increasing the cost to the consumer. The proposal sought to stabilize the industry and raise the income of the domestic producer. Some farmers and land speculators would complain about the restriction of output below the abnormally high crop of 1933, he admitted, but most farmers would recognize the advantages of controlled sugar production and marketing.

High imposts had failed the farmers, Costigan declared; it had only increased the competition from the Philippine Islands. Certainly this alternative was worth trying, he argued. Indeed, Secretary Wallace had been amazed at the coolness of beet sugar growers to the first plan in years that promised them a fair value for their crops. In the meantime, he pointed out, the tariff had succeeded in wrecking the Cuban economy, destroying Cuba as a market for American foodstuffs.[5] This bill would raise the income of the American sugar raisers and, at the same time, restore a sound Cuban market for American foodstuffs.

The sugar beet interests continued to demand that their quota be raised to the 1933 level of production, the highest in their history. The President and the sponsors of the bill were pressured to increase the domestic quota by Governor Bryan of Nebraska, Governor Rolph of California, Senator Vandenberg of Michigan, and all the representative organizations of beet growers.

While the continental producers insisted that there should be no curtailment of their output, the island growers lamented their fate. Hawaii protested that she was being treated in a manner identical with Cuba, the Philippines, and Puerto Rico, although she was a territory rather than an insular possession and was thus entitled to equal treatment with the states. Hawaiians demanded specific quotas for all areas and a larger amount for Hawaii than the President had proposed. Puerto Rico complained that the bill discriminated against her. Her representatives wanted either a fixed figure or a three-year average that did not include a year of hurricane losses. Everyone argued that only his share was insufficient.

The Denver *Post,* an old enemy of Costigan, accused "Senor" Costigan of trying to aid Cuban sugar growers at the expense of their domestic counterparts. In cartoon after cartoon, they lampooned "Senor" Costigan, in complete Cuban dress, trying to ambush the American sugar beet interests. In a field in which consumption was greater than production, he planned to reduce, not increase, the crop, they charged, and he planned to replace American sugar with Cuban imports. The bounty, the editor claimed, was a sop to American farmers so that they would agree to reduce output. The bill, they warned, would cause a crisis in the industry, for legislation would not be enacted until after planting time was past. In addition, this bill denied farmers and processing companies the power to contract, and gave this power to the Secretary of Agriculture. For these reasons, according to the *Post,* the Administration could not find a sponsoring congressman from a sugar growing state; thus, Congressman Jones of Texas had become its sponsor. "Senor" Costigan, although representing the largest sugar producing state, by sponsoring the bill had chosen to favor the interests of Cuba.

Since Cuba, Puerto Rico, Hawaii, and the Philippine Islands had no voice in the politics of the United States only the permitted harvest of the domestic producers was increased. Despite Secretary Wallace's insistence that 1,450,000 tons were quite sufficient, the continental quota was raised to 1,550,000 tons at the expense of other growers. The Secretary of Agriculture was permitted to set the figure for the insular possessions. In addition, the revised bill included two important provisions: that the contract agreement for western sugar beet fields must bar child labor and it must set minimum wages.

Steering the Bill Through the Legislature

Costigan expected the beet sugar industry to support the proposal. On April 4th the measure glided through the House with little opposition. Woodruff of Michigan, representing a beet sugar area, moaned: "A gun has been put to our heads. We must accept." Faced with the threat of a tariff reduction in any event, the sugar bloc in the House felt it had little alternative.

The passage through the Senate was not as smooth. As soon as Costigan introduced the bill, Senator Arthur Vandenberg of Michigan let his opposition be known. He quoted from *Wallace's Farmer* of June 14, 1929. The future Secretary of Agriculture had written that Cuba formed a better market for corn belt pork products than did the sugar beet farmers of Utah and Colorado. Under the proposal, Vandenberg protested, an unsympathetic executive official would make legislative decisions as to the fate of the occupation. The President, he charged, wanted to eliminate non-efficient domestic output for the benefit of Cuban sugar and of the big banks with such investments. If it so desired, Costigan retorted, the Administration could destroy this business by simply putting sugar on the free list. The purpose of the bill, he reiterated, was to stabilize the industry and aid the farmers without raising the retail price. The previous marketing agreement was designed to aid the processors rather than the growers, and lacked a guarantee for the consumers. This bill ensured the farmers a higher income.

The duel between Vandenberg and Costigan reached its climax on the final day of the debate. Costigan described how national planning would safeguard the industry. The tariff raised competitive forces which were strangling domestic producers, he said. He envisioned the cash benefits sugar farmers would get in return for quota limitations on production and imports. And then he explained how the plan was financed by a processing tax equal to the tariff reduction so that the retail price would remain the same. Vandenberg thereupon charged that the Agriculture Department "frankly admitted that in their Olympian judgments there is small place for domestic beet and cane sugar in their federal programs for the regimentation of the American farms and the American fireside."

Both Senators Reed and Adams recorded their objections. Reed of Pennsylvania imputed that the bill granted too large a quota to domestic farmers at the expense of Hawaii; he demanded, without success, a separate quota for Hawaii. Adams of Colorado, on the other hand, attempted to raise the domestic figure to that of the previous years' production. He, too, was defeated.

Two major struggles ensued—clashes over child labor and minimum wage provisions. The House had called for the elimination of child labor in the beet fields. This provision had been stricken out in the Senate committee and replaced by the Vandenberg amendment providing that only children of the proprietor's family could work in the fields. Wagner pressed for the House version, but Costigan supported Vandenberg's amendment and it passed. Costigan then called for restoration of the minimum wage provision. Secretary of Labor Perkins, he read, stated that these sections were not meant to apply to minimum wages in the producer's own family. When Vandenberg denied that wages could be raised without a raise in the price of sugar, Costigan insisted that the farmer must include his workers in increased prosperity resulting from the stabilization of the industry. Senator Daniel O. Hastings of Delaware retaliated with an attack on the very idea of a minimum wage for farm workers. The Finance Committee had recommended that minimum wages be dropped, and the Senate, despite Costigan's pleas, concurred. The Act passed the Senate with weakened labor provisions, returned to the House so that the difference in the two bills could be ironed out, and, in revised form, passed both Houses on April 25th.

Administering the Jones-Costigan Act

Although the farmers were willing to harvest the benefits from the legislation, they balked at sharing this boon with their employees. Wallace, despite the negative decision by Congress, announced on July 3rd that payments to sugar growers were conditional upon fair wages for the beet workers. The farmers protested against these minimum wages. All of the benefits of the law, they protested, would then go to laborers who should not be entitled to expect sufficient wages from eighty days' work in the fields to sustain them for the entire year. Now that only part of the farmer's income came from the price of the crop, they callously proposed payment on a share basis rather than in wages, thus avoiding the need to include their employees in the proceeds from the sugar bounty.[6]

Through sustained pressure from the Department of Agriculture the conditions of field hands improved substantially. As compared with income prior to the Jones-Costigan Act, the compensation per acre rose 43 to 46 percent. To prevent nonpayment of wages, the Department withheld benefits until the pickers had received their remuneration. All the contracts prohibited employment of children under fourteen—except for members of the producer's family—and limited the employment of children between fourteen and sixteen to an eight-hour day. While the contracts were not wholly successful, the employment of child labor in the beet fields was reduced by more than 50 percent.

As a result of the Jones-Costigan Act the beet sugar industry was stronger by 1935 than it had been in years; compared to 1933 the farmer's revenue per acre had increased between 45 and 50 percent. Senator Alva Adams, who had opposed many of its features, declared that the bill had saved the producers. J. D. Pancake, Secretary of the National Beet Growers Association and of the Mountain States Beet Growers' Marketing Association, who was one of the first to see the advantages of the bill, declared that "the sugar beet industry is in the healthiest condition it has been for many years. We now have a Government guarantee of parity prices and a Government guarantee of settling disputes over the terms of the beet contract." The law had come, he said, at a time when the income of growers was insufficient to cover costs. The sugar tariff, he argued, had been a processors' tariff; the farmers had never received a fair share of its benefits. Cooperation had brought prosperity where competition had brought chaos. Costigan had kept his election promise. He had helped to recreate a sound industry.

Costigan and War

If sugar was "not so much a food as an explosive," the Nye Munitions investigation was to prove even more combustible. While Roosevelt shunned combat, although his hands were being tied, the Nye investigations startled the nation with the revelation that our entrance into the World War was caused neither by submarines, nor by a desire to make the world safe for Democracy. We entered the war, the hearings implied simplistically, to save bankers' investments and to enrich munitions makers.

While Costigan had long been an internationalist, he had always opposed war and aggressive policies that led to bloodshed. In 1916 he had abandoned Theodore Roosevelt because of his belligerency, and had praised Wilson's moderation in foreign affairs. Even then he had hoped to contain pressures for hostilities with "private profit cut from arms and armaments through government control of the whole organization of preparedness." After the Nye investigation he declared: "We entered the war with reluctance; we look back on it now with regret." "War," he asserted, is "the sum of all villainies." "War and Civilization have always been implacable enemies. War has menaced every civilization that ever existed. . . . No Romantic glorification of courage, self-sacrifice and patriotism can longer hide war's universal threat . . . History is a race between education and catastrophe . . . between civilization and war."

Costigan was appalled by the cost of the holocaust. The First World War, he declared, cost $400,000,000,000 and 30,000,000 lives. Its financial expense was equivalent to the total wealth of the United States in 1929. With this sum every family in the United States, Canada, Great Britain, Australia, Belgium, Germany, and Russia could have been given a five-acre plot at $100 per acre; every family could have built a $2500 home on this land, and put $1000 worth of furnishings into it. With the money still remaining, all the property of France and Belgium could have been purchased at 1914 prices. The interest on the balance, at five percent, would pay 125,000 teachers and 125,000 nurses $1000 a year for all time to come. In a world gripped by a depression that was a powerful reason not to blunder into future wars.

Why then did wars take place? "One by one former incitements to war have disappeared—enslavement of labor; plundered treasuries and lands; and racial and religious rivalries. . . . Yet from their sowing of dragon's teeth newly armed warriors are ever springing; blind nationalism, economic misery and inequality; mighty armies, navies, and armaments stimulating the very fear and competitive hostility they are presumably intended to allay; and, most modern and subtly dangerous of all, insidious propaganda, inspired by limitless greed, checked by no principle of truth, honor, or respect individual, national or international."

Unlike the isolationists, Costigan singled out "the legal doctrine of lawless national sovereignty" as the most dangerous of these causes. Nations refused to settle disputes which affected their self-determined national interests. They insisted "on the privilege of being as anarchistic as they choose." While civilized man had been forced to surrender his "unhampered license to kill," nations could still "legally murder, unrestrained." To prevent hostilities, some limitations on national sovereignty must be accepted: "The age old flaw and continuously fatal defect in international relations has been the absence of authoritative agencies for determining issues in the war-breeding 'no man's land' between sovereign states which, because of their conceded theoretical independence, have felt free to proceed against other sovereign states with lawless aggression." American support for the League of Nations and membership in the World Court would aid in the settlement of international problems without resort to arms. Since wars were eventually settled at a conference table, he queried, why not go there first? "Peace will never be permanently gained until men and women are organized for fraternity, not hostility; disinterestedness, not prejudice; science, not wanton waste." The world must be organized for peace, not war.

Costigan wanted to prevent armed combat by preventing war-breeding military mobilization. Consequently, after the failure of a move to give FDR discretionary, rather than mandatory powers to raise the size of the military, Costigan voted against increased appropriations. He complained that one shot from a battleship was equal to 20,000 loaves of bread. Like the isolationists, he drew his lessons from the mistakes of 1914-1917, and hoped to prevent a munitions race that would lead to another drift towards a holocaust. To prevent conflict, he called for voluntary proportionate disarmament; he wanted to bar munitions makers from making profit out of the appeal to arms; he insisted that it was necessary to resist all war makers.

When fighting broke out in Asia, Costigan declared: "As in the days of Washington and the French Revolution, neutrality, in fact, as well as name, so far as it is possible to practice it, is sound American policy." But neutrality must be effective. Citizens must be barred from the war zone. The shipment of arms and ammunition to belligerents must be prevented. Neither contraband nor loans and credits should be supplied to combatants. All Americans traveling in warring countries should be warned that they did so at their own risk. American nationals should be kept off ships of belligerents to prevent a repetition of the Lusitania affair. Just as today, statesmen sought to prevent the previous war.

Sugar in the Courts

While the expansionist drive of the dictatorships was to make foreign policy a matter of increasing concern, Costigan continued to concentrate his attention on domestic matters.

The constitutionality of the Jones-Costigan Bill came into question shortly after its enactment. Hawaii challenged it on the grounds that the Act did not treat Hawaii as an integral part of the United States, but the law was upheld by the Supreme Court of the District of Columbia. On a later occasion, however, it did not fare so well.

On January 6, 1936, the Supreme Court, in *United States v. Butler* (the Hoosac Mills case), declared that the Agricultural Adjustment Act was unconstitutional. To steady the panic-stricken sugar industry, Secretary Wallace assured the country that the case did not affect the validity of the sugar quota. The Agriculture Department immediately promised that the allocations and the tariff would be maintained in order to prevent a heavy fall in price. Costigan announced his preparation of an amendment to the Constitution to permit crop control so that, regardless of the Supreme Court action, the government could still act.

On February 13, Costigan attacked the Supreme Court decision. He proclaimed (echoing Lincoln's comment on Dred Scott) that the decisions of the majority of the court did not have to be taken as final. "Today we confront critical legislative problems affecting the welfare of millions of farmers," he said, "because of a novel interpretation of the general-welfare clause of the Federal Constitution by a majority of the members of the Supreme Court." He quoted from the minority opinion of Chief Justice Stone to show that the Constitution, as originally ratified, authorized statutory safeguards such as the Agricultural Adjustment Act.

Despite the Butler decision, Costigan asserted, the sugar allotments were still a legal and valid use of the commerce clause. The two cases were not identical and Justice Roberts had indicated that he would not necessarily project this decision into other legislation. Nevertheless, it was necessary to prepare alternative courses of action. Costigan wrote Wallace that, as he saw it, the Department had three choices: The first and best was to announce that farmers would be paid either under a supplemental appropriations act, or by some amendment fulfilling all agreements made before January 6, 1936, as long as the growers honored their part of the contract. A second course would be to deal with the sugar beet contracts as exceptional, and not affected by the Butler decision. Since the Jones-Costigan Act dealt with the import of sugar it was part of tariff legislation and directly related to commerce, rather than primarily concerned with the control of production. (The Act had been effective in combatting child labor and he saw no reason for it to be abandoned, especially since a satisfied industry was not attacking it in the courts.) The third alternative was one for which he had little enthusiasm. The Department could treat sugar beet production adjustment contracts as part of the pending program under the recently enacted Soil Conservation and Domestic Allotment Act. Unfortunately, this Act did not provide for the regulation of child labor and the maintenance of minimum wages for sugar beet workers. Besides, insufficient funds were available to provide full parity under this Act. Costigan wanted to continue the Sugar Act with as little modification as was legally possible. He wanted to retain the progress made in providing minimum wages and reducing child labor.

In the midst of efforts to draw up a new and effective bill that would meet all constitutional objections, Costigan was suddenly made an invalid by a coronary stroke.[7]

1. Congressman Fred Cummings of Colorado and Charles Kearney demanded that Costigan wire Wallace and the President to demand immediate action, for crop prices had to be set soon. Costigan resisted their demands until he was better informed about the situation.

2. The memorandum pointed out that if the agreement succeeded in raising prices it would have had to raise the retail price of sugar a penny a pound in order to achieve parity. This would have cost consumers $120,000,000 of which only $22,000,000 would have gone to American farmers $54,000,000 would have gone to Cuban and American processors). Since the domestic price was to have been based on the London market the effort to raise prices would have failed without restriction of Cuban production. The Department would have been forced to resort to the doubtful expedient of price-stabilizing sugar purchases. The agreement could not have improved the income of sugar beet farmers.

3. Senator Alva Adams, Senators King and Thomas of Utah and Congressman Cummings favored the sugar stabilization agreement and would accept no substitute. Senator Adams had insisted that the American market belonged to the American farmer and production could not be limited for the benefit of foreign producers.

4. President Roosevelt's cabinet apparently discussed the possibility of gradually eliminating the sugar beet industry over a thirty-year period. George Dern, Secretary of War, opposed the idea and supplied written opinions of others who supported his judgment.

5. In 1928, 1,738,000 acres had been needed to supply the Cuban market with staples. By 1932 this had declined to 921,000 acres.

6. In 1934, Secretary of Labor Frances Perkins estimated that a family of six required $600 a year for minimum subsistence. If there were four employed in a family, a seven-month season brought $392. (Often they were not even paid their full wages). Migrant workers could no longer supplement their earnings with other work as they had before the depression. They lived in poorly kept two-room shacks, often sharing their quarters with another family, one farm had only twenty-eight two-room buildings to shelter forty-two families. Lacking cash, they were forced to buy on credit at higher prices. The worst feature of the system was the extensive use of child labor. Children as young as six worked in the field from nine to fourteen hours a day. As many as 85 percent of

THE JONES-COSTIGAN BILL 159

farm laborers' children between seven and fifteen worked in the fields. Consequently, the death rate of beet laborers' children was 20 to 30 percent.

7. The Agriculture Department drafted legislation that would have been satisfactory to Costigan and made an effort to have it introduced in his name. Representative Jones wanted a less complex bill. The Department felt that without the technically skilled Costigan to guide their bill through Congress it was necessary to accept the Jones substitute and Senator O'Mahoney sponsored the substitute in the Senate.

CHAPTER X

THE COSTIGAN-WAGNER ANTI-LYNCHING BILL[1]

While Costigan was still involved in preparing the Jones-Costigan Act, and was thus reluctant to undertake any other major projects, Walter White, Executive-Secretary of the National Association for the Advancement of Colored People, asked him to introduce an Anti-Lynching Bill similar to the Dyer Bill of 1922. (The Dyer Bill had been approved by the House of Representatives but its Senate floor manager, Henry Cabot Lodge, had bowed before a Southern filibuster.) White pointed to the decline in lynching after the debate on the Dyer Bill. By 1933, however, the frustrations of an extended depression had led to an increase in mob violence: twenty-three lynchings had occurred by late November as compared to ten in all of 1932. The murder of George Armwood by a Maryland mob showed the need for a federal law, White contended. When Maryland Attorney General William Preston Lane had supplied information to the local district attorney about the identity of Armwood's killers, he had been informed that the perpetrators could not be convicted in the atmosphere prevailing in that part of Maryland. In such instances only federal law could guarantee justice. And the willingness of the New Deal to use Federal power had created a more favorable atmosphere for national anti-lynching legislation. After White had dictated his letter to Costigan he received news from California which further strengthened his negative reaction to exclusive state jurisdiction. Two white youths, confessed kidnappers and slayers, had been lynched. And Governor Rolph publicly approved, promising a pardon to those guilty of the crime if they were prosecuted and convicted. White declared that lynching was more than murder; it was an anarchical deprivation of the rights of citizens. Although some lawyers doubted the constitutionality of the Anti-Lynching Bill it was important for it to pass, White said. The question of its constitutionality could be left to the courts.

On November 28, 1933, speaking from Denver, Costigan informed the nation's press that he was introducing such a bill. He emphasized the recent California affair so as to undermine the Southerner's perennial argument that this legislation was sectional. He declared: "If mob violence is to run riot in America in place of orderly justice the end of free government on this continent will have to come. The sober sense of this country does not, and will not, sanction such menacing lawlessness."

When it came time for Costigan to return to Washington to prepare for the coming session, he did not reappear. Instead he sent one note about a severe bout with influenza, and another about his wife's appendectomy. Finally, the day before Christmas, he informed White that prolonged illness was forcing him to relinquish sponsorship of the bill. Frantically, White sought another Senator. Despite the burden of other affairs, Wagner agreed to handle the bill. But Costigan had reconsidered and remained as co-sponsor. When Lee Johnson, Costigan's executive secretary, met Costigan at the Washington airport, he was shocked. Influenza had been a cover story. Costigan, the victim of a stroke, could walk only with difficulty. And Wagner became so involved with other legislation that the responsibility for the floor fight fell primarily on Costigan after all. It was a burden that ultimately proved too great for his frail body to bear.

Finding the proper Congressman to guide the bill through the House of Representatives was much more difficult. The tireless Walter White hunted in vain for a Southern Congressman to adopt the bill, hoping to minimize sectional feelings, but no Southerner would risk political suicide. Not even David J. Lewis of Maryland, Costigan's colleague on the Tariff Commission and co-sponsor of his relief legislation, could be persuaded to offer more than sympathy. The notoriety caused by Governor Rolph's statement led White to accept an offer by Thomas Ford of California, who now seemed the best alternative to a Southerner.

The Preliminary Skirmishes

The battle for the bill opened with a press release by the National Association for the Advancement of Colored People emphasizing the large increase in the number of lynchings in 1933 as compared to 1932, Governor Rolph's refusal to supply National Guardsmen to protect two prisoners, and his offer to pardon those who were convicted of this mob murder. Two days later, on January 4, 1934, Senators Costigan and Wagner introduced the controversial bill. The Anti-lynching Bill was based on two assumptions: lynching occurred only when law enforcement agents were either in collusion with the mob or deliberately neglected proper precautions; and that it could be prevented by community leaders if they so desired. Consequently, the bill proposed to fine or jail any official who did not show due diligence in protecting prisoners in his charge. Secondly, it proposed to give the taxpayers an economic stake in preventing violence by levying a heavy fine on the communities, to be paid to the surviving dependents of the victim. Finally, if the state could not, or would not, prosecute lynchers within thirty days, all persons involved could be tried in a Federal court under the laws of the state in question.

Since it was unthinkable that such controversial legislation could be passed without political pressure, White set about organizing support for the bill. As soon as Costigan announced his intention of sponsoring the measure, White worked behind the scenes to form the American Writers' League Against Lynching. During 1934 endorsements were obtained from the Conference of Southern White Women for the Prevention of Lynching, the National Urban League, the Federal Council of the Churches of Christ, the American Civil Liberties Union, the Young Women's Christian Association, the National Council of Jewish Women, the World Alliance for International Friendship through the Churches, the Geneva-Women's International League for Peace and Freedom, and the Women's Missionary Council, Methodist Episcopal Church, South. In all, organizations representing forty million people supported the bill. While the number of endorsements were mounting, White whipped up enthusiasm for the proposal through speeches and with the aid of the Negro press. Starting with its February edition, *Crisis* ran anti-lynching cartoons in every issue; each month it solicited support for the bill with an advertisement in which a handcuffed Negro was portrayed hanging by the neck. In March, White began a series of speeches to local Negro churches; at the end of the month he addressed representatives of one hundred organizations in an Atlantic City meeting observing the twenty-fifth anniversary of the National Association for the Advancement of Colored People. The NAACP mounted its campaign as it prepared to hurdle the first obstacle, the hearings of the Van Nuys subcommittee of the Senate Judiciary Committee.

For the first time hearings on a measure were broadcast. Yet, they lacked excitement for they were dominated by its proponents. Senator Wagner opened with some brief remarks on the criminal horror of lynching. Costigan followed with a detailed analysis. The senior Colorado Senator pointed out that the proposal aimed to provide the constitutional guarantee of equal protection of the law to all citizens, that Roosevelt had attacked the crime of lynching in a radio address, and that former U. S. Assistant Attorney General Goff had thought the similar Dyer Bill constitutional. To strengthen the constitutional argument, Charles Tuttle, former United States District Attorney for New York, filed a brief resting on Sections One and Five of the Fourteenth Amendment.[2] Arthur Garfield Hays of the American Civil Liberties Union thereupon cited Chief Justice Hughes' support of an anti-lynching bill in 1919. Then Hays undermined some of the opposition arguments. Legal delay had not been a reason for lynching, he disclosed. Men had been taken out and murdered after their conviction by a court of law, or while they awaited hanging. The many mob actions precipitated by a desire to save the county money would cease if financial penalties for such violence were greater than the cost of a trial. In states where counties were fined for lynching, Hays said, incidents never recurred in a penalized county. Neither the Governor of California nor the Governor of Kentucky had been interested in applying state laws against the guilty parties, Hays reminded the subcommittee. Hays and Maryland's Attorney-General, William Preston Lane, emphasized the difficulty of successful prosecution in state courts.

The testimony of Walter White was most striking. He attempted to explode the myths surrounding vigilante justice: Despite Southern rhetoric about the sanctity of white womanhood, he declared, only one-sixth of the lynchings were for crimes against white women. Thirteen of twenty-one mob victims studied by George Fort Milton in 1930 were probably innocent of the crimes of which they were accused. And, as generally known, most of the prey were Negroes. Although the Dyer Bill passed the House of Representatives, White concluded, it had been killed by filibustering Senators from the states with the worst lynching records.

Opposition and Support

The only opponent of the bill to appear before the subcommittee was Representative Hatton W. Sumner of Texas. He emphasized the historical role of lynching as rough justice, its continuance where police power was absent or where the law gave criminals excessive protection. The federal presence, he asserted, would cause community resentment, and at the same time it would create an attitude that the responsibility to prevent violence should be left to Washington. But Sumner primarily attacked its constitutionality. Basing his argument on the United States versus Harris and the Civil Rights cases, he denied that Congress or a Federal Court could sit in judgement on the actions of a state official and insisted that Congress could not establish laws for the equal protection of its citizens.[3]

Despite Sumner's testimony, the bill easily won the endorsement of the Senate Judiciary Committee. Convincing the Southern-dominated Senate leadership to permit the measure to come to a vote was another matter.

Walter White set out to obtain a vote. He used the unofficial poll of Senator's inclinations to decide where pressure could be brought to bear on recalcitrant Senators from sympathetic states. Continuing efforts were made to win popular support through speeches and articles. Charles Tuttle spoke at the Harlem YMCA. Arnold C. DeMille wrote an article in *Crisis*, "Justice, Justice," in which he described a series of lynchings where there was no evidence of the guilt of the victims. Reverend John T. Gilard of Baltimore sent two hundred letters to Catholic parish churches urging their support of the bill. By May, White was certain that the bill would pass if it could be brought to a vote, and, in an election year, he thought he had enough strength in the South to prevent a filibuster. But he needed the endorsement of President Roosevelt in order to obtain Senate consideration of the measure.

Eleanor Roosevelt was the one ally of the anti-lynching forces who was in a position to influence the President's decisions. In April, Mrs. Roosevelt enlightened White about the President's quandary. FDR was sympathetic towards the bill, but he wanted an early adjournment of Congress lest legislation be passed that would interfere with recovery. The President also feared that a filibuster would accompany any effort to pass it. The President, she briefed White before an interview she had arranged, had doubts about financial penalties on counties in which lynchings had taken place.

When closeted with the President, White assured him that states had such penalties, that state courts had upheld their constitutionality, and that they could act as a preventive. Roosevelt seemed pleased when White pointed out that the measure was sure of passage if it could be brought to a vote, and that sentiment for it in the South had lessened the likelihood of a sustained filibuster. While the defeat of the bill was unlikely, even then bringing it to a vote would have a positive effect, White contended. After eighty minutes the interview concluded, and Roosevelt said that he would speak with Costigan and Wagner. He felt that the proposal should come to a vote before adjournment but he could not hold out in the face of a long and determined filibuster.

With White waiting impatiently in the antechamber, Senators Costigan and Wagner conferred with the President. Roosevelt refused to

THE COSTIGAN-WAGNER ANTI-LYNCHING BILL 165

throw his weight behind the bill because he anticipated an extended filibuster. (Senator Hubert Stephens of Mississippi had said that the bill would come to a vote only over his dead body.) During the Presidential news conference, on the following day, Roosevelt indicated persistent reservations. In reply to a question he said: "It is a terribly difficult subject. I have been talking about the theory of it with Costigan and Bob (Wagner) and various other people for quite a long while. I don't think I had better give you any attitude because I frankly haven't got sufficient clarity in my own mind as to whether that particular method will work and also as to the constitutionality of it. I think there is a question. I am absolutely for the objective but am not clear in my own mind as to whether that is absolutely the right way to attain the object. However, I told them to go ahead and try to get a vote on it in the Senate."

White tried to alleviate the President's doubts by sending Mrs. Roosevelt a copy of Charles Tuttle's opinion on the bill's constitutionality. In addition, he asked the First Lady to show the President an article by John Howard Lawson in the New York Post describing the appalling conditions in Alabama; the article emphasized the Scottsboro case.[4]

With only limited support from the President, Costigan rose on the floor of the Senate on May 28th calling for action on a measure that had widespread support, North and South. He recalled the President's condemnation of lynching as "collective murder," and his declaration that "we do not excuse those in high places or in low places who condone lynch law." As the proposal remained dormant, Costigan wrote to the Senate Majority Leader, Joseph Robinson, reminding him that the President had authorized the sponsors of the legislation to say that he wanted the proposed measure voted upon and passed. Robinson's cooperation was essential, Costigan wrote. The majority leader did not deign to reply.

While White urged the Chief Executive to prevent adjournment, Costigan continued to press for a vote, charging on the Senate floor that the will of the nation was being thwarted while other statutes were given priority. Failing to convince the Senate leadership, as a last resort he tried to bypass them: he requested unanimous consent to bring it up for consideration. Senators McKellar and Smith refused their consent. Congress adjourned without considering the Anti-lynching Bill.

The Lynching of Claude Neal

During the summer of 1934, with Congress in recess, Costigan fought the torrid campaign against Johnson's renomination. In the midst of the post-primary gloom the tragic lynching of Claude Neal gave new impetus to the drive for anti-lynching legislation.

Claude Neal, a Florida Negro, had slain his white mistress when she threatened to disclose their affair, thus endangering his life. When the sheriff became aware of public invitations to Neal's lynching, he moved him from the Marianna jail to Brewton. But an angry mob searched out its victim and carried him across state lines. For twelve hours he was subject to the most gruesome torture imaginable. He was hung until almost dead, forced to eat his own genitals, burned with red-hot irons, slashed in the side and stomach, and deprived of his fingers and toes before he was murdered. His corpse suffered further mutilation and was hung from a tree on the Marianna courthouse square. Yet, Attorney-General Cummings said the federal government could not intervene under the Lindbergh law because ransom had not been demanded.[5]

Reintroducing the Anti-lynching Bill

Despite this outrage, White thought the struggle in 1935 would be more difficult. There were no pressures of an election year and no white victims to give the issue the universality of the previous year. White determined to intensify publicity, and to blazon the horror of the Neal murder to prevent its recurrence.[6] The bills' proponents heightened their activity.

A National Crime Conference was called by Homer Cummings. Although the President condemned mob violence in his speech before the conference, the Attorney General neglected to include the crime of lynching as a subject to be considered by its sessions. The Negro community was incensed. Pickets who marched in the cold December air in protest were arrested by the District of Columbia police for carrying signs without a permit.

Unperturbed, the anti-lynching forces once again tried to obtain the open support of the President. Eleanor Roosevelt was encouraging, as usual. She expressed hope that the Department of Justice would change its approach to the subject and assured White that in any event her husband wanted the bill pased at the next session of Congress. A petition requesting that the Anti-lynching Bill be made "must" legislation was signed by an imposing list of dignitaries and delivered to the White

House. Costigan appealed to the President to include a paragraph in his annual message urging the bill's passage to help the nation regain its self respect. Earl Wilkins of the NAACP asked Vice President Garner to use his influence with the President and Senator Robinson. Garner replied that he made no suggestions to the President on personnel and policy, but that if an opportunity arose he would so urge the President. If the latter agreed he would be glad to talk to Robinson. Despite these pressures the day after Roosevelt's annual message the front page of the *Amsterdam News* carried the following item:

"HERE'S MR. ROOSEVELT'S MESSAGE ON LYNCHING

"IN HIS ANNUAL SPEECH TO CONGRESS ON JAN. 4 THE PRESIDENT SAID

"*THIS* ON MOB MURDER

"Washington, Jan. 10 — In his annual message to Congress last Friday President Roosevelt had the following to say about lynching"

Underneath were two columns of blank space, three inches long.

Eleanor Roosevelt's assurance to Walter White that the sentence on crime in the annual message included the crime of lynching was small consolation.

Frustrated again, the proposal's supporters continued to try to build popular pressure. *Crisis*, the organ of the NAACP, devoted its entire January issue to a symposium on the subject. It included articles by Oswald Garrison Villard, Fannie Hurst, Gertrude Atherton, Pearl S. Buck, George Fort Milton, W. E. Woodward, James Weldon Johnson, DuBose Heywood, and Walter White, and the famous *New Yorker* cartoon by Reginald Marsh of a vigilantes mob with a mother holding her daughter over her head—the caption read: "This is her first lynching." Each month the magazine printed quotes from Congressmen in support of the legislation. Joseph James Ryan offered financial support for broadcasts, literature and incidental expenses. The National Broadcasting Company agreed to two free broadcasts, providing speakers of the calibre of Costigan, Wagner and Bishop Manning were available. The Columbia Broadcasting System made a similar offer soon thereafter. White prepared transcribed speeches for unaffiliated local sattions and arranged to use the talents of Lawrence Tibbett, Lily Pons, George Gershwin, Jose Iturbi and John McCormack for network broadcasts. He tried to schedule these performances to coincide with the struggle in the Senate.

As the measure's chief sponsor, Costigan made numerous speeches in the months before Congress convened in an effort to rally public opinion behind the proposed legislation. He told the American Civil Liberties Union in November 1934 that tolerance of lynching in the United States was practically equivalent to "a complete repudiation of law, order, religion and civilization." "Reason, for the time being, is dethroned and unfortunate victims are forced by atrocities, which cause them to welcome speedy death, to testify against themselves." Federal repression of interstate crime must include the crime of lynching which was usually preceded by kidnapping, often over state lines, frequently with connivance of local peace officers.

Following the State of the Union address, a mass meeting was held at the Broadway Tabernacle, an old anti-slave center in the midst of Harlem. 2000 citizens urged the President to send a special message to Congress endorsing anti-lynching legislation. Costigan, as featured speaker, told the assemblage that reduction of lawlessness required a repression of anarchic lynching; yet, while the country tolerated mob murder, it ironically continued "to eulogize ancient and venerated constitutional safeguards of American citizenship." As Roosevelt remained silent, Costigan and Wagner delivered a Lincoln Day message over CBS to an audience that included groups gathered by the NAACP. Costigan called upon the memory of the Great Emancipator and recalled Thomas Jefferson's gloomy prophecy on slavery: "I tremble for the future of my country when I remember that God is just." "At this hour," said the Colorado Senator, "13,000,000 people in this country practically dwell from sun to sun under the unlifting shadows of potential mob violence, despite all lessons taught the world by our fatal experience with human slavery."

When the new Congress convened, Costigan again faced the problem of obtaining consideration. Once again the measure was sent to the Van Nuys Subcommittee of the Senate Committee on the Judiciary where the hearings were surprisingly swift — Walter White testified for most of the day—and the proposal was again reported favorably.

The day following the hearings a startling art exhibit opened. Its subject matter was lynching. When the Seligmann Galleries bowed to unnamed pressure and cancelled the showing, interest in the show waxed strong. During the preview, famed author Pearl Buck spoke and Edward Mathews sang. Word of the contents of the exhibition spread and large crowds attended—3,000 during its two-week run. A woman fainted on opening day. Others left in a state of shock. In addition to the original of Reginald Marsh's much reproduced *New Yorker* cartoon the exhibit contained a black and white by Harry Sternberg, modeled after the Neal murder, in which a Negro victim was tied to a post completely bereft of his genitals by action of a frenzied mob. Alan Frelan's "Barbecue — American Style" depicted a distorted Negro figure burning at the stake while a crowd of whites, including children, looked on. E. Simms Campbell's "I passed along this way" portrayed Christ shouldering a cross while a Negro being pulled by a rope around his neck walked beside him. Thomas Hart Benton contributed "A Lynching," in which a Negro was being hanged while fires were burning and a door was being battered down. Other contributors included George Bellows's "The Law is too Slow," Jose Orozco's "Negroes," John Steward Curry's "The Fugitive," and Jared French's "Lynched." With all these illustrated horrors, the exhibitors had rejected the most daring work of all. It had depicted lynchers holding up the severed genitals of a prostrate Negro. The show had a vivid impact.

While the Senate leadership could resist the public demands, the reaction to the exhibition, the resolutions from state legislatures, veterans' organizations, and religious bodies, they bowed to quiet pressure from the President and prepared to consider the bill. Senate Majority Leader Joseph Robinson informed Costigan that he would not object when the measure was called up. The proposed statute's sponsors tried to have it considered on April 9, 1935, when Senate debate was limited to five minutes, but Senators Richard Russell of Georgia and Kenneth McKellar of Tennessee objected. On April 15th, Costigan learned that Robinson intended to recognize other Senators who wished to introduce legislation in order to avoid the Anti-lynching Bill. On April 16th, Costigan gave notice that he would take up the Anti-lynching Bill after the appropriations had passed.[6]

A preliminary skirmish occurred when Senate Minority Leader Charles McNary of Oregon who was to be Costigan's strongest support, requested that the status of the Costigan-Wagner Bill be clarified. Senator "Cotton" Ed Smith of South Carolina immediately jumped to the attack, insisting that the virtue of women must be defended outside of the court so that they would not have to discuss such things publicly; "the just penalty . . . should be inflicted upon the beast" who invaded the purity of Southern womanhood. He resented a proposal which was "tantamount to saying that our section of the United States is without law and is barbarous." Costigan swiftly denied that a slur on the South was intended and declared (somewhat inaccurately) that this legislation had been initiated as a result of the tragic lynching in California, and South Carolina itself, he pointed out, had legislation very similar to the proposed national measure. Senator Walter George of Georgia, while deploring mob violence, challenged the constitutionality of the proposed legislation, and warned that if it were passed, Federal jurisdiction could be extended to any crime committed by three or more persons and the state would disappear as a unit of local government. He requested a week's postponement due to an illness in his family. The preliminary skirmish ended, the Farmer's Home Corporation Bill was taken up and consideration of the Anti-lynching Bill was postponed for a week.

The Southern Filibuster

Recognizing that important Administration legislation would be blocked by an interminable debate, Costigan offered to confer with President Roosevelt on a plan to prevent obstruction of the New Deal program during the Southern filibuster. He was willing to have his own proposal laid aside *temporarily* to allow Senate action on the Veterans' Bonus, National Recovery Act, Social Security, amendments to the Agricultural Adjustment Act, and other urgent legislation. But he would not permit the bill to be shelved.

As both sides jockeyed for position in anticipation of the coming battle, Theophilus Lewis in his *Amsterdam News* column "Harlem Sketchbook" questioned Costigan's tenacity and determination:

"Southern Senators have served notice that when he calls his bill up for debate they will begin a filibuster.

"Under the Senate rules of parliamentary procedure Senator Costigan has the right to waive the right of way of the anti-lynching bill in favor of any or all of the bills which follow it on the calendar. His choice is not an easy one. The interests of capital and labor are involved in the NRA extension bill, the interests of old people, widows and orphans are involved in the social security bill, both black and veterans are interested in the bonus bill, and the Wagner labor bill will affect the welfare of all working men regardless of color.

"Senator Costigan was elected by the voters of Colorado. His Negro constituency is insignificantly small. It is reasonable to assume that his sponsorship of the anti-lynching bill was prompted solely by humane motives. . . . If Senator Costigan is more humane than human he will insist on the priority of the anti-lynching bill. If he is more human than humane, with a weather eye out for re-election, he will waive the right of way of the anti-lynching bill in favor of more popular legislation. If I were in his shoes, I would be more human than humane."

The next weeks were to test Costigan's mettle.

On April 24th, Costigan offered a motion to take up his measure and called for a record vote without debate; he indicated his desire to speak if the motion were denied. Senator Trammell of Florida announced that he would oppose the motion to consider the ordinance and Senator Tom Connally of Texas objected to a vote without debate. The Southerners hoped to prevent a vote on a motion to consider the proposal for once it was taken up it had to come to a vote. The long struggle had opened.

In his deep, melodious voice, Costigan opened the debate with an appeal to justice:

"Mr. President, high on the flawless marble which bounds the future home of the Supreme Court of the United States these words are carved:

"Equal justice — under law.

"They impress me as adequate to begin and end the argument on the pending measure."

After tracing the history of the right of fair trial, he pointed out that within the lifespan of many members of the Senate, 5071 men and women had been "summarily seized and unlawfully, privately, arbitrarily, and brutally put to death without the judgment of their peers or due process of the law." The problem was national, not local nor sectional, he asserted, and it required a national remedy; he reiterated that it was a California lynching that had led to the present bill.

Its provisions, he contended, were moderate and effective. The Federal government could only intervene if local officials failed or refused to protect suspects. And failure of a state to protect an individual, in effect, denied due process and the equal protection of the law, thus necessitating Federal action. Mob law had to be eliminated. It endangered the safety of life, property, and free government: "The progress of civilization is measured by the successive triumphs of law over lawlessness." The experience of eleven states had proven the effectiveness of a financial deterrent on delinquent counties. Penalties for negligent officials, he pointed out, were not as severe as Colorado inflicted on any law enforcement agent who allowed a prisoner to escape. Further, imprisonment for from five to twenty-five years could be imposed on officers who conspired to deliver a prisoner to a mob. Mobs rarely formed without local sanction and police knowledge, so the prospect of those penalties would stimulate preventive action by community leaders and law enforcement agents.

After a lengthy analysis of the constitutionality of the bill, Costigan summed up:

"Certain living American principles which in the long run affect our conduct and determine history should be called into action. One is that ours is a government of laws and not of men; another, that justice to human beings and the equal protection of our laws are foremost concerns of the State. The manner in which we practice these principles fixes our choice between Hitler and Mussolini on the one side, and Washington, Jefferson, Lincoln, Henry Grady, Woodrow Wilson, and Franklin Delano Roosevelt on the other.

" . . . No man can be permitted to usurp the combined functions of judge, jury and executioner of his fellow men; and whenever any State fails to protect such equal rights, I submit that the Federal Government must do its utmost to repair the damage which is then chargeable to all of us."

Senator Hugo Black of Alabama immediately denounced the bill as a potential anti-labor weapon, citing an incident in Alabama where striking miners had killed some non-striking miners while police were in the vicinity. The coal operators charged the police with excessive leniency. Black insisted that this case could be prosecuted under the proposed anti-lynching legislation. Costigan rejected this construction.

On the following day, Senator Wagner, the co-sponsor, made his initial address. He emphasized that lynching undermined American government by denying the right of fair trial and by its discriminatory nature: since 1918, 502 of 554 lynching victims were Negroes. This defiant assault on government would not die out by itself. The incidence of mob violence had declined in 1922 and 1934, during Congressional consideration of anti-lynching bills, only to rise again as the measures failed to pass. Although states had had greater success against kidnapping than against lynching, a Federal law had been passed to apprehend kidnappers. A Federal law was undoubtedly needed to prevent lynching.

As soon as Wagner had finished speaking, Senator Connally rose to lead the attack. Realizing that a comfortable majority favored the bill, a handful of recalcitrant Southerners — spearheaded by Connally of Texas, Bailey of North Carolina, Black and Bankhead of Alabama, and Byrnes of South Carolina — used the filibuster and their knowledge of parliamentary tactics to prevent it from ever being considered. Whenever fatigue affected a filibustering Senator, his colleagues called for a quorum, which could take an hour to gather, or asked lengthy rhetorical questions. Thrice Senator Robinson, the majority leader, moved that the Senate be adjourned for the day. By ending the calendar day the Anti-lynching Bill would be removed from its place on the calendar and, in effect, the measure would have been defeated. The bill's proponents countered with a request to recess; then the calendar day continued and it remained the current item of business. No effort was made to defeat the filibuster with round the clock sessions, a technique that has been used successfully on proposals that do not deal with civil rights; nor was cloture attempted. Costigan and McNary were the bill's weary watchdogs, remaining on the floor throughout the talkfest.

The major Southern attack on the proposed statute was that it was unconstitutional, eliminating state lines. Senator Connally declared that lynching was murder and thus came under state jurisdiction. He rejected a comparison with the kidnapping law for, under its provisions, the Federal government was only involved if the kidnappers crossed state lines. The Anti-lynching Bill could lead to the trial of sovereign states in Federal courts, he warned, and to a demand for equal laws with relation to marriage, divorce and labor. The elimination of mob murder required a greater sense of local responsibility, not the erosion of state government.[8] Senator Bailey predicted that this measure would lead to the creation of a Federal bureau to determine whether states enforce their own laws. Senator Byrnes ridiculed the proposal and the claim that failure of passage would lead to an increase in lynchings: "It seems that those individuals for six months had been waiting to lynch someone . . ." As to the provision to fine counties, would the Federal government take the county courthouse, almshouse or schoolhouse if not paid?

While a cry for states rights was the major defense of the Southerners, other arguments were introduced. Senator Black returned to his claim that, despite intent, the bill would be used chiefly against labor unions and a sheriff could be imprisoned for twenty-five years for neglecting to protect a mine from striking miners. After all, the fourteenth amendment had been construed by the courts to protect corporations: "Hiding behind a sentiment against lynching, it is proposed now to have enacted a law which will fit the predatory interests of the Nation, and, as I have previously stated will crucify every labor organization which exists in the United States of America." Senator Bankhead asserted that the race question was being stirred up by those living far removed from it and accused Republicans of using the bill to prevent consideration of New Deal legislation. Senator Pat McCarran of Nevada reminded him that only the Southerners were mentioning race. Finally Senator Glass of Virginia questioned whether they could realistically expect a Federal court to convict a defendant who had been acquitted by a state court if both juries were drawn from the same populace.

A suggestion by Senator Capper of Kansas, that the question of constitutionality be left to the courts, was not greeted by the Southerners with enthusiasm. Nor were they happy with Wagner's reminder that the imperfections in the proposal, loudly trumpeted by the filibusterers, could be corrected if it received consideration. Instead, after six days, with two attempts at adjournment failing by a single vote, on May 1, Senator Robinson's motion to adjourn carried by a vote of forty-eight to thirty-two. The solid South received support from Senators of different persuasions through most of the nation — the Southwest, the Mountain states, the border states, and almost half the Midwest. The Pacific Coast and most of the Northeast supported the bill to the end. Progressives as well as conservatives voted to adjourn; Borah to preserve states rights, Norris from constitutional scruples and to return to important economic legislation. The margin for adjournment was supplied by Senators who had previously abstained or who had voted in the negative; such respectable liberals as Truman, Murray and Frazier changed their vote to support for adjournment. The Anti-lynching Bill was laid aside.

Post-Mortem

When it became apparent that the Anti-lynching Bill could not be passed, Walter White resigned from the Virgin Islands Commission. He was aware that President Roosevelt had put pressure upon Senators in private conference and without the White House the majority leader would never have permitted the measure to come to the floor. Nevertheless, White felt that the filibuster would not have withstood public opinion if the President had spoken out against it. Consequently, he wrote with regret, he could not remain even a small part of the official family.

From the beginning of 1936 the proponents of the Costigan-Wagner Bill recognized that it could not obtain passage. The President thought that an investigation of lawlessness would have a salutary effect, even if it did not apply to lynchings before the case had been taken by a court and did not impose a financial penalty.[9] Costigan was quick to support a resolution to this effect introduced by Senator Van Nuys. But even such watered-down civil rights legislation met with resistance. Appropriations were drastically cut and the resolution was bottled up by the Senate Committee on Audit and Control. After three years of controversy and pressure, civil rights legislation was moribund; efforts to resuscitate it only met with frustration.

THE COSTIGAN-WAGNER ANTI-LYNCHING BILL 175

Preparations for the Senatorial Primary of 1936

As the struggle for anti-lynching legislation reached an impasse, Costigan turned his attention to Colorado politics. According to the Colorado press Costigan and Johnson were about to settle their long struggle with a direct confrontation. Johnson was going to challenge Costigan for the Senatorial nomination. Despite repeated disclaimers by Johnson the seers of the fourth estate predicted a clash between Johnson's state welfare machine and Costigan's federal relief machine.

Speculation of this nature irritated Costigan. To project a statesmanlike image he had sought to prevent political appointments to the Works Progress Administration. He stressed to applicants that the President wanted a relief program above politics and that he would make no personal recommendations to the Colorado WPA. He reminded his correspondents of the fate of Captain Shawver. In general, Costigan favored recommendations made on the basis of merit — not as a reward for past services or in expectation of any future attitude towards public affairs.[10] He bitterly resented letters from politicians who threatened to withhold blocs of votes if their demands were ignored. Similarly, he resisted pressure for legislation. Only when a legislator had endorsed a particular proposal in detail could he be held to his promise. Even the sponsor might reject a law in its final form, drastically amended. A representative could not be a rubber stamp for his constituents.

When Paul Shriver, an ardent supporter of Costigan, was placed in charge of the Colorado WPA, Governor Johnson was deeply concerned. He had just repelled an attack by the progressives and he was determined to defend his position. Having already been granted the right to pass on all new WPA programs, he resisted Shriver's administrative appointments. Shriver attempted to follow Hopkins' policy, but at the same time he was determined that Costigan's interests be protected and he cleared prospective appointments with his faction in Washington. Since WPA programs had to be approved by Governor Johnson's office, Hopkins suggested to Regional Director Clinton Anderson that administrative responsibilities be assigned to Shriver. While efforts were made to minimize partisan politics in the WPA, local officials enrolled Costigan men, just as Johnson supporters were using their positions to strengthen the Governor.

The progressives enlisted support for the ensuing campaign. John Carroll forged an alliance with Mayor Stapleton; Carroll would support Stapleton in the 1935 mayoralty primary and Stapleton would reciprocate in 1936. Ed Johnson supported Stapleton's opponent, Grant. When

Stapleton won, columnist Alva Swain predicted victory for Costigan. Johnson would, he wrote, seek a compromise whereby he and Costigan would run for renomination unopposed. Though Philip Horbein (who had supported Johnson for Lieutenant Governor in 1930 and for Governor in 1932 and had helped him defeat Josephine Roche) endorsed Costigan in a speech to the Young Democrats, and Costigan's opposition was defeated in this convention, political seers were still convinced that Governor Johnson intended a contest.

On that assumption, Chapman returned to Denver to prepare the campaign. Starting with a solid base of support from seventeen of the twenty-two Democratic district captains in Denver, Chapman began to organize the state. Soon there was scarcely a precinct in the state without a Costigan organization; they held meetings two or three times a month. Arthur Fairbanks was sent to canvass the county leaders. In county after county, Fairbanks reported, the leaders wanted no race against Costigan and had so informed the Governor. Many of them wanted both candidates renominated without fratricidal contests.[11]

In addition to political organization, the liberals prepared extensive campaign literature. Esther Lough organized a women's educational program; study kits were followed by a series of progressive lectures. The Costigan office sent newsletters on the Senator's activities, explaining the importance of the Prevailing Wage Amendment, the investigation of soil erosion, education relief and additional school buildings, the Bankhead Farm Tenantry Bill, the Silver Purchasing Act, the Veterans Bonus, and the investigation of violations of civil liberties in Harlan County, Kentucky. Question and answer sheets on the issues of social security, peace, neutrality and munitions were distributed. Oswald Garrison Villard's article in *The Nation* was rewritten with the aid of Josephine Roche so as to increase its usefulness in a Colorado primary. Costigan's partisans were confident of victory. Finally Johnson, who probably never intended to oppose the Senator, handed Chapman a written promise that he would not enter the primary against Costigan. Costigan's renomination was all but ensured.

Costigan's Illness

His renomination was never to come. The Senator had long had trouble with his respiratory system, often campaigning despite severe discomfort. He had asthma, hay fever, and chronic bronchial weakness. Early in 1933, Costigan had been confined to home for rest. He found it difficult to sleep through the night and finally vacationed in a drier climate where he could obtain relief. Later that year he requested permission from Senator Royal Copeland to use a room near the Senate Chamber for rest and brief treatment, for his own office was distant and he suffered from shortness of breath. Costigan had had his first stroke just before the introduction of the Anti-lynching Bill in 1934; upon his return from Denver he still found walking a strain. Heedless of these warnings, Costigan had thrown himself into the fight for the Anti-lynching Bill, taking the bulk of the work upon himself. In late March 1936, he had a disabling coronary thrombosis. On April 1, 1936 the Costigan office announced that Senator and Mrs. Costigan were driving to Florida for a brief vacation. Reporters suspected that the announcement was a cover for a serious illness. His condition continued to deteriorate. A week later Mabel Costigan, Josephine Roche, and Oscar Chapman announced that Costigan would not be a candidate for re-election. He was taken to Johns Hopkins Hospital but the blood clot would not respond to treatment and it was necessary to amputate his leg to save his life. Confined to a wheelchair, Costigan lived the last three years of his life in seclusion.

1. Portions of this chapter appeared, in somewhat different form, as "The Anti-lynching Bill of 1935: The Irony of 'Equal Justice—under Law'," *Journal of Human Relations,* XV (1967), 72-85. The volume was reissued as Daniel Walden, ed., *American Reform: The Ambiguous Legacy* (Ampersand Press, 1967).

2. Section 1 stated that "no state shall . . . deny to any person within its jurisdiction the equal protection of the laws." Section 5 stated that "the Congress shall have power to enforce by appropriate legislation the provisions of this article." Tuttle showed that the interpretation of these articles by the courts in a number of cases would sustain the constitutionality of the bill under consideration.

3. In the *United States v. Harris* the Supreme Court, in 1883, refused to uphold an act of Congress which penalized conspiracies to deprive Federal citizens of equal protection under state laws, and penalized infractions by individuals of the right of citizens to reside peacefully in the several states. The Court held that Article IV, Section 2 of the Constitution could be enforced only by the judicial process and not Congressional legislation, and that this law was not a valid application of the Thirteenth Amendment. But the proponents of the Anti-lynching Bill claimed its constitutionality on the basis of the Fourteenth Amendment. In the Harris case the Court had held that under the Fourteenth Amendment a case cannot be taken out of the state courts if the state had performed its duty. This bill circumvented the Harris case by taking effect only if the state failed to perform its duty.

4. The Scottsboro case involved the purported rape of two white girls by nine Negroes in a freight car bound from Chattanooga to Memphis. There was considerable doubt whether the girls had been raped, though there was no question that they had engaged in sexual intercourse. The case became a cause celebre.

5. The Chicago *Defender* accused Cummings of subscribing to the Southern belief that lynching was not a crime.

6. Thousands of copies of reports of this lynching and the later Rubin Stacey lynching, were disseminated by the NAACP.

7. In preparation for the floor fight, White sent a brief to the sponsors outlining questions that were likely to be raised and suggested ideas for their rebuttal.

8. Connally claimed that this was the conclusion of the Slaughterhouse case and the failing of the amendment as stated by James G. Blaine in his *Twenty Years of Congress*.

9. At his press conference Roosevelt said that he would not recommend the passage of the Anti-lynching Bill.

10. After the Shawver incident, Costigan warned Hopkins to be careful in choosing Shawver's successor lest the relief program be used for political ends.

11. While Johnson probably never intended to oppose Costigan, and he denied such intentions often, yet he was confident that he would have won any contest. Johnson may have released trial balloons for self-protection.

CHAPTER XI

POSTCRIPT

The progressive camp went into a state of emotional and political shock. They had lost a beloved chief and the candidate upon whom an entire campaign had been built. A mood of despondency settled over his supporters. Efforts to draft Chapman failed: overwhelmed by this personal tragedy he despaired of victory against Johnson's announced candidacy. Judge Ben Hilliard, a progressive Democrat since the days of the Denver reform movement, awaited an endorsement by Alva Adams without which, he felt, Johnson could not be defeated; it was not forthcoming. Frantically, Merle Vincent, a former progressive Republican, made a feeble effort to enter the race, but soon withdrew in favor of William Sweet. Sweet had built a progressive reputation as Governor, but he had made no effort to protect Ben Lindsey from the fury of the Klan and his refusal to support Josephine Roche in 1934 brought reciprocal treatment from a discouraged Carroll in 1936. Lacking a solid political base, failing to obtain even tacit support from the National Administration, he was swamped in the primaries by Ed Johnson.[1] At the high tide of the New Deal, progressivism was submerged in Colorado.

Costigan's career had spanned four decades, three of them pulsing with the fever of change, during which time he had worked unceasingly for that undefined progressive entity — THE PEOPLE. His life had been shaped by a philosophy of a square deal for all, here and abroad. He was as concerned with the welfare of Filipinos and Cubans as he was with the welfare of Coloradans, rejecting any domestic or foreign policy shaped by those whose vision was restricted by self interest or a narrow mind. Since he believed in a flexible, responsive government that took the initiative to improve the conditions of its citizens, since he refused to be confined by the ideas and constitutional interpretations of a dead era, he espoused both the progressive movement and the New Deal. He recognized the increasingly corporate nature of society and the weakness of the solitary individual. Thus, he proposed to tame oligopolies by encouraging the development of trade unions and by the actions of a government, directly controlled by its citizens, which used its power to improve the entire community and all of its members. With Jefferson, he believed that the object of government was to secure the pursuit of happiness for all.

Costigan had become politically active at a time when American farmers, striking out against railroads and great corporations, had attempted to forge an alliance with urban groups — particularly a labor-populist alliance. He had been repelled by their demand for free and unlimited silver coinage, only to coalesce with them in the progressive era when they no longer found monetary inflation necessary. While this alliance produced considerable reform legislation, it petered out during World War One and its aftermath, and was recreated, with a greater majority, during the early New Deal. By the time of Costigan's retirement this partnership was disintegrating. Although FDR won a smashing victory in 1936, the rural vote was already drifting back into the Republican column. And this shift was intensified by the rise of the trade union movement, by the attack on property sensibilities with the sit down strikes, and by efforts to organize farm labor. The long run national trend toward urbanization and the availability of capital for farm mechanization through agricultural subsidies resulted in an American farm population that became a well to do commercial farm lobby, while small farmers were overwhelmed by obsolescence. Costigan was sufficiently urban and labor oriented to have adapted to the new political reality, nevertheless, his career and the conditions that shaped it ended at the same time.

He was the last of his generation of Colorado progressives to hold a statewide elective office. While Lindsey created a new political life in California and the younger Colorado liberals — Oscar Chapman, John A. Carroll, Charles Brannan, Gardner Jackson and Paul Shriver — carved fruitful careers for themselves, yet, with the death of Costigan an era of Colorado politics came to an end.

1. Sweet mentioned that after his defeat for the nomination, Merle Vincent made an effort to oppose Johnson by reentering the race through a nominating petition.

NOTES ON SOURCES

The most important source for this study is the ample Edward Prentiss Costigan Collection at the University of Colorado Library in Boulder. The collection is deficient in only one respect. Costigan does not come through as a personality. In this regard the introductions to collections of his speeches and papers— *Public Ownership of Government,* ed., George Creel (New York: Vanguard Press, 1940), and *The Progressive Papers of Edward Prentiss Costigan,* ed., Colin B. Goodykoontz (Boulder: University of Colorado Press, 1941)—are also disappointing.

Possibly Costigan's correspondence with his close personal friend, Josephine Roche, might have shed further light, but she has restricted access to this correspondence and declined to be interviewed. Fortunately, many gaps were filled by contact with others who played an important role in Costigan's career. I had fascinating and useful interviews with former Senator John A. Carroll of Colorado, who managed Miss Roche's campaign; former Secretary of the Interior Oscar Chapman, Costigan's campaign manager, Denver Housing administrator Lee F. Johnson, Costigan's executive secretary; and John M. Keating, one of the founders of the Democratic Volunteers. In addition, correspondence with former Governor and Senator, Edwin Johnson, Senator Clinton Anderson of New Mexico and Benjamin Hilliard, Jr., gave some essential insights.

The *New York Times* was a valuable source for the period in which Costigan was a national figure. The *Rocky Mountain News* and the *Denver Post* supplied much background information and his scrapbooks had clippings from thirty-five Colorado newspapers.

Costigan's career has not previously been the subject of any full scale work, but interesting chapters about him appear in John Franklin Carter, *American Messiahs* (New York: Simon and Schuster, 1935), and Ray Tucker and Frederick Barkley, *Sons of the Wild Jackass* (Boston: L. C. Page, 1932). Several specialized scholarly articles on phases of his career will be dealt with later in these notes. Materials for voting analysis were drawn from Colorado, Secretary of State, *Abstracts of Votes at Primary and General Elections,* (1912, 1914, 1930, 1934), the Denver Commission of Elections, *Manuscript Election Returns* (1912, 1914, 1930, 1934), and local newspapers. Economic analysis of counties was derived from the Colorado State Planning Commission *Yearbook,* (1918, 1931). I am grateful for help I received from Colorado Archivist Dolores Renze and John Carroll in analyzing the socio-economic structure of Denver during Costigan's career.

Secondary materials on the political events of Costigan's life are much too numerous to list, but a few will be referred to in these notes. Similarly, public documents, manuscript collections, articles, pamphlets and periodicals will be mentioned.

If more specific citations are required, most of them can be obtained by referring to Fred Greenbaum, *Edward Prentiss Costigan* (New York: Columbia University dissertation on microfilm, 1962).

THE PROGRESSIVE MOVEMENT (CHAPTERS I-V)

Roland L. Delorme, "Edward Costigan and the Colorado Bar: A Case Study of the Status Revolution," *Mid America,* 49 (1967), contains a good analysis of Costigan's background and early business career, but it is marred by the then fashionable interpretation that the upper class reacted against machine politics because it blocked their aspirations to offices to which they felt entitled by status and accomplishment. Like all such diagnoses it suffers from over generalization and really does not apply to the subject. Costigan was denied a seat in the legislature in 1902, not because of machine politics, but because he was unwilling to sacrifice loyalty to personal advancement when the whole question became part of a factional dispute. For the next decade he not only abstained from the pursuit of office but his unwillingness to be drafted brought dismay to his friends.

There have been many studies of the progressive movement which contributed to my understanding of the subject. The works most heavily relied upon for background information for this aspect for the study were Kenneth Hechler, *Insurgency* (New York: Columbia University Press, 1940); Belle and Fola LaFollette, *Robert M. LaFollette* (New York: Macmillan Co., 2 vols., 1953); Robert M. LaFollette, *LaFollette's Autobiography* (Madison: University of Wisconsin Press, 1960), George Mowry, *Theodore Roosevelt and the Progressive Movement* (Madison: University of Wisconsin Press, 1947), Amos Pinchot, *History of the Progressive Party,* ed., Helene M. Hooker (New York: New York University Press, 1958), Henry F. Pringle, *The Life and Times of William Howard Taft* (New York: Farrar and Rinehart, 2 vols., 1939) and Blair Bolles, *Tyrant From Illinois* (New York: W. W. Norton, 1951). Most interpretative works try to explain the entire movement while really examining only one aspect of it. One exception is Daniel Levine, *Varieties of Reform Thought* (Madison: University of

NOTES ON SOURCES 183

Wisconsin Press, 1964). I have dealt with this problem in "Progressivism: A Complex Phenomenon," *New Politics*, VI (1968), 85-90, and "The Progressive World of Gabriel Kolko," *Social Studies*, LX (1969), 224-228.

For information about Denver I relied on George Creel, *Rebel at Large* (New York: Putnam, 1947); Thomas Fulton Dawson, *The Life and Character of Edward Oliver Wolcott* (Denver: privately printed, 2 vols., 1911), Clyde Lyndon King, *The History of the Government of Denver with Special Reference to its Relations with Public Service Corporations* (Denver: Fisher Book Co., 1911), Ben Lindsey and Rube Borough, *The Dangerous Life* (New York: Horace Liveright, 1935), Ben Lindsey and Harvey O'Higgins, *The Beast* (New York: Doubleday, 1910) and Edgar E. MacMecham, *Robert W. Speer, A City Builder* (Denver: Smith, Brooks, 1919).

In addition to the newspapers used for the entire study, the *Denver Republican* was valuable for the period 1902-1906.

E. K. MacColl, "John Franklin Shafroth, Reform Governor of Colorado, 1909-1913," *Colorado Magazine*, XXIX (1952), 37-52, supplied considerable information on the Platform Democrats.

The Manuscript Division of the Library of Congress includes a number of collections that were consulted. The Albert Beveridge Collection shed considerable light on the Costigan-John Shaffer controversy. The George Creel Collection does not contain much that he omitted from his autobiography. Many insights into Ben Lindsey and material about the Denver reform movement were found in the Benjamin Barr Lindsey Collection. The Theodore Roosevelt Collection and the Woodrow Wilson Collection were useful in limited areas of this study. The Gifford Pinchot Collection did not prove particularly productive.

Revealing letters were found in the Lincoln Steffens Collection at the Columbia University Library; Steffens acted as an elder statesman for the Denver reformers. The William Allan White Collection, in the same depository, was useful for specific areas. Less fruitful were the Charles D. Hilles Collection and the diaries of Edward House in the historical manuscripts at the Yale University Library.

The most important secondary studies about the coal strike eventuating in the Ludlow massacre are to be found in George McGovern, *The Colorado Coal Strike, 1913-1914* (Chicago: Northwestern University dissertation on microfilm, 1953) and Barron B. Beshoar, *Out of the Depths* (Denver: World Press, 1942).

The Tariff Commission (Chapter VI)

Two articles have been written on Costigan's role on the Tariff Commission. Colin B. Goodykoontz, "Edward Prentiss Costigan and the Tariff Commission, 1917-1928," *Pacific History Review*, XVI (1947), 410-419, does little more than elaborate on Costigan's letter of resignation. J. Richard Snyder, "Coolidge, Costigan and the Tariff Commission," *Mid-America*, L (1968), 131-148, contrasts the conception of the Tariff Commission held by Coolidge and Costigan, the former considering the body a fact finding advisory to the President, the latter as a quasi-judicial body. Mr. Snyder feels that Costigan's conception was erroneous and injurious to the power of the Presidency through which any progressive reform would have to come. Snyder ignores the history of the struggle to remove the tariff from politics and set rates scientifically, and he misunderstands the position of a number of progressives on this issue, particularly LaFollette. Appointees were not removable at the President's discretion, as he says, but Lewis' reappointment was only an interim one. Further, tariff fact finding can be juggled if the basis for the cost of production is shifted from case to case in order to obtain facts that will lead to an increase.

No one can understand the tariff question without reference to the body of work written by Frank Taussig. This includes *Free Trade, the Tariff, and Reciprocity* (New York: Macmillan Co., 1927), *Tariff History of the United States* 8th ed., revised (New York: G. P. Putnam's Sons, 1931), and *Some Aspects of the Tariff Question* (Cambridge: Harvard University Press, 1934). Elmer E. Schattschneider tests Taussig's ideas as applied to the tariff of 1930 in *Politics, Pressure and the Tariff* (New York: Prentice-Hall, 1935). Other useful studies include William S. Culbertson, *Reciprocity* (New York: McGraw-Hill, 1937), John Day Larkin, *The President's Control of the Tariff* (Cambridge: Harvard University Press, 1936), Thomas Walker Page, *Making the Tariff in the United States* (Washington: The Brookings Institution, 1930), *What Price Sugar?*, compiled by the American Bottlers of Carbonated Beverages (Washington: 1929), and Philip G. Wright *Sugar in Relation to the Tariff* (New York: McGraw-Hill, 1924).

For information on the commission in this period I consulted the valuable William S. Culbertson Collection, Manuscript Division, Library of Congress, as well as the William Burgess Collection, Manuscript Division, Princeton University Library, and the William Kent Collection, Historical Manuscripts, Yale University Library.

Contemporary articles pertinent to this chapter include *The American*

Economic Review, Supplement (Proceedings), XVI (1926); Silas Bent, "The Man who Threw the Tariff Bomb," *Nation* MXXII (1926), 83-84; Edward Prentiss Costigan, "The United States Tariff Commission," *The Searchlight*, undated, Costigan Collection, and "Mr. Costigan's Tariff Brickbat," *Literary Digest*, XMVI (March 31, 1927), 11-12.

Congressional hearings were very helpful, particularly the Senate Select Committee, *Hearings, on S.R. 162 to Investigate the U.S. Tariff Commission*, 69th Cong., 1st Sess., 1926. In addition, I examined the House Committee on Ways and Means, *Hearings, on Tariff Readjustment*, 70th Cong., 2nd Sess., 1929, Vol. V, and the Senate Committee on Finance, *Hearings on the Tariff Act of 1929*, 71st Cong., 1st Sess., 1929, Vol. V.

THE ELECTION OF 1930 (CHAPTER VII)

The best economic analyses of the causes of the Great Depression are to be found in Thomas Cochran, *The American Business System* (Cambridge: Harvard University Press, 1957); John K. Galbraith, *The Great Crash, 1929* (Boston: Houghton Mifflin, 1954), Broadus Mitchell, *Depression Decade* (New York: Rinehart, 1947), and George Soule, *Prosperity Decade* (New York: Rinehart, 1947).

U. S. Congress, Senate, Select Committee, *Hearings on S.R. 215, to Investigate Senatorial Campaign Expenses*, 71st Cong., 2nd Sess., 1930 provided statistics on campaign expenditures.

RELIEF FOR THE UNEMPLOYED (CHAPTER VIII)

Oscar Chapman, *Six Years with Edward Costigan in the United States Senate*, unpublished manuscript in the Oscar Chapman Papers at the Harry S. Truman Library, Independence, Missouri, while tied too much to Costigan's speeches and statements, was very interesting. The Oscar Chapman Papers helped fill gaps in the Costigan Collection.

Edward Prentiss Costigan, "A National Political Armistice?", *Atlantic Monthly*, CXLVII (1931), 258-267, illustrates his thinking at the time of the Progressive Conference and "Education and the General Welfare," *National Education Association Journal*, 63 (1935), 73-83 indicates the importance of education in his philosophical framework.

For Costigan's Senate career the *Congressional Record*, Vols. LXXV-LXXX, is a most valuable source. U.S. Congress, Senate, Committee on Manufacturers, *Hearings, on S. 174 and S. 262, Federal Grants-in-Aid to States for Relief*, 72nd Cong., 1st Sess., 1932, U.S. Congress, Senate

Committee on Manufacturers, *Hearings, on S. 4592, Federal Grants-in-Aid to States for Relief,* 72nd Cong., 1st Sess., 1932, U.S. Congress, Senate, Committee on Manufactures, *Hearings, on S. 5125, Federal Grants to States for Relief,* 72nd Cong., 2nd Sess., 1933, U.S. Congress, Senate, *Hearings, on S. 4941, Federal Loans to the Unemployed,* 72nd Cong., 1st Sess., 1932 and U.S. Congress, Senate, Committee on Manufactures, *Hearings, on S. 5121, Relief for Transients,* 72nd Cong., 2nd Sess., 1933 provided important information on economic conditions at the time.

Joanna Colcord, "Social Work and the First Federal Relief Programs," National Conference of Social Work, *Proceedings, 1943,* 382-394, is a fine retrospective of the role played by social workers in the formation of the New Deal relief program. The Costigan Collection contains the minutes of the germinal meeting on relief held in his office.

Among the collections used for this chapter and for subsequent aspects of the New Deal were the Franklin Delano Roosevelt Collection and the Harry Hopkins Collection, Franklin Delano Roosevelt Memorial Library, Hyde Park, N.Y., and the Robert F. Wagner Collection, Georgetown University, Washington, D.C.

The Jones-Costigan Bill (Chapter IX)

Edward Prentiss Costigan, "Taxes on Wealth," *Vital Speeches,* I (1935), 673-676 clearly delineates his position on Roosevelt's tax program.

The conditions of child labor in Colorado agriculture was amply described in the White House Committee on Child Labor, *Report on Child Labor in Colorado Agriculture,* and at the hearings on the Sugar Stabilization Agreement, copies of which were available in the Costigan Collection.

U. S. Congress, House of Representatives, Committee on Agriculture, *Hearings, on H.R. 1907, to Include Sugar Beets and Sugar Cane as Basic Commodities,* 73rd Cong., 2nd Sess., 1934 had many revealing passages.

On the other hand, the Henry A. Wallace Collection, Manuscript Division, Library of Congress, Washington, D.C. did not prove serviceable for my purposes.

THE COSTIGAN-WAGNER ANTI-LYNCHING BILL (CHAPTER X)

For this chapter the author consulted the files of the *Amsterdam News*, 1933-1936, the Chicago *Defender*, 1933-1936 and *Crisis*, 1933-1936.

Walter White, *A Man Called White* (New York: Viking Press, 1948), is interesting, anecdotal and helpful.

Robert Zangrando, "The NAACP and a Federal Anti-Lynching Bill, 1934-1940," *Journal of Negro History*, L (1965), 106-117 is well done.

The National Association for the Advancement of Colored People Annual reports for 1934 and 1935 supplied some information on the NAACP campaign for the Anti-lynching Bill.

Among the collections consulted were National Association for the Advancement of Colored People Collection, the Tom Connally Collection, and the George Norris Collection, Manuscript Division, Library of Congress; the James Weldon Johnson Collection and the Walter White Collection, American Literature Manuscripts, Yale University Library.

Interesting but one-sided were the U.S. Congress, Senate, Committee on the Judiciary, *Hearings on S. 1978 to Assure to Persons Within the Jurisdiction of Every State the Equal Protection of the Law by Discouraging, Preventing, and Punishing the Crime of Lynching*, 73rd Cong., 2nd Sess., 1934 and the Senate Committee on the Judiciary, *Hearings on S. 24 to Assure to Persons Within the Jurisdiction of Every State the Equal Protection of the Law by Discouraging, Preventing and Punishing the Crime of Lynching*, 74th Cong., 1st Sess., 1935.

INDEX

Adams, Governor Alva, 13, 22, 31
Adams, Senator Alva, 135-136, 138, 140, 141, 153, 158fn, 179
Adams, William, 136, 138
Addams, Jane, 49, 79
Agricultural Adjustment Act, 145-158, 170
Agriculture, 6, 70, 103, 112-117, 145-158, 170
Allen, Robert G., 10, 125
American Civil Liberties Union, 162, 167
American Federation of Labor, 76, 85, 140
Ammons, Elias, 49-51, 59-60, 71, 73fn, 74fn, 111
Amsterdam News, 167, 170
Annear, Thomas, 108, 112
Armwood, George, 160
Arnold, Henry J., 35-36, 77
Atlantic Monthly, 121, 132

Bailey, Josiah, 172, 173
Baldwin, Albert H., 92, 97, 98
Ballinger, Richard, 26
Bankhead, John H., 172, 173, 176
Barnett, John, 111, 135
Bernhardt, Joshua, 95-96, 98, 101, 118fn, 148
Beshoar, Ben, 108-109
Beveridge, Albert, 69, 79, 89
Bickel, Karl, 47, 54fn, 56
"Big Mitt", 13-14, 42
Billikopf, Jacob, 124
Black, Hugo, 126, 172, 173
Blood, H. H., 148
Bonynge, Robert, 89
Borah, William E., 56, 73fn, 104fn, 121, 127, 174
Boulder Dam, 109, 112, 116, 144
Bourne, Jonathan, 32
Brandeis, Louis, 133
Brannan, Charles, 2, 109, 180
Bristow, J. L., 28, 29, 73fn
Brossard, E. B., 92, 96-98, 100-102
Bryan, Charles W., 151
Bryan, William Jennings, 1, 11, 79
Bulkley, Robert J., 126, 127
Burgess, William, 92-96, 101-102, 104fn
Burns, Daniel C., 84, 137

Byrnes, James, 172, 173

Canadian Reciprocity Treaty, 27
Cannon, Joseph, 25, 31
Capper, Arthur, 173
Carlson, George, 58, 71-72, 74fn, 83
Carroll, John A. 2, 109, 137, 175, 179
Casey, Lee Taylor, 87
Catlin, L. D., 47, 65, 66, 71, 73fn
Causey, James, 12, 22-24, 33, 64, 66
Chapman, Oscar, 2, 107-111, 132, 135, 141, 176, 177, 179, 180
Chase, John, 74fn
Chenery, William, 69
Chicago Defender, 178fn
Child labor, 2, 5-6, 103, 144, 146, 152-154, 157-158, 159fn
Citizen's League, 27-28, 30
Citizen's Party, 12, 28, 31, 78
Civil liberties, 3-4
Civil Works Authority, 135
Clark, I. J. Duncan, 69
Coal camps, 58-59
Colcord, Joanna, 123-124
Colliers Weekly, 26
Colorado Fuel and Iron Co., 59, 76
Colorado Industrial Commission, 76-77
Colorado Springs *Gazette*, 48, 49, 57, 70, 71, 83
Commons, John R., 77
Connally, Tom, 171, 173
Conservation, 49-52
Cook, Randolph, 72
Coolidge, Calvin, 92-96, 98, 100
Copeland, Royal S., 135, 177
Costigan, Edward Prentiss,
background, 9-12; Colorado politics, 14-16, 21-24, 28-42, 45-53, 55-77, 81-84, 107-111, 131-132, 135-142, 175-179; election analysis, 1912, 52-53; 1914, 71-73, 1930, 112, 117; 1934, 139; Denver politics 9-24, 27-28, 31, 34-36, 41-42, 77-78, 175-176; description, 9-10; illness, 176-177; mine strike, 56, 60-63; national politics 10-11, 39-40, 43-45, 81-87, 88-104, 119ff.; political philosophy, 1-8, 33-34, 49-52, 108-109, 111-117, 125-130, 143-146, 150-151, 154-158, 179-180; Tariff Commission, 88-104

188

INDEX

Costigan, Emily Sigur, 9
Costigan, George Purcell, Jr., 9
Costigan, George Purcell, Sr., 9
Costigan-LaFollette Relief Bill, 125-128, 133-134
Costigan, Mabel Corey, 11-12, 87, 107, 177
Costigan-Wagner Anti-lynching Bill, 160-175, 177
Coston, S. A., 63-64, 73fn, 74fn
Couzens, James, 127
Cox, James, 86, 121
Creel, George, 35-36, 77, 82, 87fn
Crisis, 164, 167
Culberton, William, 86, 88-89, 91-96, 98-101, 104fn
Cummings, Fred, 147-148, 158fn
Cummings, Homer, 166, 178fn
Cummins, Albert, 29, 56, 73fn
Cunningham claims, 26
Curley, James, 131
Cutting, Bronson, 121, 134, 142

Dakan, Albert, 118fn
Davis, James J., 127
Dawes, Charles, 142
DeLong, Ira, 64, 74fn
Democratic Party, 13, 17, 19, 30-32, 51-53, 70, 72, 79, 81-83, 84-86, 106-111, 130-133, 135-142
Democratic Volunteers, 109-110, 141
Denison, John H., 61
Dennis, Alfred, 92, 95-96, 98
Denver, charter revision, 34-35; commission government, 35-36, 77-78; gambling, 13; home rule, 13; progressive Republicans, 6, 21; prostitution, 13, 36; reform, 12-23, 27-28, 30, 34-36, 77-78
Denver *Express*, 23, 43, 51, 65, 70, 72, 78, 97
Denver Gas and Electric Co., 18-20
Denver Law Enforcement League, 12, 18, 30, 64
Denver *Post*, 19, 23, 35, 69, 78, 136, 139, 148, 151
Denver *Republican*, 23
Denver *Times*, 23, 51, 65, 68-69
Denver Trades Assembly, 78
Denver Tramway Co., 14, 18-20, 50
Denver Union Water Co., 14, 27-28, 53fn, 68-69
Depression, 119-160
Dern, George, 147, 158fn
Direct government, 4, 30, 32-33, 36
Direct Legislation League, 32-33

Dixon, Joseph, 47, 49
Dodge, Clarence Phelps, 48, 49, 64, 66, 69, 81
Dolliver, Jonathan, 29
Doyle, Ed, 59
Dyer Bill, 160, 162, 163

Elliot, Willis V., 29
Emergency Agricultural Tariff, 88
Employee Representation Plan, 75-76
Evans, William, 21, 24, 29, 42, 43, 51

Fairbanks, Arthur, 176
Farley, James, 131-132
Farmers Union, 145
Farr, Jefferson, 76
Federal Emergency Relief Administration, 124, 139-142
Federal Power Commission, 144
Federal Reserve Board, 113
Federal Trade Commission, 96, 143
Fisher, C. E., 47, 66, 67, 73fn, 74fn
Flynn, Edward, 131
Ford, Thomas, 161
Fordney-McCumber Tariff, 88, 98, 102, 106
Fort Collins *Leader*, 142fn
Fox, A. M., 101
Frank, Jerome, 147
Frazier, Lynn, 174
Fusion, 48-49, 55-56, 63, 67-68
Fyler, James, Jr., 73fn

Gabbert, W. H., 19-20
Gandy, N. S., 47-48
Gardner, Gilson, 40
Garfield, James 37, 39-40
Garner, John Nance, 121, 131-132, 167
Garrigues, John, 31
General Electric, 105, 143
George, Walter, 169
Gifford, Walter B., 120, 122, 125
Gilard, John T., 164
Glass, Carter, 173
Glassie, Henry H., 92-99, 101, 104fn
Glavis, Louis, 26
Glenn, Otis, 127
Goff, Jonathan W., 162
Gold Standard, 10-11
Golden *Globe*, 48
Goudy, Frank, 12, 15
Green, Billy, 20
Green, William, 60, 121
Griffith, Benjamin, 45-48, 52, 64, 71
Gronna, Asle J., 40

Guggenheim, Simon, 21, 24, 29, 42, 43, 47
Gunter, Julius, 83-84
Gurley, Boyd, 24

Hamilton, Alexander, 1, 115
Hanna, Dan, 56
Hannan, John, 40
Harding, Warren G., 92, 93, 98
Hastings, Daniel O., 153
Hawkins, Horace, 61, 65
Hayes, Frank J., 60
Hays, Arthur Garfield, 163
Haywood, William, 74fn
Hearst, William Randolph, 131
Hilliard, Benjamin C., 30, 179
Hillyer, Granby, 61
Hinman, Harvey, 68
Hirsch, Gilbert, 104fn
Hodges, William, 116
Hodson, William, 123, 134
Hogback Hill, battle of, 60; trial, 61-62
Hoover, Herbert, 1, 108, 113-114, 115-122, 129, 130, 133, 145
Hoover, W. D., 115, 118fn
Hope, Clifford, 149-150
Hopkins, Harry, 134, 139-142, 175, 178fn
Horbein, Philip, 176
Horne, Robert, 104fn
House of Morgan, 44, 56
Houser, W. L., 40
Howell, R. Beecher, 115
Hoyt, Lucius, 19
Huerfano County, 58-59, 64, 72
Hughes, Charles Evans, 80-82, 87fn, 163
Hull, Cordell, 141-142, 147

Ickes, Harold, 121, 147
Independent Denver Citizens, 78
Independent Judiciary, 21-22
Investment trusts, 105

Jefferson, Thomas, 1-8, 107, 116, 168, 172, 180
Johnson, Edwin, 135-142, 175-176, 178fn, 179, 180fn
Johnson, Frank T., 19-22
Johnson, Hiram, 75
Johnson, Lee F., 2, 161
Jones-Costigan Bill, 118fn, 143, 146-154, 156-158
Jones, Marvin, 148-149, 151, 159fn
Jones, Mary Harris, 59
Judicial recall, 27

Juvenile Court, 12, 16-17, 22-23, 34-36, 87

Kearney, Charles, 148, 158fn
Keating, Edward, 67, 109, 110
Keating, John, 109
Kent, William, 86, 88
Kindel, George J., 12
King, William H., 158fn
Ku Klux Klan, 107, 117fn, 179

Labor, 2-3, 5-6, 58-63, 65, 71-72, 87, 109-110
Labor Advocate, 110, 118fn
LaFollette, Robert M., Jr., 103, 121, 123-127, 133-134
LaFollette, Robert M., Sr., 1, 29, 34, 37-41, 56, 88, 94, 100, 101, 104fn, 117fn
LaGuardia, Fiorello, 128-129
Lane, William Preston, 160, 163
Las Animas County, 15, 58-72, 108
"Law and Order," 3, 63-68, 70-72
Lawson, John R., 60-61, 73fn
League of Nations, 3, 156
Lenroot, Katherine, 146
Lester, P. P., 60-61
Lewis, David J., 86, 94-96, 98, 100, 101, 104fn, 123-124, 161
Lewis, J. Hamilton, 131
Lewis, Theophilus, 170
Lincoln, Abraham, 157, 168, 172
Linderfelt, E. K., 59-60, 73fn
Lindsey, Benjamin Barr, 12, 16-23, 27, 30, 34-35, 47, 54fn, 65, 68, 77-78, 87, 107, 117fn, 179, 180
Lodge, Henry Cabot, 160
Lorimer, William, 27
Lough, Esther, 176
Lowell, Sherman J., 102
Ludlow strike, 58-63

McAdoo, William G., 131-132
McCarran Pat, 140-141, 173
McClintock, R. M., 49, 57-58, 63
McCormick, Medill, 40, 56-57, 71
MacDonald, Jessie, 37, 41-43, 95
McGovern, Francis, 44
McKellar, Kenneth, 128, 165, 169
McKinley, William, 11, 115
McLean, N. N., 67
McMurray, T. S., 13-14
McNary, Charles, 169, 173
Mann-Elkins Act, 27
Marsh, James, 109
Marvin, Thomas O., 92-98, 100-102, 104fn

INDEX

191

Miller, Edwin, 65
Moyer, Charles, 74fn
Munsey, Frank, 56
Murphy, J. Prentice, 122-123
Murray, W. H. ("Alfalfa Bill"), 131
Muscle Shoals, 109, 112, 116, 144

Nation, 176
National Association for the Advancement of Colored People, 160-162, 167-168, 178fn
National Economic League, 106
National Industrial Recovery Act, 5, 143-144, 146, 170; Consumer Advisory Board, 143-144; Labor Advisory Board, 143-144
Neal, Claude, 166
New Deal, 2, 5, 133-134, 143-154, 157-158, 180
New York Stock Exchange, 105
New York *Times*, 97, 105
New Yorker, 167, 168
Nixon, John C., 55-56
Non-Partisan Charter League, 35-36
Norris, George, 26, 73fn, 96, 97, 121, 129, 143, 174
Nye, Gerald, 118fn, 154, 155

O'Mahoney, Joseph, 141, 159fn
Outlook, 38

Page, Thomas, 92, 98
Pancake, J. D., 154
Parks, C. C., 49
Patterson, T. M., 12, 23, 30, 36, 51, 71-72, 74fn
Payne-Aldrich Tariff, 25-26, 29, 85, 88, 89, 91-92
Peabody, James, 71, 74fn
Periodical Publisher's Association, 40
Perkins, Frances, 134, 153, 158fn
Perkins, George, 44, 45, 54fn, 56-57, 80, 84
Philadelphia *North American*, 40
Phillips, John, 32
Phipps, Lawrence Cole, 106
Pinchot, Amos, 54fn, 56, 71, 72
Pinchot, Gifford, 26, 38-40
Pittman, Key, 127
"Platform Democrats," 30-32, 81-82
Preparedness, 78-81
Presidential Organization on Unemployment Relief, 120
Progressive Conference, 121-122, 143
Progressive Party, 3, 6, 30, 45-84
Progressive Republicans, Colorado, 20-21, 24, 28-30, 32-34, 37-48; Denver, 20-21, 24, 29, 31-34, 41-42; National, 25-27, 31-34, 37-41
Prohibition, 57-58, 70, 142fn
Public Service Corp., 116
Public Works Authority, 137, 141

Radio Corporation of America, 105
Raskob, John, 121, 131
Reconstruction Finance Corp., 127-130, 133-134
Record, George, 40
Reed, James, 127, 128, 131, 153
Republican Party, 10, 14-17, 20-22, 24, 28-29, 31, 37-39, 41-44, 45-48, 52-53, 55-58, 64, 67, 70, 72, 79-83, 86, 113-117, 121
Richberg, Donald, 121, 128
Ritchie, Albert, 131
Roberts, Owen, 157
Robinson, Joseph, 97, 101, 102, 121, 126, 127, 146, 165, 167, 169, 172, 174
Roche, Josephine, 63, 103, 107, 135-139, 142fn, 175-177, 179
Rockefeller, John D., 75-76
Rocky Mountain Fuel Co., 103, 139
Rocky Mountain News, 16-17, 30, 36, 51, 56, 65, 68-69, 77-78, 87fn, 118fn, 137
Rolph, James A., 151, 160, 161
Roosevelt, Eleanor, 134, 164-167
Roosevelt, Franklin D., 1, 3, 4, 121, 130-141, 143, 147-149, 151, 154, 156, 158fn, 164-170, 174, 178fn, 180
Roosevelt, Quentin, 64
Roosevelt, Theodore, 3, 17, 24, 25, 28, 29, 34, 38-54, 56-57, 64, 68, 69, 73fn, 78-81, 84, 87fn, 155
Roper, Daniel, 86, 92
Rush, John, 36
Russell, Richard, 169
Ryan, James, 167

St. Louis *Post Dispatch*, 126
Sammis, H. M., 73fn
Scottsboro case, 165, 177fn
Scripps, E. W., 23
Sentinels of the Republic, 125
Shaffer, John C. 68-70
Shafroth, John, 30-32, 53fn, 82, 87fn, 109, 111
Shafroth, Morrison, 109-111, 118fn
Shaw, George, 110, 114-117, 118fn
Shawver, E. L., 139-140, 175, 178fn
Shouse, Jouett, 121

Shriver, Paul, 141-142, 175, 180
Shumaker, A.C., 142fn
Smith, Alfred, 121, 130-132
Smith, Ellison ("Cotton Ed"), 145-146, 165, 169
Smith, William G., 42
Smoot, Reed, 88, 94, 97, 98
Social workers, 119-125
Soil Conservation and Domestic Allotment Act, 158
Speer, Robert, 11, 14, 18, 21, 27, 31, 34-36, 77-78
Stapleton, Benjamin F., 109, 175
State Voters League, 12, 17
Steffens, Lincoln, 11, 23, 121
Stephen, Hubert, 165
Steunenberg, Frank, 74fn
Stevens, I. N., 30, 47, 66, 73fn, 74fn
Stevenson, A. M., 21, 42, 79
Stewart, Philip, 23fn, 43, 45-49, 54fn, 74fn
Stock market, 105-106
Stocker, Allison, 73fn, 74fn
Stone, Harlan, 94, 157
Stong, A. M., 48
Sugar Stabilization Agreement, 146-147
Sumner, Hatton W., 163
Sweet, William, 117fn, 179, 180fn
Swope, Gerard, 143

Taft, William Howard, 21, 24-27, 29, 37-47, 85
Tarbell, Ida, 11
Tariff, 3, 6, 10, 25-27, 42, 70, 84-106, 108, 113-115, 122, 152-154
Taussig, Frank W., 86, 88, 97-98
Teller, Henry, 10, 35, 111
Temple, J. S., 17, 22-24, 28, 39, 64, 66
Tennessee Coal, Iron and Railroad Co., 38
Tennessee Valley Authority, 144
Thomas, Charles S., 13, 30-31, 82
Thomas, Elmer, 158fn
Thurston, E. L. 100
Tikas, Louis, 60
Trammell, Park, 170
Troutman, P. H., 45, 54fn, 66, 67, 71, 73fn
Truman, Harry, 2, 174
Tugwell, Rexford Guy, 150
Tuttle, Charles, 163, 165, 177fn

Underwood, Oscar, 104fn
Underwood Tariff, 56

Unemployment relief, 119-130, 133-135; prevailing wage amendment, 140-141
Union Pacific, 18-20
United Mine Workers of America, 3, 56, 58-63, 65, 75-76
U. S. Industrial Commission, testimony of E. P. Costigan, 62-63, 75-77
U. S. Steel, 38, 56, 57, 105
U. S. Tariff Commission, 6, 82, 84-106, 122, 148-149, 161
U. S. v. Butler, 157
U. S. v. Harris, 163, 177fn
Utilities, 6-7, 27-28

Vandenberg, Arthur, 151-153
Van Nuys, Frederick, 162, 168, 174
Van Valkenburg, E. A., 40
Villard, Oswald Garrison, 167, 176
Vincent, Merle D., 16, 21, 24, 28-30, 33, 37, 43, 45-49, 64, 67, 81, 84, 138, 179, 180fn
Viner, Jacob, 97

Wagner, Robert F., Sr., 108, 113, 133-134, 142fn, 143, 153, 161-165, 168, 170, 172-174
Wallace, Henry A., 147-154, 157, 158fn
Walsh, Tom, 126
War, 3, 154-156
Washington, George, 156, 172
Weaver, A. J. S., 149-150
Webb, O. H., 115
Weber, Max, 104fn
Wheeler, Burton K., 121, 126
White, J. P., 60
White, Walter, 160-167, 174, 178fn
White, William Allen, 28, 33, 49, 71, 99-100
Whitlock, Brand, 23
Wickersham, G. W., 26
Wilkins, Earl, 167
Wilson, Woodrow, 3, 49, 56, 60, 78-79, 81-86, 87fn, 88, 101, 111, 116, 131, 155, 172
Wolcott, Edward Oliver, 10, 15, 21, 24fn
Wolman, Leo, 121
Woman Patriot Publishing Co., 125
Woodruff, Roy O., 152
Works Progress Administration, 140-142, 175
World Court, 3, 156
World War One, 78-79, 81, 84, 90

Young, Owen, 131, 132